LAND AND PEOPLE OF TIBET AND CHINA
In The Early Twentieth Century

John Weston Brooke.

FROM PHOTOGRAPH BY LAMBERT, WESTON & SON, FOLKESTONE & LONDON.

LAND AND PEOPLE OF TIBET AND CHINA

in The Early Twentieth Century

W.N. FERGUSSON
F.R.G.S.

With Illustrations from Photographs by the Author
and the late Lieut. Brooke and Two Maps

SHARADA
Sharada Prakashan
707/43, TRI NAGAR, DELHI-110035

REPRINTED IN INDIA, 1989
ISBN 81-85320-03-9

Published by
SHARADA PRAKASHAN
707/43 Tri Nagar,
DELHI-110035

Printed by
Mahindra Offset Press
Shahzada Bagh
Delhi-110035

TO THE

Memory

OF

J. WESTON BROOKE, F.R.G.S.

FENAY HALL, HUDDERSFIELD, ENG.,

THIS JOURNEY IS FIRST

RECORDED.

PREFATORY.

In offering this book to the public I must first explain its origin, and my own part in what is mainly an account of two journeys taken through China and Tibet by the late Lieutenant Brooke, F.R.G.S.

Mr. Brooke started on his first journey from Shanghai on August 1, 1906, and after crossing Tibet, returned to Shanghai in October, 1907.

He left Shanghai on his second journey in December, 1907, and travelled in Western Sechuan and Eastern Tibet until December 24, 1908, when he was cruelly murdered in the Independent Lolo Land.

On the second of these two expeditions Lieutenant Brooke was accompanied by Mr. C. H. Meares; and when that journey came to its untimely end, Mr. Meares returned to England and wrote certain articles in the Home Press on the country through which they had travelled. These created considerable interest, and Mr. Meares was urged to make of his own and his friend's experiences some more permanent record. But he had already been enlisted by Captain Scott for the Antarctic Expedition, and must leave England early in the present year for Siberia, there to purchase dogs and ponies for that enterprise; and the task which should have been his has perforce fallen to me. Mr. Brooke's parents have kindly placed at my disposal their son's diary and photographs taken on his journeys; and of these and my own and Mr. Meares's observations of a picturesque country and a singular people, never visited by white men before, I hope to make something which shall commemorate the real be-getter of this volume, and interest the general reader to whom adventure, sport, and travel in remote lands are of concern.

John Weston Brooke was born at Fenay Hall, near Huddersfield, in Yorkshire, in July, 1880, and went to school at Repton. In 1898 he joined his county Yeomanry, the Yorkshire Dragoons, and served with them in the Boer War. An act of gallantry in the field won him a commission in the Regular Army, and in November, 1900, he returned to England and joined the 7th Hussars at Aldershot. But the instinct of travel was in his blood, and in 1902 he resigned with the idea of exploration in that Dark Continent which has drawn, and yet draws, so heavily on the adventurous. An introduction to Major Burnham, the famous American Scout, then a Director of the East African Syndicate, turned his thoughts in that direction, and in April, 1903, Mr. Brooke left England for East Africa, and was sent off promptly after his arrival on an exploring expedition with Messrs. Blick, Brittlebank, and Brown. "The Four B.'s," as the party was called, travelled from Nairobi viâ Mount Elgon northwards to the western shores of Lake Rudolph, experiencing plenty of privations from want of water, and of danger from encounters with the natives.

On January 25, 1904, a report reached England that the expedition had been wiped out; but a week later this was contradicted, and proved to be the concoction of a runaway porter. Mr. Brooke returned to England the following April and applied himself to the study of scientific subjects, the more fully to fit himself for the life of an explorer. He received his diploma for survey work from the Royal Geographical Society, and was made a Fellow of the Society.

In March, 1906, Mr. Brooke sailed for India, with the

object of organising an expedition into Tibet to investigate the much debated question of the relation of the Sampo and Brahmaputra Rivers. This intention, so far as India was concerned, was frustrated by the Indian Government, in view of the Treaty just then signed with Russia, by which no stranger should be allowed to enter Tibet from India. Nothing daunted, he tried to slip across over the Assam border with only two servants; but the frontier officer, being warned of his intention, was on the look out and intercepted him.

Mr. Brooke now resolved to enter Tibet from the north, and left Calcutta for Shanghai in June, 1906, travelling thence viâ Hankow, Singan, Pingliang, Lanchow, to Siningfu. The journey was accomplished in three months, and in his journal Mr. Brooke speaks with gratitude of the missionaries, who "treated" him "with the greatest kindness and hospitality," and are "the true friends of travellers in that country." At Siningfu he stayed for about a month, gathering information and collecting ponies, yaks, and general supplies. In October, 1906, the Dalai Lama arrived from Urgu, whither he had fled when Sir Frank Younghusband's Mission entered Lhasa three years before. Mr. Ridley, of the China Inland Mission, and Mr. Brooke were lucky enough to obtain an audience of the Dalai Lama, and were the first Englishmen to see him.

Everything was now ready for the second attempt to reach the Brahmaputra, and Mr. Brooke entered Tibet by the Kokomer, travelling to the north of that lake to Baranr Tsaidan, and southward by the Tangla Pass. The journey was an adventurous one, especially so for a man ignorant of the language, and whose servants were—and proved—worse than useless. The party was several times in danger from the Goluk robbers, and on one occasion, when riding unarmed, Mr. Brooke had a hand-to-hand fight with one of these ruffians.

On arriving at Magehulla, a place about 200 miles north of his objective, he was surrounded by hordes of Tibetans, and although he held many interviews of a friendly character with Lamas, they were quite firm in assuring him that he might not travel south in that direction. As soon as he packed his camels the soldiers unpacked them, and, as he was one against hundreds, he had eventually, to his great disgust, to retrace his steps and turn again northwards. This was on April 30, 1907. The party was now reduced to two men and a few half starved camels, and with these he joined a Mongolian chief, with whom he struck up a friendship. They travelled together for some weeks, and the chief invited Mr. Brooke to go home with him, where he was given some good shooting, and secured some valuable sporting trophies.

At Tarmor he just missed meeting Dr. Stein, the famous explorer, who seems to have been in the village on the same day, but neither was aware of the other's presence.

Mr. Brooke had previously met Dr. Taffel, who had experienced many hairbreadth escapes among the Goloks, and was then himself attired as a robber, having been stripped of all his possessions.

On July 1 Mr. Brooke again arrived at the house of his good missionary friends, Mr. and Mrs. Ridley, at Siningfu, where he stayed for a few days. Then, leaving for Shanghai, he varied his route by going down the Yangtze River, and thence made a trip to Japan and Manchuria.

On his return to China, in November, 1907, he met, at Tientsin, Mr. C. H. Meares, and at once recognised in him a kindred spirit. He invited Mr. Meares to join him on his next journey, an expedition in Western China, the result of a conversation I had held with him when we met at Ichang some months before. I had spoken of the hitherto almost unknown tribes who dwell in the west of the province of

Zechwar, and among whom I had myself travelled for some years, distributing books for the British and Foreign Bible Society. An article of mine about these people, with a map of their country, had appeared in the Royal Geographical Society's *Journal* for December, 1908, being a summary of journeys taken between the years 1903 and 1907. But very much still remained to be learned, and Mr. Brooke suggested that if he should decide to go into that province, I should

CHIEF OF THE CARAVAN WITH WHOM MR. BROOKE MADE FRIENDS ON HIS RETURN.

introduce him to those chiefs with whom I had already become friends.

This expedition was subsequently carried out in Mr. Meares's company; and their route coinciding with a journey which I had previously planned, and not interfering with my own work, we travelled for a great part of the time together. In Chapters I–V the reader has what story I can make for him out of Mr. Brooke's diary, often in his own words, illustrating in detail the incidents and experiences of the itinerary which I have faintly outlined above. It was later at Hankow that he and Mr. Meares made actual commencement of their main journey. After Chentu (in Chapter V), where I joined them, I have been able generally to write of experiences which I shared.

As I write, I recall the joy which Mr. Brooke evinced in natural beauty, whether seen in the lofty mountain, with its snow-capped peaks towering on high until lost in a cloud of mist; or in the rushing stream that swept madly on, in haste to mingle its clear blue waters with the muddy Yangtze and so be carried to the ocean; the grassy plateau and the virgin forest, with their strange, exotic, sometimes unknown animals and birds—all held for him a rare and profound charm. He would revel in the beds of wild flowers which grew so profusely and so luxuriously bloomed, carpeting the entire mountain-side well-nigh to the snow line. I have seen him almost in rapture as he chased over these beds, 12,000 to 16,000 feet above sea-level, seeking out the various coloured poppies that bloom at this altitude. There we found the red, the yellow, the blue, the purple and mauve poppies of magical beauty in that setting, though only two of them have proved new to the botanist. . . . Yet a little and it was my lot to go alone into the Lolo country and identify the bruised and mangled body of my friend, then recovered from the Lolos by the Chinese officials; and beside him the body of my adopted Chinese boy, who had gone with Mr. Brooke as his interpreter, and who had remained faithful to the end. . . . But it is time to begin Mr. Brooke's narrative from the diary which he penned while he was alive and well, the picture of courage, high heart and endeavour.

CONTENTS.

ILLUSTRATIONS.

CHAPTER I.

On the Tibetan Steppes.

"After my plans for entering Tibet from India had been successfully frustrated by the Indian Government," writes Mr. Brooke, "I considered it best to try and get the support of the Chinese Government and, if possible, that of the Dalai Lama, and so enter Tibet from the north. After a most uninteresting tramp across China I reached Sining, a large town in the west of Kansu Province. Here I heard that the Dalai Lama was coming south from Urga and was to stay in a monastery close to Sining. Mr. and Mrs. Ridley, the missionaries connected with the China Inland Mission, insisted on my making their home my own, and I appreciated a rest with these very pleasant people after a lonely tramp of three months across China.

"The monastery of Tassu or Kumbum—the first name is Chinese, the second Tibetan—where the Dalai Lama was to stay for some time, had been well cleaned for the occasion, before the arrival of this great potentate. The dust of ages had been swept away, and the huge golden idols gleamed with their varied and fiendish expressions. Incense was kept continually burning in great vases in front of each. The massive doors of the building were open, and the worshippers kept coming and going, prostrating themselves on the polished boards outside, incessantly muttering their prayers.

"The palace to be occupied by the Dalai Lama was a long, low building, built on the side of a steep hill, which overlooks the whole monastery of Tassu. The golden roofs of the temples stood out dazzling in the sun, and long-robed priests ran hither and thither from one temple to another, while the devout worshippers wandered about with bowed heads, counting their beads and muttering their prayers.

"As we were at the monastery three days before the Dalai Lama arrived, we were at liberty to go almost anywhere we liked. We visited the courtyard where the Dalai Lama was to be entertained. His bedroom, which was very small, was papered with a typically English rose wall-paper; a large bed took up most of the room, and was heavily draped with bright yellow silk curtains embroidered in gold, and a counterpane to match.

"Two priests were on guard, who would on no account allow us to go into the room, and were very angry with the guards outside for letting us come into the courtyard at all.

"On October 25, 1906, Mr. Ridley and I rode out of Sining to see the Dalai Lama arrive. The roads were lined with the grotesque Chinese soldiers, armed with their very ancient guns, wearing their straw hats and pink coats made of cotton cloth, which hung on them like sacks. The Chinese on-lookers had gathered, partly because they had nothing else to do, and partly because a Chinaman must see everything that is going on; but no one was over-pleased with their guest, whom they had to supply with forced hospitality. In fact, for months past, the Mandarin of Sining had been collecting pots and pans, and even tables, from the cottages of the poor to furnish his lordship's apartments.

"As is the case with most functions of this kind, we waited for a long time for any sign of the Dalai Lama and his suite. At last, in the far distance, we heard the shrieking of the Chinese band, and then, as the diabolical noise came closer, amidst a great cloud of dust, some five or six Chinamen came up, shuffling along in a gait which was neither a walk nor a run. They were dressed as they liked, played as they liked, and shuffled as they liked, for it could not be called marching. Next came the standard-bearers, in the same disorder, and these were in considerable danger of being run down by the horsemen behind them. They carried long poles with red flags, and all manner of curiously-designed spears and tridents, which one may see outside any Chinese Yamen, and which are emblems of authority and justice. Next came the mounted Tibetans, in wonderful long yellow coats and curious hats made of gilded wood, riding rough, high-spirited ponies, which did not lend dignity to the spectacle. Suddenly a distinguished-looking Tibetan galloped out of the crowd and shouted to the onlookers to 'koutou,' *i.e.*, fall prostrate on the ground in honour and reverence before his lordship. We dismounted from our ponies but refused to do more, so he left us to harangue the Chinese, who were quite indifferent and only laughed and said rude things, as our English crowd sometimes does to our respected Metropolitan Police, who have learned, however, to take it better than did our friend this distinguished-looking Tibetan. There was more to see now, for a crowd of horsemen drew near, surrounding a large yellow cloth-covered chair, which was carried by four horses led by four mounted Tibetans, two on each side, so that we only caught a glimpse of the occupant for one second. We followed with the crowd until we reached a large camp which was prepared for him outside of the monastery of Kumbum. Here we found hundreds of tents, all pitched in a square, with one, a Mongol tent of rich yellow cloth, surrounded by a wall of the same material, where the Dalai Lama was to spend the night.

"Outside the square were crowds of many nationalities from different parts of Asia, Mongol Princes with gaily-attired camels, bringing presents from the north; wild-looking Tibetans with matted hair hanging down their backs, riding equally wild-looking ponies, driving unwieldy yaks, thin from long travelling, perhaps from Lhasa or unknown regions in Southern Tibet; Chinese in gorgeous coloured silks, and muleteers with their galled mules.

"Mr. Ridley and I donned our smartest clothes of Chinese silk for the occasion. Mine was as complicated to put on as a hussar's full-dress uniform is to a newly-joined subaltern, but no less smart. It consisted of four coats, with four different coloured silks and patterns, each being cut away a little more than the one beneath it, so that a portion of

BAZAAR AT KUMBUM.

each showed in front, dark red trousers and yellow leggings, which came half way up the leg, black boots which were most troublesome to walk in; a large black hat with turned-up brim and red tassels completed the costume. A pigtail is considered unnecessary by the Tibetan.

"We intended calling on the Dalai Lama at once, but were told that he could not see us at present, stating his willingness to receive us in a few days. We climbed up to a little tower overlooking the camp, and had taken a few photographs, when a fanatical Tibetan knocked my camera out of my hand and assaulted Mr. Ridley in the act of focussing!

"Two days after this we went up to the monastery and were granted an audience. After waiting a few minutes, sitting on little silk cushions in the courtyard, we were brought up a narrow staircase to a small room, where all sorts of instructions were given us in a whisper. Our present, which consisted of a fur coat, was taken in, and we followed; we bowed as we entered the door and again when we approached the Dalai Lama. We then placed the light blue scarf or kata (always presented on such occasions in Tibet) into his lordship's hands, and he presented us with another. He gave me a small image of Bhudda. Mr. Ridley received a bundle of joss-sticks and a roll of Lhasa cloth. The Dalai Lama asked if we had come far, and while Mr. Ridley explained who we were, I had an opportunity to look round. The room was about thirty feet long by fifteen feet wide, and the walls were draped with beautifully worked embroideries, representing Bhudda and various deities. The room was well warmed, and a mysterious scent of incense pervaded the atmosphere. The Dalai Lama sat in front of us, cross-legged, on silk cushions which were placed on a table about four feet high, so that his feet were on a level with our faces as we talked with him. His face did not show the slightest trace of expression; he greeted us with a slight forward movement of his body, but nothing like a smile ever approached his face as we conversed.

"Dr. Sven Hedin says that he had never seen such a gentle, pleasant face as that of the Tashi Lama, and I can say I have never seen such a hard, expressionless face as that of the Dalai Lama. One could not help thinking that he must have trained his features to resemble the unsympathetic emptiness of the brazen images of the country. He asked if I had come from the other side of the world, and if the

English king had sent me to see him. Mr. Ridley told him that the English were a kind people, and that he was sure that if he would come to India to meet them and learn to know them, he would not mind their coming to his country. After about half-an-hour's talk, which was mostly on our side, I asked if I might photograph him, but he refused. With a low bow we backed out of his presence; as we backed his features relaxed into a faint smile, a great relief after our grave interview.

"So ended our audience with the Dalai Lama, his first, I believe, with an Englishman." Mr. Brooke's notes and diary carry on the narrative of his experiences after leaving the Lama's presence. But, for clearness' sake, it may be well briefly to indicate what these were, leaving a detailed story to other chapters.

From Kumbum Mr. Brooke went to Tankar, a small city some thirty miles to the north, where he purchased yaks for the transportation of his party and their supplies—nearly fifty of these slow and stupid animals. Leaving this border town he plunged into Tibet, crossed the Kokonor plain, passed to the north of the lake, and after much difficulty reached Baramtsaidam. Here they found a Mongolian, who traded camels for Lieutenant Brooke's yaks, but the Mongol got the best of the bargain. Mr. Brooke refitted his caravan at much additional expense and continued his journey, crossing with considerable hardship the high passes, then covered deep with snow.

There was much difficulty in finding grass for his camels and fuel to cook the necessary food for his party.

Finally he reached a point within a few days' journey of Lhasa, and had a long interview with the intractable guards stationed at the border of the Lhasa territory. There was much delay, and Mr. Brooke made several detours in the hope of evading the guards, but was always unsuccessful.

In the end he was forced to turn his back on his goal, the source of the Brahmaputra, which, after months of weary travel, he had almost reached; with a sad heart and weary tread he turned north. On his retreat he made friends with the Chief of a Mongolian caravan returning from Lhasa and joined this party, and proceeding almost due north came out in Turkestan, and then crossed into Mongolia. He shot much game on this journey, and sent home one of the finest heads of an *ovis ammum* ever seen in England. After some months in Mongolia he returned to Sining and Lanchow and thence travelled almost due south across Kansuh and Sechuan provinces as far as Chungking.

From Chungking, in October, 1907, he took boat down the Yantze River and spent the winter in Japan and Corea.

It was on his way down and at Ichang that I first met Mr. Brooke. We had a long talk on our experiences in China and Tibet. I happened to tell him of that part of the country in which I was particularly interested, that inhabited by the eighteen tribes of Western Sechuan. "Don't be surprised," he said, "if I come up your way next spring." At Shanghai he met Mr. Edgar of the China Inland Mission, who is also interested in Western China and Tibet, and their meeting decided him to come west. Two and a-half months were spent in Japan and Corea. On his way back to China he met, at Tientain, Mr. C. H. Meares, who agreed to join him in further travel. Hankow was to be their starting point. Mr. Meares went then straightway overland, while Mr. Brooke himself went by Shanghai, to make necessary arrangements for the forwarding of money and supplies for the caravan. They met again at Hankow, and from this port they travelled together, until separated by the untimely death of Mr. Brooke.

CHAPTER II.

PROCURING THE CARAVAN.

AFTER the interview with the Dalai Lama, Mr. Brooke said good-bye to his friend Mr. Ridley, and started for Tankar to purchase the necessary yaks and ponies needed for his expedition. Tankar is a Chinese frontier town, where a considerable trade is carried on with Tibetans; it is situated on the Siho or West River, about twenty-four miles north-west of Kumbum and twenty miles east of Toba, the Mohammedan stronghold. The town is of some commercial importance, as a kind of depôt for Chinese merchants trading with Tibetans. Hither, from Lhasa, come the caravans of the Dalai Lama. That dignitary drives no small trade with the Chinese, and this town being on a direct route between Mongolia and Lhasa, large caravans pass through annually in the fourth moon on their way to the "Sacred City." To this town the Tibetans of the Kokonor (Blue Lake) district bring in their produce, which consists of salt, hides, wool, sheep, cattle, horses; and trade them with the Chinese merchants for cotton goods, red felt, wine, snuff, tea, grain, coarse hemp bags and sundry other articles which Tibet imports from China. The majority of the inhabitants of the town are Chinese, but some Tibetans and Mongolians also live on the street, and every day large caravans may be seen camping outside the gate on the grassy commons that surround the town; the writer camped there on his first attempt to reach the Kokonor district in July, 1895. Tankar, moreover, is of some political and strategical importance and was originally a military outpost.

Here the Sining Amban receives the Mongolian Princes once a year and distributes presents in the name of the Emperor. Ten miles to the east may be seen part of the Great Wall, in which the gate called Kwanmen is now in ruins, but at which a guard of soldiers was formerly stationed.

The town was once within Tibetan territory, but the Chinese have gradually swallowed up the district for its agriculture.

Along the West River are narrow gorges which make the entrance to Tankar Valley very difficult ; the Chinese took advantage of these natural defences during the Eastern rebellion to keep the Mohammedans in check.

The approach from the east is charming ; a beautiful grove surrounding a water mill near the city gate first greets one, while some beautiful temples stand out on the hills in the background.

There is one principal street lined on either side by shops, in which are to be found Chinese wares and goods for bartering ; grain and food-stuffs, beads, earrings, hair ornaments, pots, saddles, ropes, boots and so forth are all displayed. The Yamen opens out into the street, and so do a small lamasery and several wool depôts ; the houses of the citizens and representative Tibetans and the City Temple fill up most of the space within the walls of this border town. Outside the gates are small suburbs, mostly occupied by Mohammedans. Strewn along the streets and suburbs will be found the Chinese pedlar or travelling merchants with their small wares spread out on mats, waiting for their opportunity to fleece the Tibetan or Mongolian traveller as he passes through. Yaks are driven in and sold for beef, their average price being from 5 to 7 taels each, while young ones in very good condition may bring from 7 to 12 taels. A good pony costs from 25 to 30 taels. The tael up here equals about three shillings.

While Mr. Brooke was delayed here trying to secure his yaks, Dr. Taffel, a German traveller, arrived from Tibet, having been robbed for the third time by the Golok, a famous brigand tribe inhabiting the region south of the Kokonor. When Dr. Taffel arrived at Tankar he had little left but what was on his back, and was dressed like one of the famous Golok, in a sheep-skin coat, Tibetan boots and fur cap, with a girdle round his waist and his gown tucked to the knee. He narrated the story of his narrow escapes from the hands of these notorious nomads, who gain their livelihood by driving away their neighbours' cattle, attacking caravans, waylaying travellers, whether foreigners, Chinese or Tibetans. Dr. Taffel's adventures, however, did not cause Mr. Brooke to hesitate to continue his journey, and he proceeded with his negotiations for securing his caravan. Dr. Taffel gave him a good deal of information from his lengthy experience in the country regarding the price and quality of the animals required, and the day after this meeting Mr. Brooke left Tankar and proceeded to a village some twenty miles away, where the yaks were to be procured.

That night he put up in a little house occupied by a half-caste Chinaman, where he had his first meal of tsamba and buttered tea, the staple food in this part of the country as well as in Mongolia and Tibet. In these regions the frontiers are distinguished by deviations of diet. In spite of the political boundary established by the Chinese, they are constantly encroaching on Tibetan and Mongolian territory. On the other hand, while the Chinese trader soon learns to eat and even relish Tibetan food in Tibet, he would not think of living on it in China, where it is always referred to as the food of the barbarian. Tsamba is parched barley, ground into rather fine meal and mixed into dough with tea and butter; when kneaded to the proper consistency, just hard enough not to stick to one's hands, it is taken out of the wooden bowl which serves for plate, cup and saucer combined, and is held in the hand, while the cup is filled with tea, and one makes one's meal by biting a piece out of the dough and sipping the buttered tea. Buttered tea is made in this part of the country by breaking a piece of Hankow brick tea into rather small pieces and placing them in a copper pot, in which milk and water are kept boiling. This pot is kept constantly on the stove, and tea may be served at almost any hour of the day or night. When the tea is poured into the wooden basin, a lump of butter, half the size of an egg, is put in; this floats on the top and when dissolved leaves conspicuous the yak hairs the Tibetan thinks necessary to hold together and give flavour to the butter, which can now easily be skimmed off or blown to one side of the basin while one drinks from the other side. When the diner has satisfied his appetite, supposing him to have, like most Tibetans, a long tongue, he proceeds to wash his bowl by licking it clean. If, however, he is unfortunate enough to be tongue-tied, he must then use his finger to wipe the bowl out and finish by licking his finger clean; nothing must be allowed to go to waste in a country where food is so scarce and precious. Brooke's half-caste's wife did all the work and appeared very cheerful. She wore her hair in two plaits down her back. Two broad blue-cloth stoles, one attached to each braid of hair, hung down her back and were covered with stones, large cash and other trinkets, which must have weighed several pounds. This is the border Tibetan fashion, but Brooke was told the lady was of Turkish descent. Next morning, on going into the kitchen, Mr. Brooke found an old Lama, his host and four strong children all munching away at tsamba, while the old lady was making scones in an iron pot. These she heated over an argol fire. There being no wood in the locality, the excretum of the yak is dried by plastering it on the sides of the house, and when dry this makes very good fuel; that is, when one knows how to use it, but it is slow, tedious work to any one not accustomed to the use of this fuel to attempt to cook a meal on it. After the meal was over the husband spent the day in nursing the baby, while his wife attended to the work. Mr. Brooke spent the day in bargaining for yak, and succeeded in selecting twenty-five animals out of the herd at 14 taels each. The price went up as usual as soon as it was known a foreigner wanted to purchase, and unless his middleman was exceptional we may rest assured that that

WIFE OF THE MAN FROM WHOM MR. BROOKE BOUGHT THE YAK.

indispensable person did not close this bargain with an empty pocket, since every middleman expects to make at least 20 per cent. out of every bargain he drives. Mr. Brooke also engaged a yak driver, who was supposed to understand the loading and management of the clumsy and stupid brutes. After securing the animals and seeing them started on their way to Tankar, Brooke returned to Sining to pick up his belongings and say good-bye to the Ridleys. While he was there their little boy died, and he left them in sorrow. Mr. Brooke never forgot the kindness shown to him by these good people, and I often heard him speak of them while in Sechuan. Here he again met Dr. Taffel, and they travelled together half way to Tankar, where their road separated, and Brooke, not having a servant or escort, travelled the remainder of the road alone. When about five miles

CHILDREN OF THE MAN FROM WHOM MR. BROOKE BOUGHT THE YAK.

from Tankar a Tibetan overtook him, and for some time appeared most friendly, riding alongside and trying to converse. Suddenly he snatched at Mr. Brooke's reins and, pulling his pony up and at the same moment drawing his sword, an instrument which every Tibetan is provided with in these parts, he succeeded in striking Brooke over the head with it. The blow was weak and did little damage, and Brooke, slipping off his pony, kept it between himself and his sudden antagonist. Finding this defence uncertain he rushed in at close quarters and pulled the Tibetan off his pony, dragging him about on the ground, which exhausted himself unnecessarily. Finally he succeeded in securing his enemy's sword, but though he struck at him with the weapon the Tibetan's sheep-skin coat was so hard and thick that the blow did little more than cut the garment slightly. The Tibetan now rushed Brooke in turn and recovered the sword, but Brooke so kept hold of him that he had no opportunity of using it, and my friend managed to secure the weapon a second time and hurled it into the mountain stream which roared beside them. The Tibetan bolted off to try and recover it, and Brooke spent this breathing space in trying to kick up a stone out of the hard road; but the Tibetan, noticing what he was at, left the sword and rushed against Brooke, knocking him over and trying himself to secure the stone, still fast in the ground. Brooke secured another stone, but was by this time so exhausted that he had little strength left to use it and only just managed to give the Tibetan a bump on the head. They closed again, and Brooke managing to get on top, banged his opponent's face with his fist, but it seemed to have little effect. The Tibetan then got on top and pounded his enemy on the forehead with small stones. Brooke now managed to get in a stroke under the Tibetan's chin which stunned him a little, and he succeeded in getting away. His own horse was grazing close by and he managed to catch and mount him. As he rode off he looked back and saw the Tibetan do likewise, only riding in the opposite direction. Fortunately he did not appear to have any accomplices. Brooke finally arrived at Tankar bleeding and exhausted. He found his boy just lighting a lamp to come and look for him. The servant professed to be very much distressed that he was not with his master to help him against the Tibetan, but after

Brooke got better acquainted with this worthy, he perceived that he was, in fact, delighted not to have been with him. In truth, the boy proved to be a coward in every respect

Two Mandarins called on Brooke next day and appeared most sympathetic. They stated that soldiers had been sent off, soon after he arrived, in pursuit of the Tibetan, and had captured him early that morning; and they wanted to know what punishment he thought should be inflicted. Brooke said that for such a crime in his country a man would be given several years' imprisonment, with nothing but bread and water to sustain life. The Mandarins replied they had a similar law in their country; and nine months later Brooke saw the Tibetan still retained in the prison at Sining. Brooke's wounds, which consisted of a cut on his head and some bruises on his forehead, soon healed. On the 18th of November he packed the forty-five unwieldy yaks that composed his caravan, together with eight Chinamen in all, including an interpreter from the Amban at Sining, who had some influence on the robbers of the Kokonor district. It took about five hours to pack the caravan, and, as usually happens on the first day of an expedition, the loads tumbled about, frightening the yaks into a mad stampede, so that only a few miles were accomplished before encamping. The second day was most disastrous; the tent poles were broken during the night by some of the yaks smashing into it, his theodolite and plane table were also smashed during the march by the clumsy creatures. These disasters greatly affected the scientific results hoped for from the expedition. Late in the evening the yaks were tied up to the line rope, which is fastened by pegs or tied to great tufts of grass, and to this rope all the animals are attached. Senerh, his boy, foolishly went too close to one of the semi-savage yaks, whose horn came in contact with one of the boy's ribs with such force that he was compelled to ride every day for a month, and was able to do no work. The country was now covered with grass and undulating hills, on which large herds of cattle were seen grazing. The people were friendly but quite on the alert, as a dreaded band of Golok was reported to be roving about, and there was no telling when or where they might pounce upon some herd and drive them off into some secluded valley, and thus get them away into their own country, which really lies south of the Yellow River. At last they came in sight of the Kokonor and camped by the lake. During the night there was a heavy fall of snow, which had the effect of making his boys move even more slowly than the notoriously slack Kansuite is in the habit of doing. Packing the animals next morning proved a difficult job, as the men were not used to the intense cold. Their caravan moved slowly, as yaks cannot travel more than eight or ten miles per day, especially if they are on a long journey. During the march Mr. Brooke shot a wild pony called a kyang, the meat of which proved to be very good eating. It is impossible to say whether these animals are ponies or mules; they seem to be quite a distinct species and do not interbreed with the Tibetan and Mongolian ponies that roam about the plains in a semi-wild state. He only heard of one instance of a hybrid Mongolian pony and wild kyang. They are quite distinct from any species of the horse, mule or donkey, having a mule's tail, and mane, nose and ears like a horse; they can be easily caught when they join a large herd of Mongolian ponies feeding on the plains. They are very fleet, however, and when feeding by themselves would be almost impossible of capture.

Lieutenant-Colonel Waddell, in his most valuable book, "Lhasa and its Mysteries,"* thus describes the kyang:—"Passing along under the flank of Chumolhari, we found that the apparently bare desert plain, as we traversed it,

* Murray.

was freely studded over with clumps of grass and weeds between the pebbles, for the plain was thickly strewn with loose pebbles and sandy gravel like the dried-up bed of a sea or lake; and this loose gravel was very trying to walk on, and for the transport animals, as it wore out their shoes and lamed them.

"Browsing on this scanty herbage, which curiously included many thistles, were hundreds of large wild asses, the kyang of the Tibetans, in troops of tens and twenties or more. At first we took them for detachments of Tibetan Cavalry, the wild horsemen of the Changtang, as they came galloping along in a whirlwind of dust, then executed a perfect wheel-round, then extended out in a line at regular intervals, and advanced again; and as if at the word of command reformed into close order and came to an instant halt. Several of them galloped towards us and stood looking at us, out of curiosity, as near as 300 yards away, and a few trotted through the lines of our baggage mules, doubtless recognising their family relationship. They are pretty animals, more like ponies than asses, and move with great grace. They are about the size and shape of zebras, but with better heads. Their general colour is a rich golden brown with jet black points and stripes. When I was in North-Western Tibet, evading the frontier guards, I have seen these colours form startling kaleidoscopic varieties of tints in the bright sunshine, at one time bright sandy yellow, almost white, changing to golden chestnut and deep black, giving the appearance of a caravan of black-coated men moving amongst light-coloured laden animals. The Tibetans say that these animals are untameable, but they do not look so very wild. I cannot help thinking that here, in the home of these wild asses, we have a great field for breeding mules for the Indian Army, the supply for which never can meet the demand; and to obtain these insufficient numbers we have yearly to ransack the whole world, sending agents to

Persia, Spain, Italy, China, Yunnan and America, at enormous cost.

"As we march on and on across this great plain, with nothing to relieve the dulness but these herds of roving kyang and the encircling hills beyond, the eye wearies of the stretches of loose gravel with its stunted tufts of withered grass, and the monotony of it all oppresses the spirits."

Several of these animals were found at Lhalu; they had been given as a present to the Dalai Lama, who had them fed and stalled there. Colonel Waddell got close enough to photograph them, and, later, two of them were caught by members of the Mission, to be as a present to the King. Colonel Waddell classifies the wild ass as *Equus hemionus*.*

Quite early in the afternoon Brooke and his party came to an old Tibetan fort or stock yard, into which they drove their yaks and ponies for the night, as the place was infested with robbers. Four Tibetans came about, whose appearance did not inspire confidence. They were particularly anxious to see Brooke's fire-arms. He had determined not to show them unless it was really necessary, knowing that a savage's awe of a gun is always greater before he knows anything about its mechanism. However, wishing to be civil, he let his visitors each handle one of the four guns he had with him. A fourth man tried to get hold of his Mauser pistol which, after his experience with the Tibetan near Tankar, Brooke always carried in his belt. Discovering the game in time and unfastening his Mauser from his belt, he commanded the men to hand back his rifles, which they evidently intended to make their own. As it happened there were no cartridges in the magazines, even if they had known how to use the rifles; anyhow, they quietly handed them back to the boy.

Next day on the march four horsemen tried to surprise

* "Lhasa and its Mysteries," page 484.

the caravan, but seeing there was quite a large party they did not press an attack. At evening the party again encamped early and Mr. Brooke went out shooting. He had not gone far before he discovered the four gentlemen they had met during the march, sneaking over a hill not far away, their four horses tied to tufts of grass close by. The worst of this country is that every one suspects every one else of being a thief. The traveller may be out shooting when suddenly he discovers that crawling along behind him, only a few hundred yards away, are several men, evidently on his track to see what he is about. This puts an end to the hunting expedition for that day, for he has not the slightest idea who his stalkers are, but infers from their behaviour that they would as soon take a shot at the strange hunter as they would at the natural game of the country. There is a distinct difference between the professional and amateur robber—the professional is deliberate and goes in for big hauls, attacking large herds and driving off a good number of cattle at each attack; the amateur picks off small caravans, appropriating whatever goods he may obtain for the benefit of his party, but seldom taking life, unless actually driven to it. Brooke returned to camp, and during the night was aroused by a terrible barking of dogs. Turning out of his warm sleeping bag, he found the men hard at work piling the grain bags in position to fortify the camp. They all worked hard getting the bags in place, but the howls of a pack of wolves came closer and closer, and presently the camp was surrounded. Fortunately the yaks and horses were securely tethered to the line ropes, and though they made strenuous efforts to escape they did not succeed in getting loose. A few volleys from the four rifles fired from behind the grain bags so surprised the wolves that they turned and fled, leaving some of their companions dead on the ground.

The next day the party had a good deal of difficulty in

crossing a river which was partly frozen, and got most of the baggage wet, which necessitated the delay of one day to dry the grain. They next crossed over a high pass about 11,000 feet above sea-level that divides the Kokonor from the Tsaidam. There was a good deal of snow on the pass, but they succeeded in getting over without incident. They finally arrived at a Mongolian encampment and were directed to the chief, Chinghiwang, who was camped a few days' march farther on; and there Brooke hoped to spend several days reorganising the caravan, changing his slow and tedious yak for camels before proceeding on his journey.

CHAPTER III.

ACROSS THE TSAIDAM AND ON TO LHASA.

THEY reached the lake of Dulan and camped on its grassy shore in a rich pasture land, where the only difficulty was in finding firewood, which had to be carried for a long distance. Mr. Brooke called on Chinghiwang, who was camped not far away. He found him living in a tent very similar to the other Mongolians on the plain, with very little to show that he was a Prince; indeed, a Scottish crofter's cottage would have been a palace to his bare little tent. A Mongolian's tent in this part of the country consists of a framework of wood, which comes down like the ribs of a boat; only turned upside down. These ribs are joined by a sort of trellis work, and the whole frame collapses, dividing into four sections when it is desired to move on to other grazing grounds. The roof was formed of a number of sticks resting on the wall, and all were tied to a ring of iron in the centre of the roof, which formed the chimney. The whole framework was then covered with felt or a coarse cloth made of yak's hair. In the centre was a raised stone fireplace bearing an iron frame, on which an argol fire was brightly burning, and with a pot of tea always on the boil. Through the chimney hole in the roof the smoke satisfactorily escaped, and these tents are really comfortable. From the walls of the chief's tent hung several old fuse guns and skins of butter, while on the floor, around the sides of the tent, were a number of Chinese skin boxes, on one of which was placed some Tibetan Scriptures, carefully wrapped in a cloth and bound between two boards, which formed the cover. These are never opened till a priest comes, when they are read for three days continuously with great ceremony and feasting.

The Prince had recently returned from Lhasa, and as the party sat around the fire, cross-legged, eating mien which had been boiled in milk (mien is vermicelli imported from China and is counted quite a delicacy by both the Mongolians and Tibetans), he told most vivid tales of the difficulties that had to be encountered on the way, especially at this time of the year. Mr. Brooke was assured that it would be impossible to make the journey with yak, as the passes would be deep in snow and they would not be able to procure fodder on the heights, and the yak were so slow it would be necessary to camp on the passes. He felt that the Prince was paving his way to secure a good price for the camels, which he was anxious to supply, and also to depreciate the value of the yaks, which he hoped to obtain in part payment for his camels. Brooke insisted that his yak could easily make the journey, as they were young and in good condition, and added that he had paid 14 taels apiece for them in order to secure first-class animals. After an hour's interview Brooke returned to his tent, still undecided as to what was really the best thing to do. The next day the Prince invited him again to his tent. He had prepared quite a banquet and invited a number of friends. They all sat round the fire cross-legged as before, and began the feast by drinking tea and eating tsamba. The second course was boiled mutton, of which every man seized a piece in his hand, gnawing it and smacking his lips in a most appreciative way. After the mutton, Chinese wine was offered, a beverage distilled from grain, and (if no water has been added during its long journey to the Mongolian tent) usually found to contain about 65 per cent. of alcohol, though the stronger it is the more these dwellers on the highlands appreciate it. The Prince again introduced the subject of camels and promised to sell Brooke some at a reasonable price, if he would not continue his journey to Lhasa. This suggestion Brooke would not entertain, and again asserted his intention of proceeding with his yaks. The Prince insisted that Brooke should wait a few days until his caravan of camels—which had been sent to Sining laden with hides, wool and butter, and were to bring back grain—should return; assuring him that it would not be more than a few days before they arrived. He stayed.

Meanwhile he made friends with some of the people, and especially with one old man, who was troubled with rheumatism, and whom, by the use of his galvanic battery, Brooke was able to relieve. In return the old man undertook to initiate his physician in the mystery of understanding the points of a good camel. His instructions came to this :—" Old camels are not valuable, as they will not stand the fatigue of a long journey ; their teeth are short and they cannot masticate the coarse grass of the highlands of Tibet. Their hump sags or droops, and they lack spring in their gait. A young camel is alert ; he is always on the look-out for food, and is more readily startled by a stranger or by such moving objects as he may see even at some distance from the road. His teeth are long, his hump is erect and he has a spring in his movement which is easily detected."

When the caravan returned the Prince brought over four of his poorest camels, which he offered to trade for Brooke's forty-two yak : three of his original caravan having died since crossing the partly frozen river on the other side of the pass. Brooke expressed indignation at this offer, and said he had come to the Prince believing him to be an honest man, who would not take advantage of a stranger, and he demonstrated the camels offered to be old and useless. The Prince replied that as sure as God was in Heaven he could not tell a lie, and repeated that the four animals he had brought were the pick of his flock.

He departed, taking the animals with him, but returned next day, bringing four better camels. Mr. Brooke told him that if he took camels at all he would need at least ten, and that he would accept the four now brought in exchange for his yaks on condition that the Prince sold him six others at a fair price, and that he should keep possession of his yak until the bargain was completed. The Prince readily agreed, and nine other camels were chosen from the pack, averaging about 35 taels apiece, while the four young ones were about 55 taels. When the animals were packed Brooke found that he had just sufficient to carry his outfit comfortably and allow his men to ride. The last camel to be brought was one with a tuft of hair out of its side. Brooke somehow fancied the camel, but the Prince tried in every way to prove that it was not a desirable animal for such a journey, stating that it ate its own wool when it was hungry, which accounted for the bare spot on its side. He shook his head, indicating that the animal was no good, but his features betrayed him, and Brooke did not believe a word he said; and later, sure enough, another Mongolian told him that the boys at Sining had pulled the hair off. The Prince finally raised the price to 65 taels, which Brooke paid, and found the animal to be the best of the bunch.

The day before they started on their long and tedious journey towards Lhasa the Prince dined with Brooke. As a delicacy a dish made from Bird's custard powder and sugar was provided. The Prince did not seem to relish this and ate but little; his son, however, seemed very fond of sugar, and helped himself liberally.

Late in the evening of the last day he expected to spend at Dulan, Senerh, his cook, in company with his Shanghai boy, came into his tent and demanded that each of the men be given 50 taels in advance; if not they would go back. Brooke ordered them out of the tent and said he would see them in the morning.

The Shanghai boy, who up to this time had proved faithful, now broke the news that during the days spent in camp the servants, having nothing better to do, had been talking over the difficulties and hardships which lay before them, and had all decided to turn back. This conspiracy made it impossible to start next day, so Brooke sent the useless ones out to gather firewood, and kept three of the best men in camp. These he made sign a paper promising they would go on, and himself agreed to send back 25 taels to each of their families. To this plan they all agreed, much to the disappointment of the useless ones, who were the originators of the disturbance and who had hoped to gain something for their trouble. On December 28th the party set forth, leaving the rebellious and worthless men with food sufficient at least to take them back to Chinese territory. Senerh, the Sining boy, repented and begged to be taken along. The interpreter who joined the party at Tankar, and had only been engaged as far as this place, was sent back with a horse and his full wages; while the other two only got half their wages, as they had been discontented, disobedient, and lazy throughout the whole of the journey.

They found the camels a great comfort after the clumsy, slow, brainless yaks, who were always dumping their loads off by running against each other, and moved so slowly that it made the march very tedious. The camels moved along at about four miles an hour, keeping up the pace day after day during the march; they were much less trouble to tie up at night and to find when out grazing on the plain.

During the first two days' march the road led through sandstone hills, which rose from 1,500 to 2,500 feet above the valleys; the southern slopes were covered with stunted pine trees; they saw evidence of bear, but no wild yak or *ovis ammum.* On the 30th of December they crossed quite a large river, flowing through rather a deep gorge which sheltered it from the sun. The ice was sufficiently thick to allow the camels to cross it. This river is reported to be fed from Dulan Nor, but this Dulan Nor is a different lake from the one on which the Prince was camped, and its waters were more saltish, and the earth by its shores contained much alkali, which hindered the grass from growing. They were now nearing the swamps of the Tsaidam proper. Wherever the banks of the river had cut to any depth through the hills and rising ground there was evidence of conglomerate rock beneath the red sandstone which appeared on the surface. Passing through the rolling lands they entered a large sandy plain, through which they travelled as far as Baram Tsaidam, where another important Mongolian Prince had his headquarters. They were guided thither by an escort and interpreter in one, sent with them by Chinghiwang as far as Baram Tsaidam, with orders there to hand the party over to the next chief. On reaching the place they had some little difficulty in finding the Mongolian tents, and when they did find them it was to discover that the plain on which they were encamped was almost destitute of grass, and this when Mr. Brooke's camels were much in need of resting a few days on good grazing ground. The ponies suffered even more than the camels, for there was a good deal of shrubbery about on which the latter seemed to feed freely. Occasionally one of the young camels, who thought he could find better fodder further away, would start off on a journey by himself, looking back every few minutes to see if others were following him; when he found that by this means he was unable to coax them far from camp he would return, and after remaining some little time would start out on a similar search.

The day after Mr. Brooke's arrival at Baram Tsaidam he was told that the Mongolian Chief did not live there, and that it was impossible to procure a local guide. Taking the interpreter he set out to search for someone in authority, and did manage to find the house of the Mongolian Prince; but only his brother and an old Lama were at home. The village was surrounded by a low mud wall enclosing a few mud huts, which were dark and dirty. The Lama was sitting on a large shelf in semi-darkness, a butter lamp burning close by. The visitors were shown in by the Prince's brother, who motioned them to a mat, where he immediately joined them. Brooke, through his interpreter, informed the Mongolian of his recent visit to the Dalai Lama and the Amban at Sining, who had given him a passport to cross Tibet into India; and explained that Chinghiwang had received him and given him a guide to this place, where he was assured that he would receive an escort to guide him on his way.

The Lama and the Mongolian talked together for some time, and then they excused themselves on the ground that their lord was not at home, and that they could do nothing in the matter. Brooke asked them to think the matter over, for though it was not his wish to make any trouble, yet if he journeyed alone and anything should happen by the way, the Chinese Government might hold them responsible, as it was important, he told them, for him to get right through to India.

After further discussion they said they would let him have an answer in the morning, and the next day the Mongolian came to his tent with a guide who was to escort him ten days west to a place called by the Chinese, Dachinpa, *i.e.*, great clear plain. They afterwards learned that the story of the Prince being away from home was quite a true one. The day before they arrived the Golok had swept down upon his herds, and had driven away 100 of his ponies, and the whole countryside had been called out to give chase. The Golok come into the country in large bands and break up into small parties, visiting the Mongolian encampments ostensibly as traders. When they have found out where the Mongolian herds are feeding and the strength of the camp, they collect together again, and drive off the herds into some valley, and by ways and means known to them, and in forced marches, usually succeed in getting the animals clean away. A band of these Golok in disguise visited Baram Tsaidam the day after the ponies above-mentioned had been driven off, no doubt with the idea of putting the Mongolians on the wrong track of their lost possessions. Brooke tried to photograph the bunch, but the moment they saw the camera they ran off, while one member of the party sprang toward the camera and covered the lens with his hand.

When the party was just ready to leave Baram Tsaidam, Senerh, the cook, declared that he must go back as he had run out of opium. After considerable discussion the man was allowed to go. To take an opium-smoker, who had no means of securing a daily supply of that drug, could only have led to a great deal of trouble, and the man would be worse than useless; so, from this place, Brooke went forward with only five Chinese. From Baram Tsaidam to Dachinpa they travelled westward over a desert covered with brushwood about six feet high, where the camels and ponies belonging to the Mongolians roamed in a semi-wild state. Their new Mongolian guide was a most religious man, repeating his prayers continually. When they pitched camp and the tea began to boil, he would seize the ladle used for serving out the tea, and, muttering his prayers, would throw a little of the tea out of the door three times, with considerable ceremony between each swing of the ladle; then proceeding to serve Brooke and afterwards the other members of the party.

On arriving at Dachinpa the party chose a good camping ground, where there was plenty of grass for the animals, and started off to find the old Mongolian Chief who was to provide the new escort. All day they rode and at last reached a hut where they found an old Mongolian at prayers. He motioned them to sit down, but otherwise continued to chant his prayers without looking up. He was dressed in a long dirty robe and squatted in front of a little stool, his Buddhist Bible in hand; he wore large round spectacles and his head was shaven but dirty. The guide, on entering the tent, solemnly bent his head until it touched the book, waited until the old Lama placed his hand upon his head, then rose and took his place by the fire. After a considerable time the priest dropped his voice into a low murmur, and they commenced to talk. The Mongolian Chief was not at all inclined to help Brooke, but after some little conversation he accepted a present from him in the form of a tin of Bryant and May's matches. With these the old man seemed greatly delighted, as he had never seen "self-giving fire," as he called the matches, before, and he played about with them like a child. He was a fierce, fat-looking old man, much like the imagined ogre of nursery days. A large pot containing two sheep's heads was boiling on the fire, and around the tents hung quarters of frozen mutton and rolls of suet, also an old gun carefully wrapped up in cloth; just behind him were a number of young goats, tethered by strings. Most of these had light blue hair, dainty little beards, and were really pretty creatures.

Eventually the old Mongolian consented to send as guide his own son, a fine-looking boy, who was to escort the party as far as Naichi, where they were to get another guide to take them on to Nagchuka. Naichi was reported to be ten days south of Dachinpa.

After bidding farewell to the old Lama, who held the rank

of local chief, they started out to retrace their steps to their own camp. In some way the guide seemed to have lost his bearings, and after travelling some time did not come out on the path which they had been told they should find. The new guide, of course, was not to join them until next morning. Brooke, feeling the guide was going in the wrong direction, told his boy to follow him and they struck off across the plains in what he believed to be the direction of the camp. They travelled in this manner due east until they reached the river upon which they were camped; here they rested and let the horses drink, when the boy suddenly cried out, "Look over there, Master, you say you don't believe in the devil; look at that." Brooke looked round and saw a very curious phenomenon, similar to the scene which Mr. H. Savage Landor describes having seen in the Himalayas only in a more remarkable form than that seen by Brooke on this occasion. It was the planet Mars having a kind of game of hide-and-seek with the other stars, a very extraordinary sight, for the planet leaped up to an angle of 30 degrees, then down to the right, and disappeared; then up again at a tangent, now glowing bright like an electric arc lamp, now like a little star. Brooke and his boy stood and gazed in sheer amazement. Asked if he was frightened, all the boy said was, "I hope it doesn't come closer, Master." Brooke told him that he would explain about it to him later, but never got the boy to believe any natural explanation. The planet at that hour was just rising, and, when they first saw it, was behind a mountain; but the different densities in the atmosphere reflected it in various directions, according to the atmospheric power of refraction constantly changing between them and the planet.

After this experience Brooke and his boy travelled up the river, which was at this place quite a foaming torrent. The boy grumbled very much, and persisted that they were going in the wrong direction. At daybreak they found themselves within two miles from the camp, which they could see from the summit of a little hill on which they then stood, and reached it at 7 a.m.

The guide and camel driver did not arrive till 2 o'clock that afternoon, having gone many miles out of their way.

Their new guide turned up in the evening, and on January 27th they started for Naichi.

The first day they had a long march across an arid plain, intermittent with sand, quartz, volcanic rock and shingle, which was quite destitute of any kind of vegetation. They crossed over a small pass called Kokstom, which was quite difficult for camels to travel over because of the narrowness of the road. This pass could easily be avoided by blasting away a little of the rock in the gorge through which the river flows. They succeeded in making the pass without any accident, though it quite frequently happens that a camel making a false step is thrown over the cliff and dashed to pieces on the rocks in the gorge below.

They at last reached a Mongol encampment at Naichi in a terrific dust storm, and camped there.

It was a barren place, where there was little grass or fuel with which to build a fire.

The storm calmed down, their strange-looking tent attracted the Mongols, and about a dozen of them came over to call.

They chatted about the journey to Nagchuka, and asked a large sum to guide the party thither. Brooke offered 50 taels, saying that he would not give a farthing more; so they went away saying as usual that they would consult their Buddha about it, and let him know in the morning.

The natives told Brooke about some wild yak that were in the mountains near by, and next day, guided by an old Mongol, he started out to hunt them. Climbing a precipitous mountain, the granite walls of which towered above the camp, he approached the top with great care, as the creatures are often to be seen grazing under the summit on the opposite side. On this occasion, however, they were not there, and the wind blew a gale, so that it was difficult work to make way round some of the cliffs without being blown off, and only those who have stood on some of these high peaks on the roof of the world really know what a gale in Tibet means. By resting his telescope on a rock and searching the valley and further mountain side Brooke was able to pick out fifteen yaks grazing on the slopes at the other end of the valley. He and his party at once set out, and for four hours scrambled over rocks and boulders, keeping under cover that they might not be sighted by their game. On reaching a grassy knoll, which Brooke decided was near where he had seen the brutes feeding, they stopped to rest and look carefully about. The old Mongol hunter took out his rosary, muttered something, counted his beads by fives, and twisting the beads put them to his lips. This was repeated five times, while Brooke sat almost frozen in the piercing wind. At last the old prophet predicted a successful ending to their arduous stalks, but the prophecy had yet to be fulfilled, so they crept on carefully, and as they reached the top of the knoll they heard stones rattling and a great yak came tearing up the other side to meet them. When he was within 200 yards Brooke let him have it just behind the shoulder. The yak turned down the valley a short distance, then stumbled and fell over a granite rock. where they found him dead.

The poor old yaks have none of the quick instinct of wild animals generally ; they like to have a good look at the hunter before they make any attempt to get away, which may be due to the fact that they are seldom hunted by the Tibetan or Mongol. When once they do show the white flag they can make pretty good time, for a short distance at least.

On returning to camp Brooke was informed that a Mongol would escort him to Nagchuka, if two camels were added to the 50 taels offered by the foreigner.

There seemed no way out of it, and as it was winter time and the passes would be difficult, Brooke agreed to the demand on condition that the guide led them safely through the desolate track of country that lay before them, and to the famous monastery many days to the south.

So on March 6th they left Naichi, and, after travelling only thirty li (ten miles) the first day, had to pitch their tent in a terrific storm, which almost tore it to pieces, and would have done so had they not taken it down, and waited till the storm abated a little.

The following day they crossed over a small pass 15,000 feet above sea-level and came down into the valley of the Dichu, or Drichu. The Dri River flows past Batang, and is known below that point as the Chinshachiang (river of golden sand); but, after it has been joined by a number of tributaries between Batang and Hsuchowfu, is known after Hsuchowfu as the Yangtzechiang, or Yantze River. But there is no doubt that the Dichu, or Dri River, is the main tributary of the Yangtze, which is fed from the famous chain of lakes surrounding the west Kokochili range. These lakes are over 16,000 feet above sea-level, as stated by Captain Wellby and Dr. Sven Hedin.

Where Brooke crossed the Dichu the valley was about four miles wide, but only inhabited by wild beasts. His men were stricken with mountain sickness, and thought they were going to die; the Shanghai boy gave up entirely, and, letting his horse go, lay down on a sand hill in utter despair. Brooke had to set him on his horse, but he fell helplessly off. Placed on the pony anew with the promise of a good thrashing if he fell off, the boy succeeded in sticking to his pony, but Brooke knew from experience that when a Chinaman makes up his mind that he is going to die he is the most helpless object imaginable.

The following day they marched up the valley in a heavy snowstorm and camped in two feet of snow, with not a blade of grass for the poor animals, who had found it heavy work tramping through the deep snow all day.

In the morning it was still snowing and they were in absolute misery; the Chinese refused to turn out of their fur sleeping bags; there was not a stick of fuel anywhere to cook a bite of food or heat a drop of water.

Brooke pulled them out of bed, however, to make them pack the camels. The old guide picked out his two camels, or the two he would like to have had, and started toward home; but Brooke noticed him in time and made him bring them back.

Six of the animals wandered off and Brooke had to go after them himself, as the men all refused to do anything.

On bringing the animals back Brooke again pulled his boys out of their beds, and finally they got started. That night they found a camping place where the snow was not so deep, and the animals were able to scratch up a little grass.

They marched all the next day over a plain; the wind kept gaining in force all the morning until 11 a.m. The gale was running at fifty or sixty miles per hour, sweeping the sand and snow before it in a great cloud, even lifting small pebbles and lashing them against their faces. Great care was needed in holding the caravan together and in keeping their bearings, for if they got separated for fifty yards they would be doomed, as the trail was completely obliterated in places, and it was impossible to see or even hear a call for fifty yards. The temperature was 5 degrees below zero

YAK CARAVAN ON MARCH.

at 9 a.m., and with such a gale blowing it felt more like 20 degrees below zero.

To keep the party together the animals were all attached by a line; it was impossible to do more than a rough tracing of the route followed that day.

They camped that night in the shelter of a sand hill. Brooke went out in search of a grass plot, on which the animals might find something to eat, for where their camp was there was nothing but drifting sand. While out on this quest his fur cap was blown away and carried off like a balloon; it fell on a frozen pond, he pursued it, and on stepping on the ice he was swept to the other side as if he were on an ice sled. His cap turned on its edge and went racing along like a miniature bicycle, and if it had not caught in a bush about a mile further on, it is not likely he would ever have seen it again.

In this country it was with the greatest difficulty the tent was erected, for the pegs were useless in the loose sand, and the grain bags were used to hold the sides of the tent down; they were also made use of as snubbing posts for the tent ropes. If the party was roughing it, so were the animals. The search for fodder was fruitless, and the party had to share with them some of the grain they were carrying, but as there was yet a long journey before them it had to be doled out very carefully.

In the morning it was much calmer, and they got under way early. By 9 o'clock it commenced to blow again, as it did almost every day of the journey across this barren expanse. The camels seemed to know that it was worse on before, and again and again tried to turn back. They were getting thinner day by day, and it was really wonderful how they kept up in such weather with so little to eat. Indeed, they proved themselves to be much more hardy than is generally supposed, and not only able to stand the heat on sandy plains, but also to endure the intense cold, without any protection from the fierce blasts that prevail in such elevated regions.

One of the men became so ill that the caravan had to be stopped for three days. On March 17th they packed him up in his bedding and tied him on a camel. He was then still very ill, but was soon all right again.

The wonderful thing about this bleak, barren country is that although the wind is driving at from fifteen to forty miles an hour there is a clear blue sky, if the dust will allow it to be seen.

They met a Mongol caravan with 800 camels on their way to China; Li, who was still ill, was sent back with them. Brooke paid him his wages and gave him 25 taels for the expense of the return journey, which caused a murmur in his camp, for they said, "Why give a sick man 25 taels to return?" The Tibetan and Chinese custom is to leave any person who shall fall by the wayside to die or recover, as the gods may design, and in such a cruel country as this to die is the only fate of any one dropping out of a caravan.

They crossed the Dungbure, which is 16,700 feet above the sea, with little delay, commencing their march at 8 a.m. and pitching camp at 4 p.m. They experienced little difficulty, although this is the highest pass on the journey between Sining and Lhasa. On the top was the usual obo or pile of stones, in which were erected poles, and to these were attached prayer flags. Many of them hung in rags from their constant flapping in the breeze.

The top of the pass was quite flat. On the south side, some distance from the top, Brooke found hot springs gushing out of the frozen earth. They also caught several small fish, which were identically the same as some secured at Baram Tsaidam. The formation of the Dungbure range was found to be similar to that surrounding the Tsaidam, *i.e.*, red sandstone over a very hard limestone conglomerate, only in addition there were several volcanic spurs in sight, their jagged outline giving even a more barren aspect than the sloping sandstone.

At about 16,000 feet above sea-level they sighted the first Tibetan tent, pitched in a sheltered nook, and some miles further on there was a number of tents, and hundreds of sheep and yak grazing on the slopes.

The people were ragged and unkempt, with long, shaggy hair hanging down their backs; the women were very small, and the men not over 5 feet 6 inches in height. They belonged to Egla tribe, and live the whole year round at an altitude of from 14,000 to 16,000 feet above the sea-level, which may account for their low stature. They are said to be brigands, but Brooke found those whom he met quietly attending to their own herds. In the country directly south he found a great deal of granite containing large crystals of felspar several inches in length, and the large jagged boulders reminded him of some parts of Scotland.

Brooke's old horse at last gave in, and had to be left on the road; he was given to a Tibetan, who promised to care for him if he survived.

They reached the valley of Nagchuka on April 10th and found the people friendly. There were robbers roaming about who were supposed to come from a district six marches to the east; one Mongolian caravan had lost forty horses.

While they were camped in a pleasant place in good pastures, an old Lama called and warned Brooke that if he proceeded two days further south he would be stopped at the monastery there, but that if he liked he could give him a guide who would take him to Gyantse by a road which led all the way through the country of the Tashi Lamas, who were friendly to the English. Brooke feared the old man was trying to deceive him, and insisted on going on to Nagchuka Comba.

They moved on next day and arrived at the borders of the territory directly governed from Lhasa, where they camped. In the evening a number of horsemen rode up with two well-dressed Tibetans in the party. They all dismounted close to his tent. Two Turkish rugs were spread on the ground for them to sit on. Brooke walked over to them but was not invited to join the party, so he invited them over to his tent. They refused his invitation but beckoned him to be seated, and he sat. They asked him where he was bound for, and after he told them he was bound for India he learned that the two guests referred to were representatives of the Lhasa Government; one was a Lama and the other a District Magistrate, both from the monastery at Nagchuka.

The Magistrate was a pleasant looking man, wearing a beautiful turquoise ear-ring set in gold; the ring was about four inches long. His hair was parted in the middle, and a neat plait bordered the hair on the forehead. His pigtail was neatly wound on the top of his head. He wore a Mandarin's fur cap, a blue silk hood and velvet boots, and generally his dress was very similar to that of a Chinese Mandarin.

The Lama who sat opposite was anything but pleasant; his little eyes showed a keen, cruel look, and his head was clean shaved. He wore a Lama's garb that was quite smart looking, and he was really of higher rank than the Magistrate.

A gigantic Tibetan stood beside them who wore a look as if he might be the chief executioner; he was dressed in a roomy blue cloak, bordered and lined with leopard skin.

The Magistrate and Lama stated that, as this road on which Brooke was travelling led to Lhasa, the party must proceed no further until they had received permission from the "Holy City."

On leaving they promised a definite direction next morning, which meant that they were going to discuss the matter in the monastery; and after a friendly farewell they left the camp.

CHAPTER IV.

HOW HE WAS TURNED BACK.

AFTER the formal fashion associated with the state visits of potentates on alien soil, Mr. Brooke that evening returned his visitors' call, taking each of them a present. One received a cheap watch and the other a Ningsha rug. The watch caused some jealousy, as they both wanted it.

At 10 o'clock next day no reply had come as to their decision, and the interpreter was sent up to the monastery to find out what had caused the delay. He returned without an answer, so the order was given to pack the camels. This was no sooner done than a party of Tibetans came along and unpacked them again. Mr. Brooke then went up to the monastery himself to find out why the Lama and the Magistrate had not sent word as promised. He was told that they were waiting for another Mongol Prince to come and deliberate with them. His hosts were quite civil and asked the foreign visitor to be seated. While they talked, a tall man with black whiskers, sharp eyes, and rather a hooked nose, came in. They all bowed low as he entered. His bearing and looks bore evidence that he was not only a man of authority, but also a man of firmness of character and quiet decision.

The conversation of the previous day was all repeated, and the answer again was "Wait a little," with which Brooke had to depart content. At 3 o'clock in the afternoon, Lama and Magistrate appeared at the tent, bringing presents consisting of butter, flour and rice. These Brooke refused to accept until he had got an answer, and was told that he "must not go south to Lhasa but west and then to Gyantse." To this Brooke agreed, seeing that they were most emphatic on the point.

From this place the old guide from Naichi now went back, getting 65 taels and one camel as his wages. One of the boys went back with him, so that, of the original party, only the Shanghai boy, the cook from Sining, and Brooke himself were left.

They were just preparing to start when a caravan arrived from Sining, conveying two Chinese Mandarins to Lhasa. Their caravan consisted of 100 camels and 50 horsemen. They pitched their tent near by, so Brooke's party did not start that day, as the guide was afraid to join them until the Mandarins passed on.

The Chinese party cleared out the next morning, and Brooke struck camp a little later. The guide took them round by a very rough road on which they lost one camel, and now they entered a thickly populated district, where they were soon followed by small bodies of horsemen.

The country consisted of wide valleys, covered with good grass, on which large flocks of sheep and cattle were grazing. After travelling about 300 li (between forty and fifty miles), Brooke and his party found themselves surrounded by about 100 Tibetan horsemen, riding long-haired, tough little ponies. They pitched their tents all round Brooke's camp, but were quite civil.

Next morning, when Mr. Brooke began packing his camels, two of the Tibetans came forward and said they had been sent from Nagchuka Comba to stop them until they had heard from Lhasa. Brooke paid no attention to them and continued to pack, when some of the horsemen seized Senerh, the cook, by the arm, and so frightened him that he sat down and refused to help. Brooke judged it prudent to halt.

After waiting here for six days, when I suppose the gods must have sent the Tibetans a wireless message, Brooke was definitely informed that he must go back.

It seemed to be a deadlock. Mr. Brooke and his party were completely outnumbered and to resist would have been fatal; and now he wished that he had taken the old Lama's advice, or had got away before the Chinese caravan came along.

There was nothing else for it now but gracefully to give in and try in some other way to surmount the difficulty later; but the thought of having to traverse the barren track of country with thin and worn-out camels was not a very encouraging prospect, and the greatest disappointment of all was that the cherished hope of reaching the headwaters of the Brahmaputra seemed doomed, and that after overcoming so many obstacles. Brooke's one crumb of comfort was that his Tibetan guide from Nagchuka said that he would stick to him as he had received 25 taels in advance.

A body of sixteen horsemen escorted Mr. Brooke over the Tangla Pass, where they left him, and returned to Nagchuka. After continuing another day's journey north, he turned west, hoping to be able to evade the guarded district, and once more made his way south; but after travelling 200 li he was stopped again. He now went up the bank of the Dichu, and crossed the Dungbure range by a small road on the other side of the range; there was difficulty in finding the main road, but finally this was hit on. Overtaking a return caravan from Lhasa, he made friends with the Mongolians in charge, who agreed to carry part of his baggage, as his camels were almost worn out.

Brooke was able to shoot some game each day, quite sufficient, to their great delight, to keep his party in meat. He had many lonely tramps after bear, wild yak and other game that made its appearance along their line of march.

One by one his camels died off, for the long journey and

poor grazing, together with the intense cold on the passes, had made them very weak.

Mr. Brooke writes as follows about these losses :—" I have not said much about losing the animals, to me it is all too sad to think of again. I regret having lost even the rudest spitting camel, and it was a great grief to me to see the brave old beasts that had stuck to me, till so near the end of my journey, fall out of the ranks. Our three young camels are

WOMEN WEAVING TIBETAN CLOTH.

still strong, but only one of them is in really good condition ; he now has to carry a heavy load to help the others. We have still four of the original horses taken from Tankar, but I was always doubtful whether Senerh would ever get his back to China again. He had been ailing very much of late, but was a splendid dear little beast whose pluck might have saved him ; but five days before reaching the Mongol pasture lands he began to give in, and could scarcely keep up to the caravan.

At last he stopped, shut his eyes, his whole body began to quiver, and only with a great effort would he keep firm on his four wiry, weary little legs. Taking the saddle off and wrapping a rug around him, we got him a mile farther, where there was good grass. I kissed his soft little nose and there we left him. I hope he died not too cruelly. I had shot all the other animals before leaving them, but this one I thought might live. I feel as though I would rather have lost both my Chinamen, considering how inconsistent, unfeeling and cowardly they both were, compared with this fine little beast, which had carried a man for six months without either baulking, biting or kicking, his ears always talking and telling us how he hoped for grass and rest, a hope that only left him when his body refused to obey his brave little heart. My boy's black pony was another of the same stamp, but he, thank God, reached a nice camp, where a Mongolian agreed to look after him and bring him to Sining in the autumn."

One day they saw some antelope, and Brooke went after them, but the snow blindness from which he had been suffering since crossing the high passes still troubled him, and he did not succeed in getting any of them. He dropped out of the caravan to follow them up, leaving his boy to hold his horse. When he returned, they had both disappeared, and he walked 35 li and still could not find the camp. Finally he found an old Mongol, who took him on his camel to the place where the caravan had pitched for the night.

It was weary work tramping back over the same road by which they had travelled south so full of anticipation but two months before. On May 22nd, they found Li, who had been sent back sick, and also his companion. They had put up for two months in a little hut kept by an old Chinaman, who had a Mongolian wife. The coolie now joined the caravan. He would have left the old man without giving him anything for keeping him all this time, but Brooke, finding this out, gave the host one of the camels which was badly in need of a rest and could not have gone much further, together with 10 taels of silver. After all, the boy said the old man had saved his life.

The caravan kept together as far as the Kokonor, where part of it went to Tankar. The other part went north, and Brooke continued with them through a salty desert, where the salt was in thick cakes on the ground. The path was marked by slabs of this salt which was raised on end. It is

MR. BROOKE WITH THE CHINESE CARAVAN.

from this locality that a great deal of the salt that supplies Kamsu is exported, being carried out by large caravans of yak and camels.

This salt plain was about twenty miles broad; of course, neither water nor grass was to be found on the march. Another forty miles north brought them to a large lake with thousands of geese and ducks floating about on it, and here they camped. The weather was quite warm now, and the lake would soon be swarming with young ducks and goslings and many other kinds of water fowl. Mr. Brooke wanted to shoot some of them, but the old Mongolian said no; it was a pity to shoot them now, when they were nesting.

These Mongolians are a strange people; they are kind to animals, are rather averse to stealing, are extremely religious, believe it is wrong to tell a lie, and yet are always indulging in that habit.

After another four days' march the party reached the home of the old Mongolian with whom they had been travelling. His daughter was the first to meet him, and ran the last 100 yards, throwing her arms around his neck. The mother did not trouble to dismount from her camel to greet her step daughter. When they got to the tent the Mongol's old sister came out and kissed her brother's hand again and again while tears of joy rolled down her cheeks. "A funny custom to cry at meeting one's brother," grunted the Chinaman from Sining. The old woman had heard that her brother had been killed, and the joy at seeing him again brought the tears to her eyes.

On the hills and mountains in the neighbourhood was to be found plenty of *ovis ammum* and wild ponies. Mr. Brooke shot one very fine specimen. His eyes were still troubling him, or he might have bagged more.

After a great deal of discussion and bargaining with the people of the district, he secured four good horses in exchange for his few surviving and worn-out camels. The catching of the ponies was the occasion of much merriment. The people from the surrounding tents were all invited and men and women turned out. After the ceremony of tea-drinking was over, the herd was surrounded and driven up near the camp; then by means of a long rope which was encircled around the bunch, the ponies were crowded together and one by one caught and tethered to a line pegged out for the purpose.

They succeeded in catching all but one little red brute,

which Brooke had set his heart on, and which jumped the line and broke through the circle and got away. They kept the rest tied up, but this one galloped about until he got tired, then came in and stood with the others. Later they succeeded in getting the rope round him, and a clever little horseman threw a noose over his nose and got hold of him.

After patting and quieting him for an hour, they announced that he was ready to be ridden. He had never before had

THE NAICHI GUIDE WAITING FOR HIS KETTLE TO BOIL.

any one on his back and they would not put on a saddle, so Mr. Brooke mounted bare-backed. As soon as the pony felt the weight of his rider he shot into the air, his neck down and his back arched; at the third buck he succeeded in dislodging his rider. A bridle and saddle were now brought, and when all was ready Brooke again mounted, while an interested crowd looked on. The pony made six successive bucks, then galloped off. After about a three-mile gallop the pony was brought to a walk, and again tried to buck, bounding into the air, then bucking to the ground, and this he repeated twelve times. At the twelfth plunge Brooke went off, but as the long tethering rope was dragged rapidly through his hand he gripped it tight at the knot, and brought the animal down.

Remounting immediately, he put off at another gallop, and this time brought the pony home quite tame.

Finally they got all the ponies fitted out with bridles and pack saddles and made a start, but the ponies, used to freedom and new to the business of carrying a load, were, to say the least, frisky.

The boy Senerh was to ride one animal and lead the pack animals, which were all attached by a leading rope. He tied his little bundle, which a Chinaman always carries when on the road, to the back of the saddle, and mounted, but when the pony felt this bundle dangling at his side he began to kick and buck, and sent the boy sprawling on the ground; the animals all stampeded, and the baggage was scattered all over the plain.

They succeeded in surrounding the ponies again, and with much difficulty got reloaded and made a fresh start, taking this time a Mongolian guide and horseman. After two days' march over the mountain range they arrived at Uchumi, a broad valley where Mongol flocks were grazing on the plains. Large packs of wolves were prowling about and the natives kept ferocious dogs to guard the flocks. Wild camels were seen, but they could only be distinguished by being longer in the legs and slimmer in the body than the tame ones.

The first town they reached was Chichen, 130 li north-east by east from Tamar; here they found trees, plenty of grass and fresh vegetables. The latter were most welcome to men who for several months had been compelled to abstain from a vegetable diet.

They passed on to Suchow, which is a well-sized walled city, noted for its giant donkeys and mules; some of the donkeys reach twelve hands and the mules fifteen hands high. Mr. Brooke took his two Chinese servants with him to a restaurant, and they all enjoyed a good Chinese meal—meat, fish, buttered eggs, chicken with plenty of good rice, all cooked in Chinese fashion. A red wine made from dates served to wash them down, and the two servants, at least, considered that they had reached civilisation at last, although this is one of the places to which criminals are banished, and it is looked upon by the inhabitants of most of the other provinces as being the end of the earth. Kouwai, that is, "outside of the mouth of China," they call it.

The restaurant was the smartest one in Suchow, and the road to it led down a little filthy narrow street. The entrance led through the kitchen, where two cooks were busily at work over four hot charcoal fires, which burnt in a large mud range built in a semi-circle and all in one piece.

A little farther on they passed through a courtyard, filled with ducks and chickens, which wandered about amidst heaps of carrots and cabbages, all awaiting their turn to be prepared for the pot. After treading their way across this dirty courtyard, with some care, lest they should step on a cabbage leaf and find themselves sitting on the dirty cobble stones, they entered a large room, at the farther end of which they found a party of well-dressed Chinese. Some sat around a table drinking wine, while others reclined on benches sucking their opium pipes, all awaiting their dinner which was being prepared in the kitchen at the entrance of the inn.

This is the Ritz or Carlton of Suchow, and the best Chinese dinner put up in the place would consist of eight or ten courses, and for a table of eight persons, wine included, would cost about ten shillings for the whole party.

On returning to his inn Brooke found that Father Assance had just called, so he went over and spent a very pleasant evening with this priest, who was the only foreigner in the place, his sole companion a Chinese priest; yet priests like Father Assance are so wrapped up in their work that they never feel lonely and never look forward to seeing the land of their birth again, but live and die with their converts.

Brooke engaged carts to carry the baggage to Lanchow, twenty-one stages to the south-east. He travelled with them as far as Kanchow, seven stages, then went south, across grass country, where he found large herds of cattle grazing, but the people were not friendly. Gold was being washed in the river beds by Mohammedans. On the passes and slopes he found plenty of wild flowers, and finally reached Sining on July 1st, where he found Mr. and Mrs. Ridley, who again gave him a hearty welcome to their home. After a week's rest he continued his journey to Lanchow, where he found his carts and baggage waiting for him. He spent a few days at the China Inland Mission with Mr. and Mrs. Andrews, whom he found exceedingly kind and hospitable, even though he could not see eye to eye with them on religious subjects.

Mr. Brooke's impression of missions was that both the Protestants and Roman Catholics were doing good work in China, and he wrote :—

"To criticise the missionary work in China as a whole would be unfair and ungrateful of any traveller, for he receives endless help everywhere from these good people. The traveller from his short stay in the country may be unable always to see eye to eye with them, but what they do they believe to be for the best interests of the cause they represent.

"More organisation would appear to be needed in some directions. What great things might be accomplished if England would carry on mission work with as much enthusiasm as she carries on a war or builds battleships."

From Lanchow he took mules viâ Tsinchow, and passing

through a rough rocky country joined the Kialing River at Peishuikiang, the most northerly point to which boats come, which is 250 miles north of Chungking. The upper reaches of this river are only navigable in the flood season, and to Peishui boats come for wool, hides and herbs, which are brought from Kansu by mule. After the long journey on foot and horseback, Brooke found it very pleasant to be once more in a Chinese junk, and to be hurled over the rapids and through great gorges where the river had cut its bed in the limestone rocks, and rank foliage overhung the banks.

KANSU GIRLS NEAR SINING.

He was rapidly carried on down through the cultivated lands of Sechuan, where everything was teeming with life and excitement. When passing through Kwangyuen he called at the Mission Station and found two English lady missionaries at work, attending to a crowd of patients who had gathered to be treated for various ailments so common to the Chinese, and was greatly interested with the work being carried on by these women in their lonely station.

He next reached Paoning, where he called on Bishop Cassels and spent some pleasant hours with the Bishop, of whose work he speaks in the highest terms, as he does also of the medical work which is carried on at Paoning by Dr. Elliott.

Passing rapidly down the river, for it was in high flood, in six days he reached Chungking, which he describes as a dirty city, into which he had to climb up a long stone staircase by the river side before entering the gates. The roads are cut out of the solid rock and the city is perched on the side of the same.

At Chungking Dr. Wolfendale, of the London Mission, kindly entertained Brooke, who found him and his colleagues most pleasant people. While in Chungking he met most of the missionaries stationed there, and gave a lecture on his experiences in Tibet.

From here he hired another boat to Ichang. I met him first at Wanhsien on his way down and again at Ichang a little later.

He was then on his way to Japan and Corea as set forth in the introductory chapter. With that journey we are not concerned, and we will continue our story from Hankow, where he and Mr. Meares started together on that long, last journey which cost him his life.

I have written this outline of Mr. Brooke's Tibetan journey from a report he sent home, and hope that these notes will at least show the bravery, determination and character of the man, who, for the sake of science, left home and comforts, and endured hardship and danger without a murmur or complaint.

How much more should we, who believing that God has called us to go to the uttermost parts of the world, carrying with us the everlasting Gospel of Peace on earth and Goodwill toward men, be ready to suffer all things for His Name's sake.

CHAPTER V.

HANKOW TO CHENTU.

IT was from Hankow that Brooke and Meares actually started on their journey. After spending some days collecting a few remaining necessaries and securing another servant, the latter started off at daybreak, January 1, 1908, by one of the little river steamers that runs up to Ichang, in order to hire a house-boat to take them up the river as far as Chungching. Brooke stayed behind at Hankow to draw some money from the bank, and also to purchase a few more things when the shops opened after the New Year holiday.

On arriving at Ichang, Meares soon secured a comfortable little house-boat, the captain of which agreed to take them to Chungching in twenty-one days for 100 taels, or about £15. It was a more difficult matter to satisfy the Englishmen in charge of the customs. At first the officials insisted upon their producing receipted bills for all their instruments, cameras, etc.; but, as our travellers had not these bills with them, it was finally agreed to accept their statement that they had purchased them in Shanghai for their own use. The officials insisted, however, on their having a permit, for their arms and ammunition, from the Viceroy of the Province. They went round to see if the British Consul could help them in obtaining this, but he had gone off on a shooting trip and had left no one to act in his absence. This left them in rather a hole; but, on their calling on the officer in command of the gunboat, he kindly telegraphed to the Viceroy, and after some days' delay they finally got started.

Having a small boat they only had a crew of twenty men; some of the larger junks have crews of over 100 men. The junks are propelled, when crossing the river, by oars and sweeps, and if the wind is favourable they spread large sails

C. H. MEARES AS HE LEFT HANKOW, JAN. 1, 1908.

which carry them along at a rapid rate. Wherever the banks allow, they are towed up by gangs of trackers, harnessed to the end of a long rope made of plaited strips of bamboo. These ropes are wonderfully strong, and they need to be, for the weight of a heavily-laden junk at the end of a rope half a milo long in a rushing current is tremendous, and often one may see a large gang of trackers on all fours, hanging on with their hands as well as their feet, just holding their own or advancing an inch at a time.

After leaving Ichang the river in many places is hemmed in by huge cliffs more than 2,000 feet high on both sides, and high up on the face of these cliffs a tiny path has been cut out, along which the trackers crawl. This is very dangerous work, for, if the junks swerve off into the current, the men are jerked from their precarious foothold into the river, hundreds of feet below. There are several bad rapids where the river comes down in a swirling flood full of whirlpools. In these places there are hundreds of extra trackers, who make a bargain to haul the junks through. If the ropes do not break all is well, but if there is a flaw in the rope, and it breaks at a critical moment, the junk is swept away and dashed to pieces on the sharp rocks. Our travellers were unusually fortunate, and came through all the rapids without losing a rope, and tied up at Wanhsien to give the trackers a holiday for the Chinese New Year.

Wanhsien is a busy town. A British cruiser was stationed there. Not far from the city there are some interesting deposits of the bones of antidiluvian animals. These were being dug up by the Chinese and sold for medicine on the streets of Wanhsien.

On his way down Brooke spent two days trying to get some of these bones as specimens, but could not succeed in getting any complete parts, such as a leg or a skull or a large section of the vertebrae. The teeth, parts of the jaw and sections of the legs which he saw went to prove that the animal must have been very large, but he could not make out what it could have been. The Chinese were digging all about the place, and had already carried away most of the

ICHANG, WHERE MR. MEARES HIRED THE BOAT FOR THE RIVER JOURNEY.

section to various parts of China, for these mysterious bones commanded a high price as medicine.

Such things as bears' feet and heads for rheumatism and stiff joints, deers' horns and sinews for the weakness in men, are among the chief remedies of the Chinese quack, and you will hear him crying out on the streets, as he offers these medicines for sale, that there is nothing like them for a weak or sore back, and all the other ailments that the Chinese so frequently suffer from.

Chungking is situated at the junction of two rivers—the Kialing, which flows from the north, and here joins its water with that of the Yangtze, that great river which finds its source on the roof of the world, nearly 2,000 miles north-west of here.

This city, therefore, is wedge-shaped, and built on the side of a hill which at its highest point is quite 500 feet; and the widest part between the two rivers is not more than two miles, so that the houses are built on stone abutments, one above the other, like great steps in a staircase. There is no difficulty about the foundation, as that is of solid red sandstone. The streets are narrow, and are really one continuous staircase. They are kept in a continual condition of slush by the water carriers, for all the water consumed by half a million people has to be carried from the riverside in buckets suspended from a carrying pole. As the carriers wend their way up the long line of stone steps there is naturally a constant splash from the buckets. To make it worse, Chungking is like London, nearly always enveloped in fog, so that there is little chance of the streets ever getting dried up!

Although Brooke describes it as the most dismal city he has ever seen, yet it is a very important commercial centre. It is the most westerly open port in China and has a foreign community of several hundred people, including the Maritime Customs and Post Office staff, the Bluejackets and the

Missionaries. The British have three gunboats, the French two, and the Germans have one, and are expecting another soon; while the Japanese are to send up two. Chungking has many waterways as well as overland routes, by which the various imports and exports are conveyed to and fro.

Our travellers spent two days making preparations for their 256-mile march to Chentu, and all their things had to be repacked into packets of 50 lbs. each, two bundles of which were carried by a coolie, one on each end of the springing pole which the Chinese use for the purpose.

It was a bright, crisp, sunny February morning when the caravan wound round out of the north gate of Chungking. The narrow stone-paved road wound among fields of brilliant golden mustard and grey-green beans in flower; their scent was indescribable.

It was one of the mornings on which a man feels it is good to be alive, and both Brooke and Meares scorned their sedan chairs and delighted their coolies, who were glad to see them walk mile after mile, day after day, while they had only to carry the empty chairs. Yet the masters felt that they had the best of the bargain. The joy of the start at daybreak and the long march through these scenes and scents more than repaid the energy expended.

The oranges and orange-groves! Every half-mile along the road they passed a heap of the lovely golden balls, still dewy from the trees. Large, luscious, loose-skinned mandarin oranges—twelve a penny or sixteen a penny if you give the skins back—and other delicacies, huge stalks of juicy purple sugar cane, dripping with sweetness and only costing the fraction of a penny for a stick four feet long. In the cold mornings, when we started off from the inns, there was always one man waiting outside the door with hot sweet wine and an egg beaten up in it, and another with hot scones, light as snow, and with a lump of raw sugar in the middle. These refresh-

HAULING THE BOAT OVER A ROCKY REACH.

ments may not sound very tempting, but taste them after a good walk among the fields on a frosty morning, and you will think you have never eaten anything so good.

The towns of this district are all famed for their crystallized fruits, such as whole oranges, ginger, Buddha fingers, apples, plums, dates, cherries and many other varieties. If the traveller is not above eating the food of the country he can live well and cheaply here. And so Brooke and Meares marched along day after day, enjoying every hour, and rather proud of themselves when they swung into an inn fresh and hungry, after a tramp of twenty-five to thirty miles. Yet they owned that it rather took away their conceit when their miserable coolies, carrying over 100 lbs. on their shoulders, swung in behind them, also smiling and hungry.

They passed on through lovely fertile valleys, then up over rolling hills covered with fir trees and bamboo grooves. All along the road they met numbers of coolies carrying baskets of coal. Brooke, dropping behind, thought he would like to find out where these men came from, and followed up one of the coolies who was returning empty-handed. After going about a mile from the road he came to a shaft sunk in the ground where a Chinaman was turning a ventilating fan. A ladder descended into the bowels of the earth, by which he reached the main shaft, where miners were dragging little sledges full of coal along a gallery five feet broad by three feet high. One of the sledgemen was induced, for a small tip, to pull Brooke along the gallery on his sledge, and did so for some distance, till the seam suddenly dipped down into the earth. Here he bolted, leaving Brooke in the dark on the edge of an incline, until another miner, with a lamp in his hat came along, and, "tipped" in his turn, allowed Mr. Brooke to hold on to the back of the full sledge which he was dragging out, and so brought him safely from the shaft, where Brooke was greeted by a friendly crowd, who brought him hot water to wash his hands. The coal was of a splendid quality, the mine was neat and clean with timbered and whitewashed walls, and the Chinese miners were well-dressed and healthy-looking.

Brooke caught up with Meares and they had breakfast. In the afternoon it began to rain and the stone road which had been in such good condition for walking in the dry weather became like a sheet of ice.

They passed several duck farms on the road, and a wonderful sight they were. The duck farmer, by some means, gets thousands of ducks' eggs and hatches them by artificial heat. As soon as the ducklings are a few days old he drives them out in the fields to forage, and it is most interesting to watch him shepherding a flock of several thousand little ducks with the help of a long bamboo rod.

Some of the farmers were beginning to prepare the fields for planting rice, and the fields which a few days ago were covered with sun-burnt bricks, had now been changed into muddy sloughs. Scarcely has the water been turned on the fields than the fisherman is at work, wading about in mud up to his knees and with very little on but his hat. He carries in his hand a large round bamboo basket without a bottom. This basket he suddenly plunges into the mud, and then feeling round inside with his hand he draws out a little fish three or four inches long.

Next day was wet. They passed a string of coolies carrying the mails from Chentu to Chungking. These men make wonderful time, averaging sixty to eighty miles a day, while they carry bags of mail averaging from 50 to 60 lbs. in weight.

Some of the towns they passed through were very picturesque, and were all decorated for the Chinese New Year. One in particular impressed Brooke. The scheme for the decoration of the whole town was dark red, the streets were roofed in with the same colour and were lined with rows of

DUCK FARMER HERDING HIS DUCKLINGS.

red silk lanterns. The inns, too, were above the average, that is to say, they were as good as a poor European stable, instead of being worse than a bad pigsty, as usually they are.

Near here they met strings of coolies carrying what they thought to be very dirty sandstone. On asking them where they were taking the stones they replied "that it was salt, and that the blacker it was the better." This salt is obtained from the brine wells in this district, and these wells Brooke thought were one of the most wonderful things in China. The wells are about six inches in diameter, and some of them are 3,000 feet deep. They are drilled out by a steel bar slung on the end of a long bamboo rope, and jerked up and down by a cow, and you may imagine they take many years to sink. The brine is drawn out of these wells in a large bamboo tube with a valve in the bottom; this is lowered into the bottom of the well, and when full is raised by being wound round and round a horizontal drum turned by water buffaloes.

Some of these wells give off natural gas, which is used for illumination and for evaporating the brine into salt. A sight of these wells arouses admiration for the first man who sunk one of them. How did he know that the brine was there? Even if he was so far certain, he must have known that it would not be reached during his own lifetime, nor perhaps, in that of his son. Yet there the wells are, for all to see, and the blacker and dirtier the brine the more valuable the well, for the Chinaman thinks that white salt is unhealthy, and that the dark colour has superior medicinal qualities.

And so they passed along through the fruit district, the sugar-cane district, over mountain passes and beautiful plains, sometimes following the river-bed, sometimes climbing hillsides, and over stone steps cut out of the solid rock. Everywhere the busy farmer was to be seen working on his farm from before sunrise till dark, with a short interval to eat his boiled rice and pickled turnip, and drink a cup of tea. Not only are the fields in the valley irrigated, but even the hillsides are terraced in many places and cisterns are made on the tops of the hills, which are filled with water during the rainy season, and hold it most of the year. From these cisterns water is let down into the terraced fields on the hillsides, and it is wonderful how they keep many of these small fields submerged for the greater part of the year. At last they ascended a mountain about 2,000 feet high from its base, and quite 5,000 feet above the sea. From the top of the pass they got a grand view of the Chentu plain. It looked like an immense forest, for the whole plain was covered with trees, and large feathery bamboo groves enclosed most of the farmhouses. When they reached the plain they found that it was simply a Garden of Eden. Every farmer took as much pains, in working up and fertilising his wheat field, as most of our gardeners in Europe or America do their vegetable plots, when catering for some large city trade.

The Chinese system of fertilising may not be a very pleasant one, but there is no doubt that the secret of their success as cultivators of the soil is the fact that they let no particle of fertiliser go to waste, and use it in a liquid condition. Our farmers in England have here a great deal to learn from the Chinese. We prefer to send millions of dollars worth of the richest fertiliser through our sewers into the ocean every year, and to buy our wheat from abroad, rather than find a plan of utilising it on the land from which it originally came.

Brooke and his party finally reached Chentu, after passing through about ten miles of beautiful flat farming country, which looked like a forest from the pass above the mountain.

Along this road are several very busy market towns, but the road itself showed by far the worst condition of any part

THE OLD FORT FOUR MILES WEST OF CHUNGKIN

of the 256 miles they had tramped from Chungking, a condition due to the large quantity of stone brought in on wheelbarrows from the quarries at Lungcheni at the foot of the pass.

Chentu is a very large city, and they walked for miles looking for a decent inn. So many officials come to this city that all the best inns are kept occupied, though even the best are nothing to boast of, for a large city like this. Finally they found a half-respectable one, and there, though the rooms were small and dirty, they decided to remain for a few days while they completed their plans.

CHAPTER VI.

CHENTU TO WENCHUAN.

ON the following day they called on Mr. Fox, His Britannic Majesty's Acting Consul-General, and had a talk with him about the country they hoped to travel in. He did not give them much information.

In the afternoon they called on the writer and we talked Mantze Land over a cup of tea, which our two visitors seemed to appreciate very much after their long journey across China, where they had not the latest convenience for making cake, and had very few opportunities of enjoying home-made bread and butter. They seemed to have enjoyed the Chinese food by the way, but it had by no means destroyed their appreciation of 5 o'clock tea, even when served in the humble cottage of a missionary nearly 2,000 miles west of Shanghai.

We talked about the people and the country, and as they seemed anxious to do some big game hunting I promised to introduce them to So Tussu, the Prince of the State of Wassu, where large game is to be found. These tribesmen are great hunters and spend most of the year in the chase; except for a month at seed time and another when the grain is being harvested, which is their close season. At that time the Prince issues a proclamation that every one must be in the fields.

As I had never taken a day off to enjoy a hunt since coming to China, I arranged to join the party for two weeks in the Wassu Forest.

They spent several days in Chentu, making the necessary

preparation for the hunting tour. Coolies had to be engaged, the loads repacked and made lighter; for the mountainous country into which they were now about to enter was much more difficult for the porter, and they were anxious to have no complaints after they started on their journey. I gave them all the help I could, securing for them a good head

A CHINESE PEASANT GIRL LEADING A BUFFALO TO GRAZE.

coolie, which is a most important item in starting on an expedition of this kind.

The head coolie is responsible for the conduct of all the porters; he keeps their time sheets, pays them their wages, engages new men by the way, should one by any chance fall out of the ranks or get "baulky" and refuse to do his work, as they often do. Much of the success or failure of every expedition depends on the conduct of the porters, for if they are obstinate they not only hinder the progress of the expedition, but often make it very unpleasant and even dangerous for the whole party.

It is advisable when one is starting on a long journey in a rough or mountainous country to have the loads comparatively light, *i.e.*, 10 to 20 lbs. below the standard weight carried by coolies on the main roads. The coolies will then travel up to thirty miles a day if necessary and always be cheerful. Long stages are very seldom called for in the Tribes country, for much of the transport is achieved by "peitze," *i.e.*, a load carried on a man's back. The men's loads are made fast to a frame or human pack-saddle and fit down the back, and have straps coming over the shoulders; in this way they carry 250 to 500 lbs. per man, and travel about forty li (ten miles) per day. Usually every three miles, at most, along the routes there is an inn, or a stopping place called an inn, where passengers can put up. When the traveller gets off these main roads into the small paths that lead through the country, there are no inns; one has to make other arrangements, and get into a private house if possible.

It is a great relief to the traveller to know that his men are not too heavily laden and that he may have no fear of delay on their account. The average load for a coolie who has to pass over high altitudes should not exceed 60 to 80 lbs. per man; if this rule is adhered to, there will seldom be any grumbling or disputing in the ranks.

On February 27th Meares started off to Kwanhsien with the coolies and servants, while Brooke remained behind to secure an interpreter. Unfortunately the man he brought as interpreter from Shanghai developed heart disease, and on arriving at Chentu was in a very bad condition indeed, his legs and body being much swollen. The doctor strongly recommended that he should be sent back, saying that he

MANTZE CASTLE AND TOWER; KIAKOS (ON RIGHT) FOR DRYING CORN.

would be certain to die were he taken to higher altitudes. They decided the best thing they could do was to send him home and run the risk of getting a local man at Chentu. Here, again, I was able to come to their aid, and, knowing a number of students who spoke English, helped them to secure the services of a very respectable man. Unfortunately he did not prove to be quite what was wanted, but rather elegant; and affected long finger-nails, beautiful silk gowns, and rode in a sedan chair wherever he went. He was useful, however, in translation work, and the travellers kept him for about a month in their employ.

Meares reached Kwanhsien in two marches, a distance of thirty-four miles, while Brooke, starting the next day at 12 o'clock, did it in nine hours; feeling his way for the last five miles; for it was pitch dark and he had no lantern, and did not know the road, which winds its way between swift-running streams for a great part of the distance. He finally reached the city at 9 a.m. and called at the Mission Station, which is just outside the city, in a nice little semi-native house on the banks of one of the irrigation streams. They directed him to the inn where Meares had put up and found the place not very large or clean. The inns in this city are for the most part occupied by merchants, who come here to buy up furs, hides, wool and herbs, which are brought from Songpan, Tsakulao, Mongum and other centres of trade on the Tibetan frontier.

Kwanhsien is a busy little place on the Min River and is the frontier town between China and the Tribes country. It is the point at which most of the big Chinese firms trading with the Tibetan and border tribes have their head depôts, which are most interesting places, almost like museums; one finds all kinds of strange medicines, horns, birds, skins, furs, etc. Some of the skins are of animals almost unheard of in England.

They were very much struck, on the road from Chentu, by the constant stream of wheel-barrows conveying produce to the capital, grain of all kinds, huge bales of tobacco, black pigs which are trussed like helpless bundles, and packed on each side of the barrow; besides many other commodities. There are also passenger barrows which carry one along very

CONVEYING PIGS TO THE CAPITAL.

comfortably at five miles an hour, at a charge of about a penny for five miles.

They spent the next day exploring the town and examining the irrigation works. They naturally wondered where all this water comes from; along the road various dams and sluices are run, by means of which the water is turned into the various

ON THE YANGTZE ABOVE THE ICHANG GORGE.

courses, yet not until they reached Kwanhsien did they discern the wonderful piece of engineering work, which has been stated on good authority to be equal to anything accomplished by our modern engineers. A great volume of water comes rolling down from the snow-capped mountains of Tibet. Just as the river leaps from the slopes and gorges through which it has come, and is about to enter the plain, it is caught and parcelled into seven artificial beds, any of which would make a good-sized river. These divisions, again, are subdivided into thousands of small streams, so arranged that the water in them flows as high as ten feet above the surrounding fields.

Sluices are so arranged that, at will, the entire plain, consisting of over 100,000 acres, may be irrigated or left dry, as the owners choose. A large part of the water thus diverted from its original course is carried northward, and along the foot of the mountains, and through a cut in another range nearly 1,000 feet high; and so flows on for nearly 300 miles and joins the Yangtze at Lucheo, instead of returning to the Min River from which it was diverted.

To accomplish this feat the water of the Min is not only diverted from its natural course, but is brought over two water-sheds and joined to the Hanchow River, which finds its course on the opposite side of the mountain range. Thus the water taken northward from Kwanhsien, by being kept near to the foot of the range, is brought across the water-shed which separates the Kwanhsien and Hanchow waters, and is conveyed into the bed of the latter.

The plan for performing this piece of work was conceived by a Chinese Mandarin named Lee Ping, in 300 B.C., and the whole plan was put into operation by him.

For this famous piece of work Lee Ping was deified, and his memory is still kept fresh by a fine temple erected to him at Kwanhsien, where the officers and people worship him every year. A great fair is held annually in this temple to which the people gather from far and near. Lee Ping left to be observed throughout future generations this motto: "Keep the banks low and the beds deep." The motto is still to be seen engraved on a stone in the temple at Kwanhsien, and, if it had not been scrupulously obeyed, the country would have been deluged long ago. About 60,000 taels (about £8,000) are expended annually in cleaning out the beds and repairing the dams; and the people willingly pay this tax, which is assessed on all the lands benefited by the irrigation system.

It would take too long adequately to explain the plan by which the immense volume of water is successfully carried out of its bed, and sent glistening and dancing over the large and fertile plains: watering thousands of acres so that they are entirely independent of rain, and enabling this track of country to bring forth sufficient food to support many millions of people annually.

The next morning they started early, and about a mile north of Kwanhsien, came to the temple dedicated to Lee Ping. This is one of the most beautifully situated temples in China, and is kept in better repair than any other temple in the country. All the gilding and lacquer work looks as fresh as if it had only been put on yesterday, and the whole place is kept in beautiful order—very unlike most of the temples in China.

At the entrance of the temple, carved in stone and gilded, is Lee Ping's motto for the keeping in repair of the irrigation works, and the Chinese show that they have not forgotten his instructions. Every winter they employ a huge army of tribesmen to divert the river from the irrigation canal and dig out the sand and stones, brought down by the summer floods, until two huge iron bars are exposed. These were first deposited by Lee Ping to show the proper depth of the channel.

Almost opposite the temple is an immense suspension

bridge, over which much of the traffic between Chentu and the Western Tribes passes. It is about one-third of a mile long, and is made of huge hawsers of plaited strips of bamboo, which stretch from bank to bank and are pulled tight on big wooden windlasses. Loose planks are laid on these hawsers, and it is ticklish work leading a horse across the gaps, especially when the whole bridge is swinging and oscillating in the strong winds which blow every afternoon in this part of the world.

REPAIRING THE WENCHUAN SUSPENSION BRIDGE.

The march was continued up the Min for some hours, past many coal mines and coke works, until a small stream was reached flowing from the east, which at this point ran through a narrow gorge, with huge cliffs on either sides ; after following this stream for some distance the road again turned northward and led over a pass at a height from its base of about 3,000 feet, or 5,000 feet above sea-level.

The view from the top of the pass is superb, but this was

not the time of year to loiter and admire. It was bitterly cold; every hair on every leaf of the bamboo and cryptomerias was encrusted with masses of crystal ice, and the whole place looked like fairy land. Swinging down the long sloping road, and returning to the Min at Yinhsiuwan, the party found a comfortable little inn perched amid the most beautiful scenery, and almost overhanging the river on a balcony of tree trunks.

Yinhsiuwan is a small town of about 100 families, and boasts several inns, but only two of them are really fit for habitation; the others are patronised by the tea and medicine coolies who tramp this road. The place itself is specially noted for its timber market, most of the square timbers and coffin boards, cut farther up the river in the Wassu country, are carried on men's shoulders to Yinhsiuwan, thence they are sent on rafts in the summer months to Kwanhsien, Chentu and other large centres.

Yinhsiuwan is also a tea station, and much of the tea that goes to Songpan and Matang for trade with the Tibetans and Tribes passes up this way. It is the first stage; the coolies have to carry the tea to this place before they get any pay for their work; thence it is carried from stage to stage by different coolies.

At this point the party had now really entered the mountains, the scenery of which surpasses description, peak after peak towering to a height of 6,000 to 8,000 feet; there was evidence of profuse vegetation, though just then everything was in its winter coat.

The route lay along the banks of the Min, which was now a rushing, roaring torrent, and the road was rough and stony and walking was most difficult. On both sides the precipitous snow-covered mountains rose sheer from the river, and only a narrow strip of blue sky was visible overhead; yet even these steep mountains are cultivated, and one wonders how the farmer can ever get the scanty soil to stay where it is wanted, and not be carried down into the river with the first shower of rain.

After travelling for two days in this most picturesque valley a new kind of dwelling, not of Chinese origin, came into view—great three-storied buildings, solidly built of stone and mud for mortar; and great water towers like factory chimneys rose in all directions. On inquiry it was found

CHENTU TO WENCHUAN—WHERE WE LEFT THE MIN AND ENTERED THE GORGE.

that the people living on the east bank of the river are called Chang Ming, and are supposed to be the remnant of the aborigines of the country; while the people on the west bank are the Wassu, descendants of the tribesmen brought by the Chinese from South-Western Tibet more than 800 years ago to help conquer the Chang Ming.

The whole stretch of the country is interesting, and it is well wooded for the most part, though every available spot is cultivated. Along the road came thousands of coolies laden with furs, wool, medicines, deer sinews, brought from the Tibetan border towns, where these commodities had been taken in exchange for salt, sugar, wine, rice or bamboo and hemp sandles. The road runs parallel to the river all the way, and every two miles are found rest houses, very poor looking homes, in some cases covered only with split clap boards or undressed shingles; the frame structure, often as not, leaning at such an angle that one would expect the buildings to fall at any minute on their tenants, occupants, and on the travellers who are to be seen drinking tea and eating their food in many of them. There are, of course, exceptions; but most of the buildings certainly impress one with the fact that the inhabitants have a hard job to make a living. The average hut, called an inn, is filthy, and the pigsty and its inhabitants have the most prominent and honourable position—a room or pen at the upper end of the enclosure.

Reports of game were heard along the road, yet nothing was seen but one raccoon, which some of the natives had trapped and chained up. The country was very wild and rugged, and so steep were some of the cliffs that formed the river bank and so high did they tower, that the road builders, at points, had cut a passage out of the solid rock. In other parts mason work is built, or a wooden bridge is thrown across a chasm, sometimes several hundred feet above the foaming stream. Yet over these narrow and dangerous places the pack-mules plying between Kwanhsien and Songpan pass continually, and hardly ever with an accident. Often they have to walk within a few inches of the edge of these precipices with not more than two inches of space between the load and the solid rock on the inside, while a sheer drop of several hundred feet is between them and the water or the rock as the case may be, on the other side. Yet these wonderfully sure-footed animals seldom make a mis-step or even bump their loads on the rocks, though you would not care to have your hand between the loads and the rock, so little space is there to spare.

SO TUSSU, HIS SON, AND SECRETARY.

On the evening of March 6, Wenchuan was reached, and a fairly comfortable inn was found in which they made their headquarters for some time. I started from Chentu several days after them, but making a quick journey on my frisky little horse, overtook them the evening they arrived.

Next morning we called on So Tussu, who had just come down from his palace on the mountain of Tongling to meet a new Chinese official who had just been appointed to Wen-chuan. He was very friendly, and arranged a small hunt for us next day, to test our sporting capabilities.

CHAPTER VII.

SPORT IN WASSU.

NEXT morning we were up early, but by 8 a.m. no hunters had arrived, so we went over to the chief to ask if they were coming. A little later two ruffianly-looking hunters appeared, dressed in skin coats, and armed with long gaspipe guns, with coils of fuse made with bamboo fibre. They all wore bamboo or hemp sandals, and we did the same, as leather boots were quite useless, not to say dangerous, on the crags where we were to hunt. After leaving the village behind us we followed a small path which zigzagged up the precipitous side of the mountain, and, after some more climbing, found six other hunters with their dogs awaiting our arrival.

We still climbed higher, to take our positions for the hunt, while some of the hunters with their dogs remained below to drive the game. Before we reached our positions we heard the dogs barking, and the hunters shouted up to us that a musk deer had got away.

After a tremendous struggle up the precipitous cliffs, over which we scrambled, dragging ourselves up, by catching hold of the brushwood and shrub bamboo which covered the face of the mountain, we finally reached a position, far up the mountain side, where we had a most wonderful view of the surrounding country. Here we halted for a little, to gain our breath and enjoy the panoramic view unfolded before us. Away to the west a great snow range seemed to blend its glistening peaks with the clear light blue of the western sky. The lower slopes were dotted with the dull grey stone dwellings of the Wassu and Changming peasantry, and the great towers, erected in these villages, looked like church spires in the distance. Above the cultivated fields rose green forests of bamboo, white fir, birch, shrub and prickly oak; and just below the snow line the rhododendron forest and higher yet the grassland topped by great craggy rocks, their peaks covered with eternal snow.

In the valley beneath us, 4,000 feet below where we stood, the Min, like a little stream of silver, glistened in the sunshine. To the south the view was not so extensive, but not less beautiful and interesting—the mountain wooded almost to its base, and, far up its sides, small openings in the forest where the perpetual smoke of the charcoal-burners showed and the potash-makers were at work: the trees bending under their load of snow.

We looked northward to see if we were nearing the summit of the mountain, which we had been toiling up for the last two hours; but on looking to the valley beneath us, from which we had just come, and then toward the top of the slope that contained our hunting-ground for the day, we decided that we were not more than one-quarter way up. We had climbed 3,000 feet already, and the valley whence we started was 5,000 feet above sea-level, so that our position was quite 8,000 feet above the mighty ocean.

Our hunting-ground was covered with shrub bamboo, but there were many open spots and run-ways here and there, so, by choosing good positions, we had command of a considerable stretch of mountain side.

Prince So's head hunter allotted us our position, and we were all placed by 12 o'clock.

It was bitterly cold, for a strong wind had sprung up, and the heat of the sun did not seem to have much effect.

We knew from the barking of the dogs that game was

NEAR SO TUSSU'S CASTLE; MOUNTAIN AT END OF VALLEY SIXTY MILES DISTANT.

moving, but no shots had yet been fired; everyone was expectantly waiting, for there was no telling where the game might pop out.

The dogs kept zigzagging back and forth up the mountain side, at times coming near, again turning and apparently driving the game right away and round the farther side of the mountain. It was then the cold wind seemed to pierce us, chilling us even to the marrow in our bones, and my own hands got so cold that I don't think I could have held my rifle steady if the dogs had brought something to my feet.

For a long time they had not come near my side of the mountain, and their bark became almost indistinguishable from the murmur of the wind. One second I imagined I could hear them coming nearer and nearer, then the sound would die away. Knowing that the game in this part of the country are not afraid of smoke, so used are they to the charcoal-burners, with their camps everywhere in these mountains, I gathered at last some dry wild grass and bamboos, and made a fire in a little nook under a rock close by my station.

Finally, just as we were giving up hope of seeing anything coming our way, we heard a shot round the corner of a hill, and Mr. Meares rushed round just in time to meet a large wild boar and give him a charge of buck shot at ten yards. This bowled him over, but he recovered sufficiently to scramble down the steep hillside for a distance. Mr. Brooke glided down the hillside after him and gave him the *coup-de-grace*—rather dangerous work, as a steep hillside covered with thicket, in which a wounded boar is taking shelter, is not the safest place in the world.

The hunters soon collected round, and were much pleased to see a mass of pork, which they cut up and packed on their backs. We then descended 3,000 feet back to the river bed by one of the steepest tracks we had ever traversed.

We found it quite as difficult work safely to descend the mountain side as it was to ascend it. The path was narrow and covered with small round pebbles that rolled under our feet, and we all took turns in unwillingly and somewhat suddenly sitting down.

We had not yet got used to our new footwear, and the coarse hemp ropes of our sandals seemed to find tender spots in our feet, and especially as we found our way down the steep mountain side. Our toes would insist on finding their way through the strands of rope, which felt as though they were cutting ruts into the bones. We were glad when at last we arrived at the inn and found a good supper of boiled rice and curried chicken awaiting us, and I am sure the cook was pleased with himself, for we licked the platter clean that night.

We all felt quite proud of our first day's hunt, for although we had not got anything remarkable for our arduous climb, yet we had found there was something in the neighbourhood worth hunting, and our first day was not a blank. The carcase of the wild boar, which we had divided among the men, had put them all in the best of spirits, and they all joined in earnest expectation for good success on the morrow.

When the hunters collected next morning they brought the report that a ngaelu (cliff donkey), which we afterwards discovered was a serow, had been seen near where we hunted yesterday, so we set out early; it had snowed some in the night and the paths were quite slippery, but it was wonderful how our hemp sandals gripped the rock. By 10 o'clock we were all in our places, for we did not go quite so high as on the previous day.

Meares and I were posted in the river bed, and Brooke went higher up on the mountain side with the hunters. Old Wang, the head hunter, kept with Brooke, and they took up their position on a little ledge of rock with cliffs on

PRINCE SO (IN CENTRE), MR. MEARES AND MR. BROOKE.

two sides of them, on which the serow might at any moment appear, should it be pressed hard by the dogs.

Hardly had they got to their places when some of the dogs began to give tongue, and in a short time the beaters sent down the cry that a serow had gone to bay on one of the crags on the opposite side of the cliff from where Brooke and old Wang were located. But before any of the beaters could get near enough to get a shot, the serow broke through the dogs, and started up the mountain in quite the opposite direction from what those experts had expected, and, getting in the deep snow, was clean away. Another pack of dogs that had been started simultaneously raised another serow, and brought him round the lower end of the cliff. He was too far away from Meares and myself to get a shot, though we could see him like a little speck on the mountain side.

Old Wang rushed down the mountain side by leaps and bounds, and called to Brooke to follow on. Endeavouring to keep up with Wang, an expert mountaineer, he soon found himself in a sitting position, and came sliding down, rather to the damage of his trousers, but got off without a scratch. The serow turned just as he was about to enter the open ground, crossed his track, and went off in pursuit of the first one. It was now getting late, and we thought the sport was over for the day, but old Wang said there was still a chance, for when they were coming up in the morning they heard a goral blowing on the mountain side. He declared these creatures did not travel far at this season of the year, unless they were hunted, and that they would be out feeding at this hour of the evening.

They called the dogs in by a shrill, long cry, followed by several shorter ones, which echoed and re-echoed through the mountain side, and the weary disappointed little creatures were soon seen coming slowly back from three different directions, just as the men had all collected in the valley where Meares and I were posted.

One little stray dog, which the beaters had begun to grow anxious about, lest it had pursued the serow too far up the mountain into the deep snow, and had got eaten by a panther, appeared; and just before him, far up the mountain side in the clearing, a little coloured creature was seen hopping along, almost like a rabbit. This the hunters declared was a chitze, *i.e.*, a chamois. He was over 1,000 yards from us, and though we sent a few shots after him he escaped without injury, and the dog left him in answer to the call of his master.

The dogs were sent home by one of the hunters, who took us along on the other bank of the small stream. We followed a narrow path, which led up to a potash-burner's hut, then on, round the face of the cliff, and crossed over a precipice bridged by rotten logs. These were pinned to the side of the cliff by wooden pins as rotten as themselves; for it was many years since they were placed there by some venturesome charcoal-burner, to enable him to collect suitable sticks for burning in his kiln farther up the mountain side. The timber, suitable for this purpose, having all been cut, the road was long since discarded, and only these risky, fearless hunters now pass over it. It would only bear one person at a time. Old Wang said "siaosin, siaosin" (carefully, carefully), but there was no need for his advice. In places there was a sheer drop of 500 feet, and the only footing was a single rotten log, not more than six inches in diameter when first placed there, but now wasted to half that size, and we never knew just how sound the remaining portion might be. Then there was some snow lying on them in places, which added to the treacherousness of the situation, and there was nothing to hold to but the side of the rock, with here and there a small brushwood that had grown out of some crevice on the cliff's side, and on which one could not put much reliance.

The only thing was to look aloft, keep steady, and try not to think of the danger, for if one's nerves go for a second one's head would begin to swim and the danger be increased many fold.

After about 500 yards of this we came out on a more sloping hillside, but still not a place to slip on, for it was a long way to the bottom, and soon came to a flat place, where there had been an old hut. Here we stood still to scan the rocky cliff on the opposite side of a small ravine just in front of us; it was here the hunters had heard the goral in the morning.

The keen eye of Wang soon picked out something which he declared was a living creature; but though he tried to point it out to us, even with the aid of a good pair of binoculars, we could see nothing but rocks and trees. Some of the men were sent away round, to beat the side of the cliff, and drive the goral our way; but how they were to make their way was a mystery; in fact, it seemed impossible, but these men are like flies, they stick anywhere they set their feet.

We were a long time waiting. At length some of the beaters got beyond, and came down near where Wang kept telling us the animal stood; we saw an object move. It started to come toward us, suddenly it disappeared into a hole in the rock; the hunter followed, but could not find where it was hid; threw a stone into the hole, and out it came within a few yards of him, and went sliding along the face of the cliff across the gulley from us more like a panther than a goral.

When the goral came opposite to us he stopped; the light was failing when Brooke fired at about 200 yards, and wounded him badly. He fell straight off the cliffs and turned several somersaults before reaching the rocky bed of the stream, and we expected to find the beast a mangled mass at the bottom. With great difficulty we got down the face of the cliff, but when we came to where we expected to find him, up he jumped and escaped without further damage from the volley of shots which followed him. After running about 500 yards he halted, and Mr. Brooke bowled him over again, and now we thought that he really was killed, and sent up a hunter to carry him down. No sooner did the hunter approach the spot where he lay than up he jumped again ; we had given our guns to the hunter to carry, and he escaped.

It was now getting very dark, and the paths were terrible, so we thought that we had better get down to the level as soon as possible. The hunter put a dog on the track of the goral, saying he would drive it down, but we saw nothing more of him that night. When we got safely back to the main road we could still hear the faint sound of the dog baying the goral in the pitchy darkness, right on the face of the perpendicular wall of rock 2,000 feet above us. We never expected to see the dog alive again, so sat down to wait events. Suddenly from the face of the cliff shot out a flash of sparks and a bang, then silence ; then the dog barked again, then another flash and bang, then a final silence. After waiting some time the other hunters said we had better get home, though there was neither sight nor sound of their companion who had gone after the goral.

The brave little hunter followed the goat along the face of the cliff in the dark, and had shot at it by hearing, and then returned safely along those terrible tracks in the pitch dark. Few foreigners would have cared to undertake so much in broad daylight.

On returning to the town we spoke to the chief about what had happened, as we were quite anxious about the man, but he only laughed and said, " My men are not Chinese."

The goral was brought in next morning badly bruised from its fall over the cliff. It had stuck in the brushwood on a narrow ledge, some 500 feet below where the hunter had given it the *coup-de-grace* the night before; and to get the

THE HUNTERS SCANNING THE MOUNTAIN SIDE FOR GORAL.

beast one of the men was roped and suspended over the side of the cliff and attached the rope to the dead goral, which was drawn up, and the rope again let down for the man; who clung to the narrow ledge by the few bushes that grew out of a crevice in the rock. We found that three shots had been sent through the beast—one through the intestines, which also broke one hind leg, the other not far behind the heart; and the little hunter's buckshot, one of which hit him in the head, had bowled him over the cliff.

The vitality and agility of these animals is incredible. The horns were so badly broken from the fall that the skin was useless as a specimen.

The next day Meares and I went out on the other side of the river; the road was much better, but the game not so plentiful.

Just as we were giving up, for we had patiently waited for some hours, the dogs drove a chitze (chamois) down to Meares. It came out of the undergrowth just behind him, but turned before Meares got a shot, and came towards me, the dogs hard after, one of them not more than ten paces behind. I let drive at the chitze at about seventy yards, while he was on the run, and shot him through, breaking a front and hind leg; so he did not go far, but managed to get down the mountain side some little distance before the dogs got him.

One of the hunters and myself were soon at the spot and recovered our prize from the dogs, who would have torn it to pieces. We had each now bagged something, and felt that we had also some experience in shooting in a mountainous country.

Tussu now insisted that we should come up and spend the next day with him in his castle on Tonglin, so we went, and he had a feast prepared for us, and entertained us royally. Brooke took his phonograph up, and the whole countryside gathered in to hear it, so we spent a lively evening.

The following morning we went over to the chief's private temple, over 600 years old, and filled with the most obscene idols I have ever seen. At the right of the door as one enters the temple is the idol of Sakti, wife of the god Siva; while inside are the obscene idols of the Bön sect, the most vile form of nature worship.

"The Tantras," or Sakti Bible, which presents Hinduism at its worst and most corrupt stage of development, and identifies all force with the female principle in nature, is no longer used by this tribe, as their religion has been reformed by the Lamaism of the Red Sect; yet there is still much of the Sakti superstition practised among all these tribes, and there are some who still retain the old Tantras writings as their standard of morality and holy living; but I will write of these things in another chapter.

The head Lama is a cousin of the chief, and is a pleasant young fellow, but not inclined to give away much information, or he may not be well acquainted with the early writings to which I have just referred. The old Lama, who is really dying of consumption, was well up in the subject, and gave me a good deal of information, but this is not the place to deal with this subject.

There were shelves piled with books written in Tibetan character, but they did not look as if they were much used, or as if the cobwebs were often swept off them. Old scrolls with paintings of Buddha and the saints, or incarnations decked the walls and hung from the beams. Candles were kept burning in front of some of the idols, but many of them were quite neglected.

The tribesmen seem to be losing confidence in the power of these idols to perform the mighty things claimed for them by the priests, and while they do not really profess Christianity, they are a happy, jolly people, who deserve something better than they have; and, when the missionaries commence to work among them, they will prove themselves to be a people worth working for.

We enjoyed our visit to the chief, and learned to understand him better, as he was more free, when away from the Chinese. He is a heavy opium-smoker, however, and is always proposing to go to the hospital at Chentu and break it off, but has not the courage to make the attempt. He is rather a weak man, and the Chinese play a good deal on his good nature. He fears that the chieftainship may soon be taken from him, and the whole country put formally under the Chinese official. This will probably take place in the near future; as the Chinese are certainly planning to replace all the hereditary chiefs of all these border states by Chinese officials, appointed by the Emperor periodically, as in other parts of China.

I should be sorry to see a people like this lose their identity and be completely absorbed by the Chinese, but it might be the best thing for them, as they are at present despised and down-trodden by their conquerors, as well as oppressed by their chiefs and princes. The position of the ordinary man and woman is that of vassal or slave, and they can never expect to possess anything of their own. To eke out an existence is about their only ambition under the present system.

CHAPTER VIII.

HUNTING THE PANYANG.

WE heard of a strange kind of sheep called "Panyang," by the Chinese. It was reported to have long curved horns and to live on the grass lands above the tree-line, which in this latitude is 11,000 feet.

The Prince showed us some skins, which were incomplete, the native hunters having cut off the legs and head, considering them of no value. The horns and skulls also were left on the mountains where they were shot; so that these skins were of no use as specimens, but we were able to get some idea of the animal and its coat. The hair was of a greyish blue or drab colour, white on the flanks and belly, and black stripes bordering the flanks and down the front of the legs. The hair was rather coarse but soft and thick, more like a deer's coat than a sheep's, and could by no means be called wool.

The description of the habits of these sheep, as given by the natives, was sufficient to arouse our curiosity and we determined to secure a specimen. The chief declared the snow was too deep on the mountains for us to ascend to their haunts, but on offering a reward for a skin in good condition three hardy hunters volunteered to attempt the task. The chief recommended that we should go to Tsaopo, a small place lying back from the main road where his old palace is, and which was once the headquarters of the Wassu Chief. He put this old castle at our disposal and sent in word to his retainers that we were to be well looked after. No foreigner had ever lived in this locality and only two or three had ever visited it. The chief sent ten of his hunters with us, and we were to wait in the valley near the castle, while the three hunters, who had agreed to go up the snow-clad mountain to secure a panyang, returned.

The next day, March 13, we set out, retracing out tracks down the Min about seven miles to Sohchiao, where there is a very long rope bridge suspended across the river.

Here a good sized stream coming from the west joins the Min. We followed up this stream for about ten miles, crossing it several times. For the coolies this was easy enough, as there were rope bridges over which foot passengers can make their way; but, I having my horse along with me, and the planks being set so far apart that it was impossible for him to cross the bridge, I had to take the pony down to the river bed, and almost swim him through the swift waters. The natives said it could not be done, or rather that it had never been done; but my pony was in good condition, and knowing how to handle him, we soon crossed over and overtook the party again. I had thus to cross the river several times, as there were many places where the path ran along the side of the cliff, where it was so narrow that it was impossible for the horse to pass. At last we reached the junction of two streams, the one still coming from the west, the other from the south-west. Here the valley opened out more. There were several water mills along the stream, and a great part of the valley and part of the hillsides were cultivated; but the mountains towered up from 7,000 to 10,000 feet, and the tops of them were deeply clad in snow.

We made our way up this valley by a zigzag path, and about 4 o'clock arrived at the old castle. It is situated on the spur of the mountain about 100 feet above the stream. I found an old keeper in charge, who showed us the three rooms we were to occupy.

The ground storey was really a stable, or large pen for sheltering stock, but there were very few animals about, as the people are very poor. They depend for a livelihood on the timber trade, which is the chief industry of this section of the country. The men also get something out of the hunting, while the women do most of the farming and attend to the water mills in which they grind their grain. We went up a long stone staircase and entered a courtyard about twenty-five yards square, and surrounded by a parapet which on the inside was about three feet high, but when you looked over the wall you saw it was quite twenty-five feet to the ground on the outside. Passing through a long hall or corridor, we turned to our left and found a suite of rooms, which were very dark and dirty. The whole castle was unoccupied, except for the caretaker and an old Lama. He performed the priestly rites in the presence of the castle idols which have their lofty abode on the fourth storey of the building, and which are of the same obscene character as those found in the temple at Tunglingshan, where the Tussu lives.

The interior of the castle was exceedingly gloomy; the dust and cobwebs of ages hung from every beam, the floors had not been swept for years, let alone washed—a thing indeed entirely unheard of in this country. Three of the best rooms in the castle were filled with maize-cobs and husks, which were stored for fuel: when these were turned out and the rooms cleaned up a bit, they were quite habitable. In this country, where for at least seven or eight months of the year but little rain falls, every place is infested with fleas; and when we began to move about in the dust that had been lying undisturbed for so long, it was like stirring up a bee's nest, the fleas attacked us in earnest, and in the morning we were all as much spotted as if we had had measles.

Soon after our arrival the chief's brother, who lives near here, called and chatted till late. He partook of supper with us, which consisted every day of bacon and eggs, or boiled rice and bacon with Chinese scones: when we wanted a change we reversed the order and had scones and bacon. During the last two days the weather had been very fine, and the hunters thought the snow might be melted off the grass country above the tree-line, so we decided to go with them to the top of Chienliangshan, where the panyang was to be found. The hunters were not anxious to take us along, as they knew the road was very difficult and in places dangerous, which indeed we afterwards found out for ourselves. After fitting out three light loads of 20 lbs. each, which contained our bedding, a few extra garments and some provisions consisting of about 5 lbs. of bacon, 10 lbs. of rice and 20 lbs. of flour to make scones, with three tin cups, frying pan and tea kettle, at 9 o'clock we left the castle, and followed the stream till we came to the last habitation, where we stopped for the night. It was a miserable, dirty little hut; but by stretching the bamboo mat across the tie beams in the roof, which were about two feet apart, we succeeded in making a place to spread our beds on. Fearing we might not have sufficient food, we here bought some maize, and during the evening amused ourselves and others by grinding it in a hand mill. This we turned by means of poles attached to the stones, and walking round and round till we were quite dizzy, we finally managed to turn our maize into meal.

Next morning we started out at daybreak, and soon got into deep snow drifts, some of them very treacherous, not to say dangerous. The banks of stone along the river bed were covered with a smooth coating of snow, which would break through after one or two persons had passed over; we took turns in disappearing through the snow into the pits below, but fortunately no one got hurt. Farther on, we had to make a road through the thicket of dwarf bamboo bearing a load of snow which bent the trees almost to the ground.

This was cold wet work, for the moment we touched one of these trees a load of ice and snow was deposited on our heads and necks. The path next ran along the face of the cliff, on slippery poles, sometimes horizontal, sometimes at an angle of 10 or 15 degrees. These poles were pinned to the rocks or suspended by the vine ropes. Next, we had to cross and re-cross the stream on bridges, and what bridges! Just a tree eight inches in diameter, lying from bank to bank and on top of it a crust of snow and ice six inches thick. If this crust broke or the passenger lost his balance, the only issue was a leap of thirty feet into the rocky bed of the roaring torrent. The hunters walked boldly across these bridges and we followed, treading in their footmarks. The brave coolies, with 20 lbs. on their backs, followed in our steps, and seemed to think little of it, so that we could not feel proud of our performance. We struggled on thus for miles, crossing and recrossing the stream, and at last turned sharply off and climbed a zigzag path up the side of the mountain, the incline of which could not have been less than 60 degrees. The snow was not so deep here, but quite enough to make it very slippery walking. However, by much struggling on hands and knees, we gradually reached the belt of white firs, which begins at about 8,000 feet above the sea, and continues to 10,000 feet. Then we passed on through the rhododendrons, some of which were showing a few buds.

A few months later the forest of white fir would ring with the sound of the axe of the woodman, who comes all this way to fell these trees, which he roughly squares into coffin boards and sticks of timber, and carries on his back to one of the towns on the banks of the Min, there to sell them for a few shillings apiece to the wood merchants. But now all was still, and in silence we toiled on till we emerged from the rhododendron thickets into the grass land. We hunted about for some time, seeking for a place where we could spend the night, and were about to camp under a shelving rock when some of the hunters, who were higher up the mountain side, shouted for us to climb on; so, after tramping through deep snow drifts and over cliffs for another hour, we found the remains of another hut, which had been made by the herb diggers the previous year. Here the snow had almost disappeared, and the tufts of grass, yellow from the frosty winds

OUR CAMP AT CHIENLIANGSHAN.

of the past winter, stood out against the barren crags that dotted the mountain side.

Far above us towered a great range, its peaks covered with eternal snow. The coolies arrived shortly after us, but one of them had fallen over a cliff and had knocked out most of his front teeth. Just after dark it grew bitterly cold and began to snow, and as the coolies had no bedding with them, and none too much clothing for this temperature, they had to take most of the wood off the roof of the hut in order to keep a fire burning for the night. Next day it was still snowing heavily, but the men decided to go out and get some firewood, so putting on their sandals and climbing irons, they descended to the tree level and later returned with huge bundles of wood. It was impossible to see any distance, and we remained in camp all day. By the following morning it had ceased snowing, and although the sun was not visible from where we were, we could see its rays flashing with dazzling brilliancy on a huge ice peak which shone up behind us another 8,000 or 10,000 feet. After some hours the sun drove away the clouds which had hung over the lower ranges in the early morning, and by 10 o'clock was shining brightly on us. Our camp was about 11,600 feet above sea-level, and from here we set out for the haunts of the wild sheep still thousands of feet higher. The newly-fallen snow was knee-deep, and the glare of the sun on it was so powerful that after going about a mile, Meares became perfectly snow-blind, and returned to camp, finding his way with great difficulty by feeling with his hand the track we had made in ascending. Brooke, two hunters and myself climbed on over some very rough ground and came upon a flock of peimuhchi, a bird as large as a turkey, which lives on these mountains. Brooke had a shot at them, but as he, too, was almost snow-blind by this time, he did not succeed in killing one. The light was such that it was impossible to judge the distance. We found afterwards that the birds were not more than 60 yards away, but thought they were more than 100 yards when he fired. The mist was now closing in on us again, and seeing that it was useless to attempt to hunt in such weather we decided to return to camp. The little hunter who was our guide said, "This is the shortest way back," and sitting down on the steep snow slope, he shot off into the mist and disappeared. This was all very well, but in a country which is mostly precipitous, the longest way round is often the safest way home, so we retraced our steps by the way we had come, and returned safely to find that the little hunter had arrived long before us, and after having finished his evening meal was comfortably warming himself by the fire. The next morning it was still snowing, so we determined to retrace our steps to the foot of the mountain. We packed up our things, and cut for ourselves strong alpine-stocks in preparation for the dangerous descent. It was a difficult task to find our way back as our track was completely obliterated; but it took much less time to get down the mountain than it did to ascend it, and in many places we shot quickly down the slopes in a sitting position, holding on to the branches of trees to keep ourselves from going too fast. On our way back we passed a wonderful hot sulphur spring which was building for itself a marvellously coloured basin; its waters were so hot that we could scarcely bear to dip our hand in them. We reached the castle at Tsaopo the same day without anything to show for our trouble. The next morning we went on to the hills near the castle, where there were a number of goral about, one of which I picked off the top of a rock at 1,000 yards, much to the admiration of the natives, and Mr. Brooke shot another a few minutes later, which the dogs brought to him. The following day was a blank, but we enjoyed life while waiting on our game-runs in the warm sunshine, with snow mountain piled upon snow mountain in view, contrasted with a brilliant blue sky. Many a man has travelled thousands of miles to see a sight not half so magnificent. We discovered that the panyang we had gone after was the "blue sheep" (*Ovis-nahura*), or the Tibetan Nawa, "the Bhural of India." These are common all over this part of the country between the tree-limit and the snow-line, that is, from 12,000 to 17,000 feet. The old males leave the females in June or July and live by themselves.

Both sexes have horns, but the horns of the females are much smaller than those of the males. They have the habit of always grazing near rocky ground, in which they take shelter when startled by any strange object. And they always post a sentry when feeding. He stands amid some jagged rocks where he has a good view, and where it is impossible to distinguish him from the surroundings. He does not move his head, and one is attracted to him, if at all, only by the sudden bound he takes when leaving his watch tower, and which is the signal to his companions that it is time to be off. The natives first told me this story, and later, when crossing a high range in July where these animals were feeding, I had occasion to prove its truth.

Although I joined the hunting party for a few days, I tried not to forget my own special work among these people, and always had books with me to give to the mountain dwellers, whenever I came in contact with them. While in the old castle, I found the Lama had procured a copy of the Gospel from me on a former visit, and had read it frequently, for it was well thumbed and worn. This copy he took from the shelf, and, turning up several passages which he could not understand, I tried to explain them to him. During the past two weeks I had learned to understand these people better than ever before, and they had come to look on me as a friend. We had many long chats about their difficulties and social problems which constantly confront them. Some of them expressed the hope that the Chinese would soon do away with the existing feudal system, and accept them as Chinese subjects. Many of them say the burden imposed on them by their chiefs and princes, together with the tribute that has to be collected by the Chinese Government, is greater than they can bear. Some of them would gladly make friends with the missionaries and even join themselves to the Church in the hope that they might be in some way released from their bondage of feudal service imposed upon them ; but, of course, the missionary can offer them nothing in this direction. These were burning questions with them, but they would only speak of them in a whisper, and to those who are their friends. What these people need is education, that they may be able to take their place in the nation, and that they may find their place in God's kingdom.

I had now to return to my work at Chentu, and left the party to continue their wandering alone.

CHAPTER IX.

Hunting the Serow.

Messrs. Brooke and Meares decided that they must try and get a serow before leaving this part of the country, so on March 25th they started off with some hunters and their dogs to Taokwan valley, which is a famous place for these animals. They pitched their tent in a nice little spot near the banks of the stream and hunted for some days, but shot nothing but a few small deer. There were plenty of serow about, but the dogs were afraid to tackle them. Finding it useless to continue with the dogs they had, they struck camp and went down to Taokwan, a village from which the valley derives its name, and there secured two good hunters with four excellent dogs. One of these men had been with us on Chienliang mountain. Thus equipped they returned to their camping ground, and hardly had they set out when the dogs got on the track of a serow. The hunters were all waiting on the game-run on the top of the ridge, when Meares thought he heard the sound of an animal in the brushwood below; but his hunter declared there was nothing, and suggested that he should go down and watch another game-run on the other side. He did so, and subsequent proceedings interested him no more.

Hardly had he left, than four dogs, closely followed by a hunter, dashed past him through the undergrowth; an animal had passed quite close without their having seen it. Wang at once drew his curved knife and slashed his way down the steep hillside through the briars and thorns. Brooke followed him, sliding, running, falling, anything to catch up with the dogs, which were now chasing the serow down the river bed toward Taokwan. Around a waterfall which poured over a huge boulder they found four dogs barking, and made a cave underneath. Wang declared that the serow had taken refuge under the boulder, and Brooke nearly drowned himself trying to get under to see. Another hunter now arrived on the scene, and immediately stripping off his clothes made another attempt to get into the cave, but without success.

They then dammed up part of the river with stones and turned aside enough of the stream to allow him to get under the rock, but found nothing. The owner of the pack now arrived on the scene, and declared that the serow had gone down the stream, so they again raced on and came to a group of Chinamen staring in the vacant way they sometimes have when greatly surprised. On going across to inquire if they had seen anything of the animal, there, lying in their midst, they found a fine serow, with its throat cut and its legs badly hacked, and beside it a Chinaman badly gored. Brooke did what he could for the poor victim and had him taken to a neighbouring house. He wanted to send him into the hospital at Chentu, but the man refused to go, and, after lingering for some days, he died. It appears that the two dogs bayed the serow, and the Chinese, thinking that there was money to be made, attacked the animal with clubs. It charged, and drove its horns through one of them. One of the party succeeded in ham-stringing the animal, and in some way they managed to kill him. In the meantime Meares had gone to the top of the mountain opposite and returned to camp in time to meet them coming in with the dead serow.

Next day they hunted up the left hand valley, and early in the morning sent out hunters to act as stops along the tops of the hills. Meares was posted at a point half way up the mountain on one side of the stream, and Brooke was higher up on the opposite bank.

As Meares was going up into his position he again got a glimpse of a serow dashing through the trees, but could not get a shot at it. The dogs soon got on its track, and after a long chase drove him right past Brooke, who dropped him at forty yards. It was a fine female, and a good match for the male they had secured the previous day. One of the dogs was still hunting something, and finally drove another serow past Brooke, which also he shot; but this one was immature.

The following day Meares stayed in camp to prepare the skins, while Brooke went out in the neighbouring hills. After working a short time Meares heard a tremendous row, and picking up his rifle went out to find the dogs driving a serow right towards the camp, and it went to bay on the ledge of a rock not more than 100 yards away. He tried to get a shot at it, but could not for fear of hitting the dogs, which were all over him. Finally one of the hunters shot the beast at close quarters.

This finished the serow hunt, and they struck camp and returned to Wenchuan. The Mandarin prepared a great feast in their honour, and gave them the chief seats, making himself very agreeable. He plied them with many questions—no doubt his chief object being to find out their business and their intentions regarding their future movements. They had the advantage of not being too familiar with the language which he spoke, he being Cantonese, and, as their interpreter was at another table, it was a very simple matter to say "Putong," that is, "I don't understand," to any question they felt was unnecessary to answer. As it was important for Brooke to go to Chentu to have some dental work done—for he had suffered much during the past month with his teeth—it was sufficient in reply to their host's question to give this as their purpose, and to add that Meares was going down as far as Yinhsiuwan, the lumber centre, two days to the south. It rather relieved the Mandarin's mind to feel he was getting rid of these strangers, who had been wandering about on the hills and valleys of this neighbourhood for more than a month. He was politeness itself, however, and they parted on the most friendly terms.

On their journey down they met two hunters who had just

MR. BROOKE AND HIS FIRST SEROW.

caught a young takin, which they offered for sale. Brooke jumped at the chance of securing the first specimen of this animal, for when he left England there was not a live one in the Zoo, and this wonderful little creature was very much prized by us all. He was low set, had very heavy legs, and was about as large as a three months' old lamb, only much heavier, rather clumsy in his gait, but not at all wild or timid : there was not much trouble to teach it to take its food first from a bottle, and later out of a dish. Brooke had him carried to Chentu, where we cared for him for nearly three weeks. He grew to be a most affectionate little creature, and would follow us all about our compound like a little dog, even coming into the house at times. Meares sent down a young goral a few days later, so we had both these animals going about the courtyard, and they became really good friends. The young goral soon made friends with our cow, and was most anxious to help milk her. One morning, unfortunately, the cow stepped on the goral's leg and broke it; we did all we could for the poor beast, but after lingering a few days he died. The takin seemed to do well for quite three weeks, when suddenly one morning, after taking its breakfast, it appeared sickly, and that day refused to take any more food, and died during the night.

For the loss of this most valuable animal Brooke blamed his boy, who had given it some sour milk the morning it took ill, and had not been careful about scalding out the dish from which it fed. We found this out, however, when it was too late.

Meares soon secured a hunter to go with him, who proved himself an excellent cliff climber as well as a good marksman. He knew every inch of the country, and thought nothing of going into the most precipitous places, penetrating every nook and cranny where the game peculiar to this country is likely to hide. He was also quite a naturalist, knowing the habits of the various animals, as well as their haunts and calls. Meares found him a most congenial companion and a good sportsman, his one fault being that he smoked opium, though only at night when they returned from the chase. He writes of his hunting expedition thus:—

"As my new guide believed in still hunting we started off without dogs, taking nothing but a small lunch in our pockets. Our object was to follow the goral to his own hunting ground on the face of the cliffs. This is very dangerous work, as they make their homes on the most precipitous places, and hide in the caves and crevices of the rocks. The only way to get to them, when still hunting, is to walk along the narrow ledges, sometimes with a sheer drop of 1,000 feet and only a few inches of shelving rock to stand on ; but generally there are small trees and shrubs growing out of the cracks of the rocks, that afford one a hand hold while carefully treading one's way along these dangerous ledges. The little hunter was so used to his work that he could trot over places that made my head swim, and he would lean his body out over the side of the cliffs in search of game to such an extent that I often feared for his safety, and expected to see him go dashing on the rocks below at any minute. There was no need for alarm, however, on my part, so far as his safety was concerned, for I soon found out that he knew his business thoroughly, and that my whole concern need be about myself and the game we expected to see at any minute. He would place me on an important game-run, then circle round. If he started anything and could not get a shot at it he drove it towards me, and we never returned empty-handed during the days we hunted in this locality.

"One day I hit a big wild boar and broke his shoulder. He went to bay in some long grass. The little hunter at once rushed in after him and gave him a charge of buckshot at close range, which so disgusted the boar that he threw himself over the cliff, and we found him dead and very much mangled on the stones at the bottom. He was the largest wild boar I had ever seen ; one of his hind legs had been broken at some time but had mended again.

"The hard hunting on the cliff day after day was too much for me, and the tendon of my heel got strained and swollen to double its size. With a great effort I managed to get to my inn and had to lie up the next day. So Tussu arrived in the evening and put up in the same inn. A little later a runner came in with the news that So Tussu's castle was being attacked by brigands, and begged him to hurry to the rescue. The Chief pleaded with me to accompany him and bring my rifle along, offering his horse for me to ride on. Seeing he was in trouble I decided to go along; so blistered my heel to reduce the swelling, and next morning we started off early. After two days' forced marching we reached the castle where the old Tussu, So's father, lived. On our arrival we were told that the robbers had heard of our coming, and had retreated into the mountains, and we heard nothing more of them during my stay. The old castle is situated at Sanchiangkou [*i.e.*, Three Rivers Mouth]. The castle is hid away in the mountains in a very picturesque place, where three streams, one coming from the west, one from the north, and one from the east, join. This was once the southern capital of the States, and is quite a typical Mantze castle. Over 100 years ago the Prince was asked by the Viceroy of Szechwan to move from here to Tunglin, where the northern capital now stands, so as to be near the Chinese official at Wenchuan, who is nominally responsible for the affairs of the Wassu State, and through whom all reports to the Chinese Government is made.

"I spent a few days getting some very interesting fossils, which are quite plentiful in these valleys. The country is very mountainous, with out-crops of limestone, and in some places granite, quartz and mica schist are to be found; but as I am not a geologist I will not attempt to give a full description of the geological structure of this country, but I feel sure it will prove a very interesting field for the scientist.

"I started back to the inn in Yinhsiuwan on horseback, but on the second day my horse broke down and I had to finish my journey on foot, and arrived very much of a wreck. I laid up for some days, and watched the rafts being built which were to shoot the rapids for a distance of thirty miles down to Kwanhsien. The square sticks of timber are fastened together into long narrow rafts, the logs being laid overlapping each other, and then fastened together with ropes of twisted bamboo, which are lashed up tight and then driven firm with wedges. The result is a raft that is firm and yet

THE GORAL SHOT BY THE AUTHOR AT 1,000 YARDS.

pliable. One long oar is mounted on the bow and another on the stern. When all is ready six men are lashed to each oar, the ropes are cut, and off goes the raft dashing through the rapids, water breaking over the heads of the men, who are straining at the oars to avoid the rocks that crop up everywhere. I saw one raft strike a rock, and not only was the raft broken apart, but the very logs were snapped into pieces like so many dry twigs, and only three out of the twelve men on the raft got ashore; the rest were drowned. The men who do this work have wonderful nerve, but a large number of them annually find a watery grave."

While Meares was waiting at Yinhsiuwan some hunters brought in another young goral alive, and he sent it on to Brooke at Chentu; but, unfortunately, it also died, the heat of the plain seeming to be too much for it. Another hunter brought in two golden-haired monkeys he had just shot. These were carefully skinned and forwarded to Chentu, and one of them is now mounted in the South Kensington Natural History Museum. These monkeys are remarkable animals: they have bright blue faces and dark brown eyes; their nose looks as if a bright blue butterfly was sitting with its wings open in the middle of their face; they have a long golden mane down their back. At Kwanhsien I saw a skin with hair eighteen inches long and valued at £12 15*s*. These skins are collected and sent to the Imperial Family, and when made up into garments are allowed to be worn by them only.

CHAPTER X.

HAUNTS OF THE BUDORCAS.

WHEN I returned to Chentu at the end of March I found plenty of work awaiting me, but by working hard early and late I soon overtook it, and on May 10 again set out on one of my long tours through the semi-independent States, called by the Chinese Mantze Land (the Land of the Barbarian). This trip had been planned in the previous autumn, when I made out my annual report. Mr. Brooke, on learning of my intention to take this journey, was anxious to accompany me, so made his plans accordingly. When I reached Wenchuen I found him and Mr. Meares awaiting my arrival. I immediately went to see Prince So, to try and get a letter of introduction to some of the princes of the interior States through which I wished to travel. I was much disappointed, however, to hear that he had not yet returned from his southern capital, but his secretary informed me that he expected him any day, and that he had sent word that he had already started for home. It was important to have a letter from him, as the territory through which I hoped to travel had not previously been visited by any foreigners, and the letters he gave me on former occasions had been a great help while travelling in the Central States of Somo, Drukagi, Ranga, Damba, Chos-schia, Bawang, Bati, Gaishechia, and also on my journey over the Hungchiao Pass and in the Muping State. This time my plan was to get farther north and cross through Ngaba, Ngolok and Youkoh States, then down through Gaishechia, a journey which would take at least three months. I had a large supply of Scriptures with me to distribute among the priests and any people who could read. The Tibetan Scriptures are taught throughout this section of the country, but the spoken language would not be understood in Tibet proper. I had a friend at Tsakalao who, I knew, would give me a letter to some of these chiefs; but on former journeys I had started from this point, and kept my connection right through by being handed from one prince to another, thus going from State to State; and I felt it very important to adhere to a plan which formerly had proved so successful.

Having decided that it was best to wait the return of the Prince, we planned to spend a few days visiting the Changmin villages, which are to be found far up the mountain side. Many of these villages are also hid away in deep valleys, where they cannot be seen from the main road. On hearing that another party was on their way up to hunt the takin in these mountains, we thought it might be worth our while to see if these Changmin people knew anything about these strange animals, the budorcas or takins, and their haunts, as it was reported that they captured a great number of them every year.

On the street we had a Mohammedan friend, who has a great deal to do with the Changmin people. At the present time he owns much of the land occupied by them, having taken mortgages on their property, which they have not been able to redeem; their deeds have fallen into his hands, and they now find themselves renting their lands from him. Indeed, he has almost as much power over the Changmin as Prince So has over the Wassu people.

This Mohammedan started life as a poor boy, selling scones on the street at four a penny. Having shrewd business capacity, his fortune has grown until, at the age of 65, he owns over 200 mules, which carry much of the goods passing between Songpan and Kwanshien. He buys up all the gold and musk

THE INTREPID HO, MR. BROOKE'S COOK, WITH TWO HEAD COOLIES HAVING DINNER IN CAMP.

of the district, supplies the farmers with seed grain, and in the autumn buys up any produce they may have to dispose of. He is also squire of the country side, and tries more cases than the magistrate, since every case which reaches the higher officials must first pass through his hands; and many cases are settled without going further, he receiving a small fee for his trouble per case. He is now very wealthy, and by far the most influential man in this part of the country; and even the mandarins borrow large sums of money from him when they wish to purchase billets. Mr. Ma has been very friendly to me for some years, and to have him on one's side implies practically the whole of the Changmin and Chinese community.

We inquired of him about the haunts of the takin and the people who live in the valleys and mountains to the north-west. He at once supplied us with a guide and sent word to the headman of one of the Changmin villages, hid away in a deep valley surrounded by lofty mountains. Though no foreigner had penetrated this valley before, we found the headman and many of the people awaiting our arrival on the commons outside the village; they gave us a hearty welcome, and escorted us to apartments provided by the headman. We spent a pleasant afternoon chatting with the people, who freely gathered about us; and as they offered to supply hunters to guide us to a place where they claimed that the takin roamed in herds, we decided to go up with the hunters and see if we could secure some of these animals.

The next morning we started early, taking supplies for three days, and followed up a small stream which we crossed and recrossed hundreds of times, having to wade sometimes nearly waist deep through the cold water, which came rushing down from the snow-clad peaks all about us. By noon we came to a deserted lumberman's hut, and as it was raining, our men took possession of it to prepare dinner. But before they had got the fire well kindled they came rushing out as if they were possessed, some of them rolling on the grass, others beating themselves with their caps, others tearing off their clothes in such a wild way that we thought they must have stirred up a nest of deadly vipers. What they had actually deranged was in fact a nest of fleas, but such fleas I had never seen before. They were as large as the small black fly of Canada and quite as ferocious. The faces, hands, feet and clothing of the coolies were literally covered with these creatures, and every bite left a great red blotch; nor could they have made more fuss if they had been attacked by a nest of hornets. Needless to say, we chose another camping ground and ate our dinner in the pouring rain.

By 4 o'clock we were in a dense forest, where there were plenty of takin tracks, but these not very fresh. We climbed up to the snow-line and there found an old woodcutter's hut, built out of coffin boards and roofed with bark; in this the coolies took shelter. We cut some spruce boughs, and by propping up some of the coffin boards, managed to make a flat place on the side of the mountain on which to spread out our beds, and put up our tent as best we could; but it was impossible to get room to stretch it tight enough to keep it from leaking. We were a forlorn-looking lot; our clothing was wet through and even our bedding none too dry, and the tent was leaking. Fortunately there was plenty of wood, so we built a huge fire in the coolies' hut and sat round it, everyone trying to dodge the streams of yellow water that streamed through the leaking roof.

After our evening meal we turned in, and our bed of wet boughs seemed really comfortable after our arduous tramp. Towards morning we heard the screeching of a wild animal of some kind, but none of us were sure what it was.

After breakfast we all started out in various directions, each with a native guide. I went up through the firs to the rhododendron forest, and along the top of one of the ridges where the snow still lay deep ; but all I could find were tracks, most of which were several days old, and two old traps set to spear animals as they passed over the game-ways. These were made with a spring pole, on the end of which had been attached a sharp knife ; there was a trip spring which the animal would strike with his feet and release the spring pole, which would drive the knife through his side, presumably just behind the front shoulder.

These traps had been set by the woodcutters or hunters the previous year. The knives had been taken away, so that when we saw them they were harmless ; but one of our guides showed us a mark in his thigh where one of these knives had been driven through one thigh and into the other by one of these spring poles or traps, and the hunter needs to be on the look-out when tramping through a forest.

One day, while we were sitting on the top of one of the ridges eating our lunch, there came suddenly a great crash and roar as if the earth had split in two, and even the hunters looked aghast; but it was only a landslide, and part of one of the mountains was seen sliding down into the valley. In some places the path would lead us along a narrow ridge where a slip of the foot on either side would land us at the foot of the precipice several hundred feet below. Again, we would climb high staircases made by notching a log and setting it on end against the cliff; in other places sticks of wood were tied to uprights by creepers, and up these we had to climb until it made our heads giddy to look down. How the takin makes his way about in such a country is a mystery to me, but in the early spring here he is to be found, during his short period of migration from the sheltered valley in which he has passed the winter, to the grassy plains where he feeds during the summer months. We saw plenty of fresh tracks, but unfortunately did not meet one of these wonderful creatures.

The spell that sometimes comes over one, standing on some lofty peak admiring the work of nature, is indescribable. People say it is necessary to go to church to recognise the sublimity and omnipotence of a Supreme Being; but they can have no idea of the meaning of the words till they have gazed on such wonderful scenes as are unveiled before one's eyes in such a country as this, where nature has been untarnished by the hand of man. There is no cathedral in the world which can compare with God's handiwork, and one often feels His presence nearer in the open church of nature than in the buildings and dress of conventional religion.

We had received word that Prince So had returned to his castle, and we immediately struck camp and returned to Wenchuan, that no further time might be lost. The stream which had been so difficult to cross when coming up was now flooded with heavy rains, and was rushing shoulder deep over the boulders, so that it was only with much difficulty and danger that we succeeded in getting our coolies safely over. On the way down I called at So Tussu's castle to see the Chief and try and get the letter of introduction that we had been waiting for. On this occasion, however, he flatly refused to give one for the Ngaba and Ngolok chiefs, as he declared there was war going on between them and Somo. Of this trouble I had previously heard something, but thinking it might not be very serious, I was anxious to try and get through that country if possible. Prince So was quite friendly and gave me a similar letter to the one of the previous year on condition that I should not try to enter the territory where the fighting was going on. Then we said good-bye, and I went down to the city to make our arrangements for a forward movement on the morrow.

Brooke and myself continued our journey westward, following the valley of the Min as far as Weichow, where we crossed the rope bridges that span the Min and the Siho

West River, and followed up the banks of the latter, passing through a barren-looking country where the only sign of anything green was the cultivated fields along the valley and hillsides. Sage brush was the only natural vegetation.

On many peaks were to be seen the villages of the Changmin scattered along the mountain side. These villages were often scarcely distinguishable from their surroundings, being built of the native stone which is the same dull colour as the barren-looking mountains, but in this section of the country between Weichow and Lifan there are at least 50,000 of this remnant of the ancient occupants of the province of Sechuan. They are now under the Chinese Government, and have had no chiefs of their own for nearly 1,000 years. They are still looked down on by the Chinese, though they have adopted Chinese customs and habits to a great extent. They dress in a coarse woollen cloak which is suitable to protect them from the cold winds that continually blow in these mountains. The women speak their own patois, which is not understood on opposite sides of the river; the men all speak Chinese, many of them "broken" enough; and very few of them are able to read the Chinese character. They have no written language of their own. The Chinese Government is establishing schools in some of these villages, and the coming generation is encouraged to attend them. I visited several of these schools, and the people were most friendly.

We next visited Lifan or Paongan, where there are two Chinese officials, one a civil and the other a military, who nominally have authority over a large section of the country to the west and north, but being located in the south-east corner of their jurisdiction they have little or no power over such remote parts as Somo, Drukagi, Ranga, Damba or Ngaba, which are entirely governed by their own princes and chiefs.

However, they claim the same right as the Chinese do in Tibet proper, *i.e.*, that these States must supply the Chinese with free transports when travelling through the country, and once in seven years visit Peking with tribute which consists of the natural produce of each State.

At Lifan we visited my old friend, Mr. Wang, the Chinese civil official. He was most friendly, but tried to persuade us not to go north into Ngaba, and said he could not give us any permit into that country. Indeed, he showed us an order from the Viceroy to keep foreigners out of all the semi-independent States, on account of a German traveller having got into serious difficulty with the Golok the previous year.

As I was an old friend, he consented, after a lot of talk, to give us a pass. It stated we might go where we wished, in terms so vague, that it appeared we might go where we would; but Wang added a verbal warning to us to be very careful and not get into trouble, and to keep clear of any districts where there might be any local feuds going on.

He sent the same old Lingpan or escort with us who had accompanied me on my former journeys, so I felt pretty safe, and was very glad that the German gentleman's troubles of the previous year had not blocked the way for another journey into a most interesting country.

At Lifan I met my old friend, Colonel Kao, who was down from Tsakalao on business, and who gave us a pressing invitation to stay with him at his yamen.

On the way to Tsakalao we spent the night at the home of another friend, Colonel Gou, who has command of the Kamba military camp. They were delighted to see me again, and the best they had was not too good. These officers live in old feudal style, having many servants who have been born on the estate, and who are practically members of the family, or at least in many respects are so treated as such; yet they preserve a certain distance all the same and have great respect for their master and mistress and family. These servants appear to be perfectly happy, and are given their clothes and food, besides a little spending money when they go to the city, but they have no stated wage.

One member of every family must hold himself in readiness to bear arms for the Chinese Government, whenever they should be called on, and they receive the small annual allowance of about five shillings during times of peace, and fifteen shillings per month when called to service.

There are five of these camps, each under a colonel, and are called by the Chinese Wutun (five camps), viz., Shangmungtun, Shamungtun, Kintzechai, Kamba and Tsakalao, the latter being the most important.

There are between 600 and 800 men on the road at each camp. I have visited each of these, and found all the colonels and people most friendly. At first they were suspicious, but now we are the best of friends, and I am always taken into their castles or yamen and treated with entire kindness.

As this is mainly a narrative of travel I must not go into any detail about customs and habits of these people, but will just say that at one time the strongest of all the tribal chiefs controlled the affairs of this valley. He rebelled against the Chinese Government, and a large army was sent against him. He was overthrown, and his castle, which was located near the place where the town of Tsakalao now stands, was razed to the ground. The Prince was captured and put to death, and five Chinese colonels were placed in control of the five camps above mentioned. They took to themselves wives of the daughters of the native chiefs, and later were given hereditary colonelships, on condition that they kept the people loyal and peaceable. To-day we find a mixed race. There is a good deal of Chinese blood in them; as each colonel marries the daughter of one of the semi-independent princes of the eighteen tribes, the Chinese strain in the families of these hereditary colonels is considerably lessened; but they are all loyal to the Chinese Government. After spending two days visiting the district and the large monastery here, we moved on to Tsakalao and stopped with my old friend, Colonel Kao, who would not hear of our putting up in the inn.

No word had arrived of Meares, who was to have met us here. But a short time after we left Tsakalao he arrived, quite broken up after the rough time he had during his search for the takin. He sent a coolie after us, who overtook us about ten miles out, and Brooke returned to Tsakalao to see the skins Meares had secured, and to arrange about their being forwarded to Chentu. I continued my journey alone until they overtook me by making forced marches. Meares separated from us on May 17th, and started off with three hunters and a coolie, a little bedding, and a limited supply of food. After three days' hard tramp up a most terrible path, he reached a spot where the takin was supposed to abound. The mountains were so steep that it was difficult to find a level space on which to pitch their tent, and so they all camped out under an overhanging rock. After unpacking the loads, Meares took his rifle and went out for a stroll. He had not gone more than 200 yards from the camp when he found the fresh tracks of a takin cow and calf. He followed these tracks for a long way until they crossed a stream, on the other side of which they left evidence that they had very recently moved away. He followed them on through the bamboo thickets until darkness closed in and he had to leave them and return to camp.

Next day they again got on their tracks and followed them up to a salt spring where the takin congregate, and where they had made broad, beaten-down paths running in all the points of the compass, but their quarry had not stopped long here, and they followed it on over the mountain tops till evening began to fall, when they had to abandon the chase. For the next week, from daylight till dark, they were out scouring the mountains without seeing any trace of the takin.

One day was like the next. They rose every morning as soon as it was light, cooked a meal of rice and bacon, and then off to the mountains, always climbing upwards, pulling themselves up by the rhododendron roots, and sometimes falling back again, and so on upwards to the heights where it was hard to get one's breath. The most depressing part was that there seemed to be no living things in the mountains; only once or twice they saw a tiny mouse-rabbit, and on one other occasion, when high up on the mountains, Mr. Meares was surrounded by an army of angry little birds, tiny tits and small brown birds, which suddenly appeared from nowhere, When he was sitting on a stump resting, about fifty of them collected on the branches all round him; and then, when he kept quite still, they got bolder and bolder, till first one sat on his rifle, then another on his shoulder, then others, all jumping about and using terrible language at this strange giant who had invaded their country. At last he had to move, the spell was broken, and the wilderness was birdless again for days. But there was no sign of a takin, except once when the hunters were alone, they said they saw one, but their guns were wet and would not go off. All the time it poured in torrents day and night, except high up, where it snowed.

After ten days of this, provisions got low, and as Meares had to cut across unknown mountains to meet us others, he gave orders to pack up the camp, and went out for a last look at the salt springs. That reached, he found fresh tracks of a cow and half-grown calf, and at once went in chase, and after many hours climbing got a sight of them, and put a bullet into the cow. She was hard hit, but managed to get down the hill some distance, and he only just managed to give her the *coup-de-grace* on the edge of the cliff 100 feet high.

The hunters went off after the young one, and soon brought it down on their shoulders. By the time they had photographed and skinned the takin it was dark, so they felled some huge fir trees, and made an enormous bonfire around which they sat all night, roasting and eating the meat. The young takin meat is like the very best veal, and by morning there was very little of the smaller carcass left but the bones.

TAKIN SHOT BY MR. MEARES.

Meares told us later that he will never forget the morning following. The camp was high up among the pine trees and the sun rose in a clear blue sky, painting the circle of snow peaks around them the most brilliant colours. Everything was perfect, and he felt at peace with the world. He had been rewarded for his trouble by being the first person to shoot an animal which had hardly been seen alive by a European before, and last, but not least, he had had a real good feed. He returned to the cave, and the hunters carried down the skins and heads and bones of both animals and all the meat that was left. How they managed to do it Mr. Meares had no idea, as there were no paths whatever, and each man's load must have weighed over 100 lbs.

Next morning they started off with their bedding and the skins and bones to cross the mountain range to join us.

It was a pouring wet day, and they trudged up the valley, most of the time wading almost waist deep in the stream itself, for there was no road along the bank.

Meares was at the head of the party when suddenly he caught sight of a hump-backed, grey-coated, black-horned, short-legged object crossing an open space on the hillside about 300 yards away. It was a bull takin. He at once sent a bullet after it, and though it appeared to be hit, it went off at a good pace. On arriving at the spot he found a good deal of blood, showing it had been badly hurt. They followed its trail some distance, but the rain was coming down in such torrents that it soon washed away all trace of the animal, and finally they had to give up the chase.

They toiled up the mountain side till darkness overtook them, and pitched their camp under a pine tree, where they spent the night. At daybreak they started off again, leaving the stream and striking straight over the mountain. After a hard climb for several hours they reached the tree-line and entered the open land beyond, where a bitter cold gale was blowing, which froze their clothing and cut right through them. He saw some of the large yellow mountain poppies, which were already in bloom, but, the day he passed, every hair on every petal was encased in a coating of ice, which shows how hardy these wild poppies are. When they topped the pass, and had reached the northern slopes, they escaped the bitter wind, but found in front of them a field of deep snow, but no path or track was visible.

The snow was more than knee-deep, the coolies were heavily laden and almost frozen, so Meares had to go ahead and break a road. His rope sandals were worn out, and he had to finish the journey almost barefooted. After much difficulty they reached the timber-line, and were able to make a fire and warm themselves; here they found an old timber slide, down which they quickly slid, and soon found themselves in the warm, sunny valley in which Tsakalao is situated. On arrival he found that Brooke and myself had left the day before, but having no money with him to pay the men, he sent a coolie after us to call Brooke back. On the latter's return he found a fine takin skin, which delighted him much, for since he had not been able to shoot it himself, he rejoiced that his companion in travel had been the first Englishman to shoot this strange and coveted animal, the inhabitant of these almost inaccessible mountains.

This little-known animal stands as high as a small bullock, but is much more heavily built. Its legs are especially short and thick, and its feet are shaped like those of a goat, only much larger. I have seen some tracks as much as six inches in diameter. They have Roman noses, black curved horns, and short cut-off ears; the hair of the cow is creamy white, but most of the bulls have a reddish-grey coat, a short tail like a goat, and to some extent resemble the musk ox. In the springtime the cows travel about with their young, who can follow their mothers anywhere at three days old, and are weaned at one month old. In the early spring they seem to feed almost entirely on a plant which looks very much like rhubarb or burdock and grows along the bottoms of valleys. In the month of June they all collect about the salt licks, toward which they make broad, regular, beaten roads, and a little later collect into large herds, and graze in the grass lands above the tree-level.

The natives are very much afraid of these animals when

HUNTING THE TAKIN; A BIT OF THE ROAD.

they have congregated in herds, and say that if one of the group is wounded, the whole company will charge right over the hunter. Each herd has an old bull as leader, and they follow him everywhere ; an old hunter told me that on one occasion he met a small herd on a narrow path and shot the leader, who fell over the cliff, the others immediately threw themselves over after him, though there were some tens of feet of a sheer drop. Judging from the skins I have seen, some of the bulls must grow to a tremendous size.

CHAPTER XI.

FORWARD TO SOMO.

WHEN Messrs. Brooke and Meares had finished drying and packing the budorcas' skins they crossed the river over the big cantilever bridge to visit Colonel Kao. While they were talking and drinking tea with him they heard a crash and a roar, and on going out to see what it was they discovered that the bridge over which they had just passed had collapsed. It had been standing for forty years, and, as the Colonel apologetically remarked, "It never did that before." This entailed their marching five miles down the river to the nearest bridge before they could recross.

On June 4 Brooke and Meares set off to overtake me, and by fast travelling caught me up in two days, as I had been doing much visiting by the way. The road they took is most picturesque, and keeps close to the banks of the Siho (west river), crossing from time to time from one side to the other to avoid the great cliffs that rise sheer up from the river side in many places. We overtook a pack of mules laden with tea for Matang. This tea was the worst rubbish I had ever seen going under that name, it looked more like dried birch leaves and half rotten twigs than tea, and smelt very musty; but the tribespeople seemed to prefer it to a better quality. We passed several Mantze villages during the first twenty miles' march, and there were a number more up the ravines to the north and south which we could not see from the main road. Leaving the cultivated lands behind, the road ran through a deep gorge close to the side of the river, and the mountains seem to rise almost straight up for 6,000 feet, so that the sun can only cast its rays in the narrow valley for about two hours each day. This is, indeed, a lonely place, and the roar of the river and the song of the birds are all that breaks the stillness. Passing through this gorge we came out to a small clearing, in which stood a solitary house, called Sintientze (new inn), but I have no doubt it had stood there for at least a hundred years, as the smoke from the fireplace in the middle of the main living-room had long since turned the rafters and ceiling the colour of ebony. Passing on through a widening valley, in which stood isolated farmhouses, built of stone, we soon passed the boundary line between Tsakalao territory and the State of Somo. We were at last on ground completely governed by an independent hereditary Tussu or Prince, with many chiefs under him, who direct the local affairs throughout his kingdom. From the boundary line of Somo to Kouerhkou, where we hoped to spend the night, we passed through wheat and barley fields. The people were very friendly and came out as we passed through their little settlements. We were able to have a kindly word with them. It was 7.30 when we reached the little wayside inn, located within half a-mile from the Mantze fort of Kouerhkou, where the chief of this district has his palatial home, built on the spur of the mountain. The town looks quite impregnable, but we decided to take it by a strategy, being determined not to spend the night in the miserable little hovel by the wayside. It may be necessary to explain to the reader that it is most difficult for a stranger to find hospitality in any of these forts, and for the accommodation of the Chinese coolies and travellers little wayside inns have been erected all along the main road so far as the medicine digging enterprise is carried on ; but these huts are so filthy that it is next to impossible for a foreigner to live in them, even for a night, though on many occasions when I have not had a tent with me I have been compelled to lodge therein. On this occasion, however, I made up my mind I would try for something better in the fort, and sent my interpreter up to the head man of the Chaitze,

THE INTERPRETER KAO.

while I remained at the Chinese hut by the roadside. My interpreter was a native of Damba State, and was also a relative of my friend Colonel Kao, so that he would have no difficulty in procuring lodgings for himself. The plan was that he should first secure lodgings and then inform his host that a friend of Colonel Kao's was stopping at the inn and would also like accommodation, but not to intimate to him that this friend was a foreigner. I could trust my interpreter to play the game, for he had been with me the two previous journeys, and had proved himself adroit. When he had secured the room he was to shout down and I would come up, so that I really entered the house before the old chief knew I was a foreigner. As arranged so things befell. At first the chief was somewhat sulky; but when he found that I was the person who passed through last year he became more friendly, and in less than half-an-hour we were on the best of terms. He gave me a very nice little room on the roof, where I spread out my bed and made myself comfortable, and after supper I came down to the family apartment, a large room in the centre of which a huge fire was burning, while on large iron tripods stood three great pots used for cooking purposes. We all sat round the fire tailor-fashion, for they never use chairs or benches in this part of the country, and there we chatted till midnight. The old lady was very anxious about her daughter, who had run away some weeks before because she had been punished for disobedience. The mother was quite anxious that I should divine, and tell her if her daughter would ever return! She was sure I could, and when I explained that no one could really tell the future, and that it was only a way the Lamas had of making money, she half agreed, but still thought there was something in it. The tribespeople are also strong in palmistry, and as I had read a little on the subject I greatly pleased the old lady by looking at her hand, and telling her she was to live to a good old age—as she was now between sixty-five and seventy, and there was little danger of my not telling the truth. We were good friends now, and I was urged not to go on the morrow, but spend the day with them. As I was anxious to visit the valley that runs north from here I gladly accepted. Before retiring tsamba and tea were provided. This is the usual Tibetan food, made of parched barley meal and buttered tea. As explained before, the meal is mixed with the tea into a thick paste, then kneaded dry, until you can hold it in your hand much as you would an uncooked

COLONEL GOU AND HIS FAMILY.

cake; but as the meal has been previously parched it tastes quite good when one is hungry, and in effect buttered tea is much like soup. Strange as this food may seem to the stranger it is very nourishing, and the people seem to thrive on it. After thus refreshing ourselves I retired to my apartment on the roof, and, as I went, the family stretching themselves out with their feet toward the fire, which still burned in the centre of the room, wrapped themselves in their woollen or sheep-skin gowns and seemed not to mind the hard boards of the flooring, which is the best bed they know of.

Next morning, after an early breakfast, I started up the valley to visit another chief. For some hours we walked up the path which lay along the bed of the stream, on which were built several flour mills, also a number of large prayer cylinders turned by water-power. These cylinders are filled with rolls of parchment, on which are carefully written the prescribed formulas, such as "Om! ma-ni pad-me Hung!" —*i.e.*, "Hail! The Jewel (Grand Lama) in the lotus-flower!" which is the standard prayer of Lamaism. Of course there are many other formulas of a similar character used to fill in the miles of parchment neatly rolled on these cylinders, which are kept constantly turning by the sparkling streams Nature has so bountifully provided in this wild and fascinating country. The banks of the stream were covered with thick brushwood and flowering plants of many kinds; the perfume of the lilac and other sweet-smelling flowers filled the air; the humming of the bees, the song of the birds, could not but arrest and charm; but there was less of the song of the busy tribesmen, and I was disappointed to find so few people in what I had assumed to be a thickly populated valley.

On arriving at the village I found that most of the houses had been burned down the previous year, and nothing but the charred walls of most of the buildings now remained. The only sign of life was a few women busily weaving their coarse hempen cloth, and some girls beating out the flax. Most of the inhabitants, both male and female, were away on the mountains with the cattle, or on the heights near the snow-line, gathering herbs, an occupation general among the inhabitants of this region during the months of June and July, while their crops are maturing in the fields. Return in August and the hills and valleys will resound with the merry song of the young men and maidens, as they ply their sickles to the beat of their weird chanting.

The people were very timid, as they had never before seen a foreigner. After a little inquiry I found the chief, with whom I chatted for a few hours. He did not invite me into his home, but was quite friendly, and when he learned I was stopping with his neighbour chief at Kouerhkou he told me of a road which led from here over the mountains to the Black River valley, occupied by the famous Hei Shui (black water) tribe, who hold the valleys of the Black River. That is a country never yet visited by any European, but I hope some day to tramp these hitherto forbidden reaches, as I have an invitation from the chief Daerhwangchen to do so.

After partaking of some refreshments with the chief I retraced my steps down the valley, and the only people we met during the march were some woodcutters returning with huge bundles of faggots on their backs, and two Chinese wine merchants making their way toward the villages we had just left. These people are passionately fond of wine, and while they make a mild drink locally from barley, they are very fond of the Chinese fire-water, which is about sixty-five per cent. proof, and will burn readily if you simply set a match to it. Water is sometimes added both by the Chinese merchant and by the people themselves after they purchase it; but the liquor is also frequently imbibed in its pure state through the little terra-cotta syphon quite like a small jug, with a teat on the handle for the lips. The syphon is usually sucked from after heating it, for while they do not mind eating cold food they like their wine hot. When a tribesman is intoxicated, the best plan is either to give him a wide berth or let him have his own way, and say "yes, yes," to all his suggestions. To oppose would only provoke him to a free use of the small sword or dirk which he always carries in his belt; and though perfectly friendly when sober, the man may suddenly turn one's bitterest enemy when intoxicated. Few of them eat opium, though this curse has found its way into a few homes, and with consequences even more marked on the tribesman than upon the Chinese. Immediately he adopts its use the former surrenders himself completely to the habit, and in a very short time becomes a complete wreck. Two causes suggest themselves: firstly, the opium sold to the tribesmen is largely made from opium ash and refuse from the Chinese opium dens, and is adulterated for the tribal trade; in the second place, these people have little to occupy their minds, and when once they become addicted to the habit, have little to oppose to its influence.

When I started on our forward march next morning the chief provided me with an escort, composed of one old woman and two girls. It is customary in this part of the country for the females to escort visitors from one chief to the other. The only reason I can give is that the men are usually away on a hunting tour, and the women are left to look after the homes and crop. The women and girls of this part of the country are very different from the Chinese, and are more like the American, French or Scandinavian girl in their freedom of conversation. Our escort marched along with the caravan, freely chatting to the interpreter and myself, as though they were the happiest people in the world. On one occasion I made a remark about their aversion to the free use of water, saying they would be really good-looking if they would only keep themselves clean, and by way of contrast pointed to my neck, saying, "Yours might be as white as mine if you would only use soap and water." Her neck as I spoke was black as an African's. But for all that she was a sharp witted, rather good-featured lass, of about eighteen, and the quick reply I got was, "Yes, your skin may be white, but your heart is blacker than my neck." I was not aware that I had said or done anything to merit the remark, but I had to take it in good grace; and by the time our journey was ended I hope she realised that my heart was whiter than she suspected, for they all returned to their homes with a small string of cash and a thank you for their help in carrying our belongings over the five miles of rough but beautiful country. To receive pay and a kind word was

TIBETAN PLAYERS IN COMEDY.

rather a surprise to them, for if they had been escorting a Chinese Official they would probably have returned with curses for thanks and abusive language for pay, these being the attentions of his followers, even where the Official himself was polite. Kindness is something which surprises these people, so little of it do they receive from strangers; yet they are very kind and affectionate among themselves, and

I have never yet seen or heard any quarrelling in their ranks.

We followed the west bank of the river for twenty li (about five miles), when we again crossed another cantilever bridge, and entered a fertile valley which supported four villages, with a population of 300 families. Lodgings were found on the roof of one of the houses in the village of Cheoti, and we spent the night in fairly comfortable apartments. Here

TIBETAN PLAYERS IN TRAGEDY.

Brooke and Meares overtook me, and we travelled together as far as Chowser, the capital of Chosschia State.

About an hour and a-half after our arrival a Chinese Wei-yuen arrived from the west, sent out by the Viceroy of Sechwan in the interest of education, his business being to establish schools for the study of Chinese throughout these semi-independent States. His style and bearing, however, was not such as would give him much prestige, or command the respect and sympathy of this independent people. He rode on to the street with an air of superiority that was quite resented by the people, and seeing us on the roof of one of the houses he dismounted and walked in, feeling his way through the smoke, which was making use of the staircase for an outlet. When he emerged from its columns and stood on the roof beside us tears were in his eyes, but not the tear of sorrow or sympathy. He cursed the smoke, the houses and the people that lived in them. After he had finished and recovered his breath he demanded of me my business, how it was I had secured rooms in this house, and where I was going, and so forth.

He next informed me of the hostility of this barbarous race, saying it was not safe for a foreigner to be in their country, and tried to impress me with the importance of returning with him to Chinese territory. In reply, I asked him, "Whose jurisdiction this country was under; if, on their maps, it was not included in the province of Sechwan? for which I held a passport." When he found he could do nothing with me by arguments of this kind, he changed his tactics, and informed me that the road ahead was impassable, the rivers being swollen to such an extent that it was impossible to cross them, and that the mountain passes were deep in snow, and we would surely be frozen to death if we attempted to cross them. I listened to his story until he had poured it all out, then asked the question, "Where have you come from?" He told me how he had left Chentu and had travelled up the Siaochin Valley and over the pass to Drukagi, then up through Somo, over the Chiku Pass, and down to this point, all in the interest of education; but said he had not been able to establish a single school. I sympathised with him in the difficulties he had encountered during his arduous journey, and then asked, "How did you succeed in overcoming them?" When he told me a long story of how it was done I thanked him for his information, saying we would do likewise. He suddenly realised that he had given his case away, but I informed him there was no need of feeling badly, as I had been over the entire route that he had just travelled more than once, and knew it quite well. When he found he could make nothing out of me, and seeing the rooms were all occupied on the roof of this house—the best in the village—he bowed in farewell and went through the column of smoke down the crude staircase, and after seeking accommodation in the other houses of the village, where he was refused admittance, mounted his horse and with his companions rode off in search of accommodation in the next village, where he was told he would find it. I hope he was successful, but as the village was five miles away, and a rough road separated him from that place, I should not be surprised if he found himself compelled to spend the night under the open canopy of heaven or under some green tree. By 6 a.m. we were on the march, our road led us on through the valley, in which were cultivated fields to the right and to the left. The path kept near the river's brink, which here flows in a south-eastern direction, the early morning air was wonderfully refreshing, and almost in every direction the mountain tops glittered in the sunlight, many of them clad in a mantle of snow, while their lower slopes were covered with forests. Near the river's brink soft, maple, birch and ash trees abounded, while here and there a prickly oak warned us that we are approaching an altitude of 9,000 feet. Cultivated fields were seen dotting the mountain side, surrounded by rank foliage, and stone houses adorned some of the hillsides facing south. We reached Jiapi at noon. This is a village of about fifteen families; on a spur not far away stands a massive stone building, belonging to the prince, which he occupies during his periodical visits through the country. Away to the north the wide valley leads up to extensive pasture lands, on which we could make out through our glasses large herds of cattle grazing, and far above them the peaks capped with snow.

A little further on it was necessary to cross the stream, but here the bed of the river was broad and there was no bridge. The rain which fell during the previous night, together with the melting snow, had much increased the volume of the stream, and we had a great deal of difficulty in finding a suitable ford. On several occasions while endeavouring to cross my pony was almost carried off his feet by the swift current. Finally, we found a place where the water was not over three feet deep, and by stretching a guide-rope across for the pack coolies to hold to and steady themselves as they forded, we succeeded in getting the whole party safely over on the other side. About 4 o'clock we arrived at Miala, a group of stone houses built on the side of a hill, which boasts itself of supporting two chiefs and a population of 1,500 families in the surrounding district. It was difficult for us to discover where all these homes were located, as the village itself had not more than thirty houses, but scattered about on the mountain side are many isolated dwellings, which cannot be seen from the main road. There is also a large monastery on the wooded mountain to the south, which boasts itself of having about 1,500 lamas, or a proportion of one lama to each household—a rule which they try to live up to wherever Lamaism prevails.

On arriving at the town we were very much surprised to find all the doors shut in our faces. The interpreter and the Fusong were not able to obtain access, even to the home of the chief, the doors being locked and barred, with no sign of any life within. I had told the Fusong to go ahead and secure a place before our arrival; but as he had stopped for two days in this same town the previous year, and had left them so far as I knew friendly, I had not insisted on his doing so, while the interpreter, thinking there would be no difficulty whatever, had dallied behind with the coolies, and only arrived when we did. It began to look rather serious, and there seemed to be no way of getting in touch with the people, so I accompanied the interpreter and escort to the home of the second chief, who lived some little distance away. There the outer door was also locked; and though we rapped loud enough to be heard for some distance, the interpreter repeating the well-known call, "A friend has arrived, open unto him the door," there was no response. The wall was not very high, so Kao, who was an expert climber, scrambled up the side like a rabbit, and standing on the top called aloud to the inmates. At last a servant came out, and announced that there was no one at home, which we knew very well was a lie. The servant disappearing and leaving us to make the best of the situation; my interpreter quickly descended the wall on the inside and unbarred the gate, which was made secure by a great wooden cross pole, but not locked. And both he and I passed through the courtyard and through the stable that occupied the first storey of the castle, and ascending a broad staircase found ourselves on the flat roof, which formed the courtyard of the second storey.

When the inmates found the castle had been taken by storm, and that we were actually in possession, heads appeared over the balcony above us, and through windows on the second storey, declaring that they had no accommodation for travellers. My interpreter informed the old lama, who seemed to be the chief spokesman, that we were quiet and peaceable people, and that he had been sent by Colonel Kao, his master and lord, to escort and protect us from all harm, and that all we wanted was accommodation for the night, for which we were prepared to pay. Showing his military coat, as evidence of his authority, he took it off and hung it on the door; and according to the tribal custom, to refuse to open the door to that coat, or to insult it in any way, meant open revolt against the Colonel, whom they all respect throughout these States. There was nothing for it now, so they opened the door, and we were shown to a small room at the north side of the flat roof upon which we stood. The Fusong was sent down for the rest of the party and our things, and in a very short time we were comfortably settled in our little room. In less than half-an-hour the whole town had congregated on our roof. There were lamas in their scarlet robes, the layman in his brown yak-hair homespun gown, women clad in their hempen accordion-pleated skirts and short tight jackets. They were all curious to see the strange people who had come in their midst so unexpectedly. We were not long in making friends and gaining their confidence. Each of the lamas, and such laymen as could read, were supplied with books. It was interesting to see them collect in groups examining the clear type and passing complimentary remarks on the quality of the paper and the writing. We trust they understood the message these books brought to them. They soon began to gather around me, reporting their aches and pains—some toothache and rheumatism, others with ulcers and skin diseases of every kind. I was kept busy till dark extracting teeth, washing and dressing sores. Their fear of the foreigner had vanished, and old men and women and young maidens alike pressed for their turn of attention. One old lady sat down on the floor and let me extract two roots and one badly decayed tooth, all of which were giving her a great deal of trouble. She did not even groan; and when I had finished, though the blood was flowing freely, directed my attention to two other roots on the other side, which she was anxious that I should remove. But fearing that she might lose too much blood I advised her to wait until the morning to finish the operation. When the party broke up it was well on to 10 o'clock, but each with a polite bow said "good-night" before descending the staircase. We found the report of the Chief's absence was quite true, and some weeks later we met him at Drukagi, where he was trying to solicit help from that State against the people of Ngaba, with whom he and his expected to engage in war at any minute. The Chief's wife and family were extremely friendly, and sent letters by us to her husband. These I personally handed over to him, and he seemed greatly pleased with their contents, and was a good friend to us during our stay at Drukagi.

Here we were supposed to get ula; but, on account of our Fusong wanting to make too big a squeeze, the people would not bring their animals in until we promised to pay for them.

We now found out the reason why the doors were closed in our faces on arrival. I was told in confidence that my Fusong, on my previous journey had demanded fourteen horses and ten carriers to convey me and my belongings to the next chief, and that when the animals were brought in he had refused to take them, saying he must have the money instead. The price of a horse for a stage in the country where ula is used is three chien of silver per animal, and one chien for each carrier. This meant that the Fusong had extracted about fifteen shillings from the people, besides getting a free ride over the pass. Of course I knew nothing of it until after we had passed the place several days, and then only discovered it through a quarrel between the interpreter and the Fusong. On this occasion, however, I made it very clear, both to my escort and the people, that when I asked for animals I expected to pay for them, and that on no condition would I allow the Fusong to extract money from them on my account. When this was understood the people felt quite differently towards us, though I cannot say the Fusong was altogether pleased, nor did he exert himself on our behalf as on former journeys. I believe that much of the trouble experienced by so many travellers in China and Tibet is due to these blood-suckers, who, while they are serving the foreigner and extracting all they can from him, do not fail to do likewise to their own people, placing the blame on their innocent employer.

On the morning of June 7 we left the village of Miala behind and climbed up 2,000 feet, only to descend again to the river bed on the other side of the spur. We followed the stream, which for five miles flowed through a dense forest, and on emerging from this we entered a cultivated plain, on which were five small villages or groups of houses, all surrounded by green fields. The chinku (a kind of huskless barley), about the only crop grown at this altitude (for we were now quite 10,000 feet above the sea), had not yet grown to more than two inches above the ground and would not be harvested till September. For the last five miles of this stage it rained hard and we all got wet to the skin. On reaching Chintouchai, the last village before ascending the pass, we were able to secure rooms in the same house that I had stopped in the year before, and the whole party were soon sitting round a great fire in the large kitchen, steaming ourselves dry, for even our bedding had got wet, so heavy was the rain. All through the night it continued to pour, but towards morning it turned to snow, and when we awoke it was falling so thickly that we could not see any distance. The hills were covered a foot deep by 8 o'clock, and there was quite six inches in the valley. What were green fields the evening before were white fields now. The men said it was impossible to cross the pass, so we turned in again as there was nothing to be done, and one's pukai (a Chinese quilt), which serves the purpose of both mattress and bedding, was by far the most comfortable place in such weather.

I was not to enjoy this very long, however, for at 9.30 the

interpreter came into my room in great excitement, and reported that my horse had broken loose and got out of the stable, and they could find no trace of him. I sent the interpreter and head coolie in search of him, and neither of them having returned by the time I had had breakfast I too joined in

THE LI FAIR—CHINESE MANDARIN.

the hunt. I could track the horse by his shoes, and soon found that he had taken the road toward home. After I had followed him thirty li (ten miles) through the mud and slush (for the snow had now pretty well melted) I met some coolies who reported they had seen a horse near Miala, some ten li further on, and that he was still making toward Tsakalao as hard as he could go. I had run most of the way, but I now increased my pace down the mountain side, hoping he might turn into the place where he had been stabled at Miala; but on arrival there I learned that he had galloped straight through the village, and that my coolie had gone after him. Some five li further on we could see the horse, like a little speck, coming towards us, nibbling a bit of grass and then trotting forward a little. Later we could distinguish the coolie hobbling along behind him, driving him towards us. The road ran through the plain below Miala, and I knew there was no use trying to catch him there, so went back and waited for him in a stone lane near the village, and, just as he came round the corner, caught him. At the village I got some food and borrowed a saddle. In trying to catch the pony the coolie had been knocked down, and was so badly hurt that I had to put him on the horse's back and lead them both toward Chintouchai. At the top of the hill we met one of our muleteers coming in search of us, and on his mule I put the coolie, and mounting my horse galloped him all the way back, and got in nearly three hours ahead of the others. I was determined to pay the pony back for the tramp he had led me, but I am not so sure that I did not get the worst of it. The saddle I borrowed was an old hard one, which did not seem to fit me very well, and my horse seemed as fresh at the end of the run as when we set out. It was 4 p.m. when I returned, and we had perforce to spend the night in camp.

Next morning by 5.30 we were on the march and soon entered a thick forest, through which the road ran for fifteen li. Then we came out on the grass land at the foot of the pass, and soon overtook a caravan of some sixty mules, laden with tea, which had camped for the night, and was just loading up to start on the steep and arduous climb over the pass called Chiku Shan ("Eat-bitterness Mountain" the pass is called) ; and when the snow lies deep on its slopes, and especially in the "saddle," through which one goes on reaching the top, it is quite worthy of its reputation, and has claimed many victims during the winter seasons. There are many wild tales told of how the Black River people raid the caravans while crossing this pass, and muleteers always club together in large bands, and will scarcely ever venture over when there are less than twenty in a party. Some small caravans wait for days just above Chintouchai until a large caravan arrives and there joins them. While crossing this pass 12,000 feet above sea-level the grade is quite gradual, and the climb is only a little over 2,000 feet from the base of the mountain to the top ; but by the time the traveller has reached it he will imagine it to be several times that altitude. At the top there were still deep snow drifts, but these were melting away, and we found the purple and yellow poppies and many other flowers in bloom almost at the edge of the snow drifts. A drop of 2,500 feet in about four miles took us to Matang, a little tumbled-down trading station where the tea is deposited, and where the Tibetans and tribesmen from the upper Kermer and part of the Ngaba bring in their wool, hides and animals, in exchange for Chinese commodities. The inhabitants of Matang are nearly all Mohammedans. This place is too high to produce even vegetables, and the only occupation of the people is to trade with the natives in the surrounding country.

Ta-erh Wang Chen, the Chief of the Black River district, had arrived some hours before us, and was in his Kunghuan, or private residence, in which he puts up when passing this way. His lordship called on us soon after our arrival. The main object of his call, however, was to see if we had a gun for sale ! He was on his way to see the Somo Tussu and discuss the war that was imminent.

At 8.30 he sent his men up and invited us to come and

see him. We had called before but they were in council, and had asked us to wait till later. We were ushered into a room, at the head of which sat Ta-erh Wang Chen and his brother on rich Turkish cushions. In front of them was a large handsome brazier, on which were pots of steaming tea made from the coarse Kuanhsien leaves, with plenty of milk, and a goodly supply of salt added thereto.

The walls were covered with fuse guns, swords, daggers, spears and armour; while along both sides of the large room sat, or rather squatted, some fifty of his retainers and followers. All rose to their knees and bowed their heads as we entered. I was given a seat one place below the Chief at his left hand, which is the seat of honour. Hot wine was offered first, and when I refused it hot tea from the steaming pot before us was poured out, and we sipped and chatted till after 10 o'clock.

Ta-erh Wang Chen has a peculiar voice, more like the quack of a drake than anything I can think of. He understands and can speak some Chinese, but most of the conversation was carried on through an interpreter. He took a fancy to my little pony and I let him have it, though it was an old friend, on condition that when I wanted to go through his territory he would give me a pass and escort, which he promised to do.

CHAPTER XII.

THE JOURNEY TO CHOSSCHIA.

ON leaving Matang we descended an easy grade and soon reached the Kermer River, a stream flowing from the north. At Changku, the point where we crossed, it is spanned by a cantilever bridge, and there turns west and continues this general course, until it joins the Kwanyin River at Damba, and from this point, Changku, the united stream is known as the Tachin Ho (Great Gold River).

We followed the right bank of this stream. All the way to the capital of Somo the river was a foaming torrent, and for the most part of the way we passed through a dense forest, which extended from the river's bank to the lofty peaks, several thousand feet above our heads. Here and there where the valley opened out a little, some lonely farm houses were seen nestling at the foot of the cliffs, or perched on their sides. About 4 p.m. we emerged from this forest and got the first view of the fertile valley of Somo, dotted with its many villages, the houses of which are all built of stone; most of them three-storey high, and some even running to five storeys.

While we were resting and admiring the view that had opened out before us, we heard the war cry of the Black River warriors, which rose above the deafening roar of the Kermer. Their cry came nearer and nearer, so we decided to wait and let them pass, as the road was wide where we were. It was not long until the leaders appeared, some of them riding very fine mules and ponies, others at a half run holding to the tails of the animals, which were laden with their camping outfit and instruments of war. The cavalcade was a very extended one, and they came in bunches of threes and fours, and were spread out over about two miles.

We could not wait any longer for them and started off and marched in their ranks for some distance. They were a jolly lot. Once, when the advanced guard stopped to wait for their caravan, which was at the rear, and had not been able to keep up, we attempted to pass on. Some of them, out of fun, turned their animals across the road and tried to block it, and at first we were not quite sure of their intention, but soon discovered it was only play. No doubt they wanted to see if we were easily frightened. Finally we passed the whole cavalcade, which stopped to wait until their chief overtook them.

After a five-mile walk through cultivated fields, in which was a good crop of barley and wheat just coming into head, we found ourselves at the little bridge at the foot of the spur on which stood the castle and a group of houses, mostly occupied by the Tussu's retainers.

Several of the houses are also owned by representative men of districts throughout the realm.

On my former visit I lodged in one of the houses inside of the palace enclosure, which belonged to the Hei Shui Chief, but on this occasion he would need it himself, for he and his followers would fill every bit of available space, and we wondered where we would get accommodation.

I went on ahead to secure lodgings, and on the green near the bridge I found most of the inhabitants, both old women and young maidens, old men and boys, together with local headmen or chiefs, all kneeling on the grass, while Tibetan rugs were spread out, on which they were to entertain and welcome the Chief of the famous Black River people. I was riding along with two of Daerh Wang's heralds, and, according

DAMBA CASTLE.

to custom, we all dismounted when we drew near and were saluted by the waiting party.

I inquired where we were to lodge, and a man was told off to guide the way. We were led to a fine large stone house at the back of the palace, and about half-a-mile to the west of it, where we found comfortable quarters.

After passing up a long stone lane we entered a large court-yard, surrounded by a stone wall, where the animals were put up.

On going through the heavy doors, over which the skull of a bear was hung to keep away evil spirits, we passed through an opening in the thick wall of the house and, turning to our right, entered a large room forty feet long by thirty feet wide, in the centre of which was the usual fireplace, and a great fire burning under huge pots that stood on iron tripods, each pot holding about fifty gallons of water. This was the general kitchen and living room. We did not stay here, but were led up two dark stairways to the third floor, and shown to a very nice room in the centre of which also was a fireplace and a pot almost as large as those below. Wood was provided, but as there was no chimney, and the only way for the smoke to escape was through the two small windows, which did not afford much light to the room ; we preferred to be without a fire, and to have our food cooked in the kitchen below.

Although we did not have a fire in our room, we were not without our share of the smoke, for when all the coolies arrived, each group wanted a fire to themselves, and the smoke came in clouds up the stairway ; and, not being able to escape with sufficient rapidity through the windows in the outer wall, much of it found its way into our apartment. This made life so miserable that we had to go down and put out some of the fires, and inform the coolies they must be content to use the one general fire, as they would have to do in a

Chinese inn, or else buy their own wood and go outside to burn it.

We spent all the next day here. A number of people came about, but we were not able to see the Tussu ; he was some distance away, worshipping in a temple, and imploring the idols to endow him with wisdom before attending the council of war.

Next morning our ula arrived and by 9 o'clock we were on the march. For the first four miles the valley was cultivated, then we again entered thick undergrowth with a few large trees scattered about. Fire had run through some parts of it. There was nothing of particular interest until we reached Mami Chiao. There were a few houses here, in one of which I had put up for the night during my travels in 1907.

The cantilever bridge that spanned the river was leaning at quite an angle, and we had to be careful lest it should collapse like the one at Tsakalao ; however, we got safely across and the bridge was still standing when we left it.

A stiff climb brought us to the top of the spur, and here we had a fine view of the town of Drukagi, as well as of a good part of the State.

After a long detour down a zigzag path we reached the town. The interpreter and escort had gone on ahead, but when we arrived they had not succeeded in securing accommodation, so we had to stand in the street for some time.

Finally a house was put at our disposal, but the people refused to sell us wood. They had not been very friendly when I passed through here before, but they seemed more sullen than ever this time.

After a little some of the people became more talkative, and we found out that our Chinese friend, in the interest of schools, had left word with the Tussu that if any foreigner ever passed through this way again they were to take him

THE BRIDGE OF MAMI, WHICH THEY TORE DOWN TO KEEP MRS. BISHOP (MISS ISABELLA BIRD) FROM CROSSING.

prisoner and escort him out. My letter from So Tussu and Colonel Kao had rather put a different aspect on things, and they felt they must at least give us a place to sleep in. The Tussu, who is a Lama, left early next morning for a temple situated some distance up the stream, flowing from the south-west. He told our interpreter that he had no time to get us ula or an escort, and had left no one with power to act. The interpreter went up several times to try to get an escort and had for his pains a blank shot fired out of one of the windows of the palace at him.

We spent the day here, but were not able to do much more than make friends with a few of the people on the street, and next morning we left. Following the river which here runs a little north of west, we arrived at a large monastery called Maerhkang Cumba, five miles below Drukagi. The people and Lamas were quite friendly and we spent an hour chatting with them, but they would not let us enter the monastery.

From Maerhkang a road leads up one of the ravines to the grass land of Drukagi and on to Ngaba. From here we continued down the right bank of the stream, passing through a cultivated valley with groups of the usual stone houses on the hillsides, on both sides of the river. At last we sighted Runga on the spur of a hill, and the great castle in which the Princess lives, by far the most prominent edifice in the town. The Princess refuses to marry, lest the reins of government should be taken from her. She is greatly influenced by the Lamas, and spends a great deal of her time in a large monastery on a mountain some five miles from her castle. A report has it that she is not as virtuous as she would lead people to believe, and spends a good deal of her time with a favourite Lama in the temple. The rest of his time is taken up reciting prayers before the castle idols and acting as prime minister in temporal affairs. A Lama will probably succeed the Princess in the near future. The Lamas already have control of several States and are aiming at greater things. It is strange that these shepherds of the flock are not satisfied with the control of the spiritual welfare of the people, but are anxious to grasp the State and all its property and completely control it.

A very nice place was put at our disposal, and the people soon gathered round. Many of them came for medicine, and brought vegetables, eggs, meat and barley meal as a thankoffering; those who could read were given books and we were kept busy. Several of the headmen or local chiefs came and spent most of the time with us, partly to see how we treated the people, and hear what we had to say to them.

Mr. Brooke and Mr. Meares went over to the monastery at the other side of the river, and gave some small mirrors to the people, trying to make friends; but their effort was not very successful, for some of the priests objected to the maidens being able to see their own faces in the small glasses presented, lest they should really know how pretty they looked. So the priests had the mirrors all collected and broken up, saying that by means of these reflectors the foreigners would get possession of their souls. There is a belief current that to look into a looking glass will cause an abortion, which is why so many of them object to being photographed. To avert this influence the priests called all the holy men together, and, in chorus, from the roof of the temple, they clanged their cymbals, blew their trumpets, read their holy books, and poured out all the curses in their ritual on the foreigner's head, for his attempt to harm the people under their care. They were surprised that their curses seemed to have but little influence on the bearing towards us of the common people who had become used to us and had received our medicine, and certainly we did not seem to mind their cursing in the least. The next day many who had been helped by the medicines they had received the previous day came to thank me, and

SOME POPPIES NEAR THE SNOW-LINE.

brought friends along to have their troubles attended to; even some of the Lamas came for medicine. As we passed the temple on our way to the State of Damba they all gathered on the roof of their temple again and in loud chorus continued their most impressive ceremony of yesterday; but with no better result, for we quietly stood by and photographed them, much to their amazement.

Passing up a broad valley, covered with grass on which were many horses and cattle feeding, we came to a small monastery, called Tawei. Here we turned due west, and started up a steep incline. After climbing for about a mile, the grade became more gradual and we came to farms where they were just sowing their buckwheat. It came on to rain, and the pass that was still far above us was white with new-fallen snow, so we stopped for the afternoon and night in an old farmhouse, used only in the autumn, when the farmers come up to reap the harvest.

Next morning it was fine and we made an early start. Before going far we entered a thick undergrowth, which soon gave way to a dense forest of scrub, oak, birch and a few white firs intermingled. All were draped in fairy scarf, some of which must have reached a length of thirty feet. This fairy scarf is a kind of lichen, a cellular cryptogamous plant, which clings to the bark of the trees and hangs in long streamers from the limbs and branches. This lichen is almost like fine hemp or flax fibre, and rope made of it is quite strong.

For hours we travelled along a narrow pathway on the side of the cliff, arched over by branches of shrub oak, which grows from ten to fourteen inches at the trunk, and these were all draped in the same silvery green ribbons. On we marched till we came out on a grass valley where we had dinner. To the west was the snow-capped range and pass, the other three sides covered with forest. The cry of large flocks of grouse, as they flew up on all sides of us, was the only sound that broke the stillness.

After lunch we set out for the final climb, and toiled for another three miles, up through deep snow drifts, in which the animals almost floundered, and we had much difficulty in reaching the top. It was a beautiful day and well worth while to stand on this pinnacle of Pewa Pass, the dividing line between Runga and Damba State, and gaze upon the panorama that opened out before us. From here we could see over a great part of Damba State, which is not a very large one, being only about forty miles square, the most part of which is mountainous and uninhabited. The valleys are quite fertile and thickly populated, and in many secluded spots lonely houses were hid away from general view. The people of Damba are very proud of their reputation, and tradition says they were famous warriors and most fearless men.

Three hours' hard march brought us down the steep mountain side, first, through beds of wild flowers, then through another dense forest, and finally out to cultivated fields on to the village of Drozer, where we put up for the night and changed our guide and ula. It was a beautiful clear night and we got a latitude, after the inhabitants had all retired, for we had to be careful not to arouse their suspicions by doing much star-gazing.

Word was sent out to the people on the mountains, whose turn it was to escort us, and early next morning they were waiting before we had finished breakfast. It was a new thing not to have to wait for ula, which is the only drawback to the system, so far as the traveller is concerned, for not only does it ensure a safe transit from one tribe to another, but the charge is quite moderate. The Chinese seldom give them anything, but I believe in always paying a proper price for their help.

We only travelled some five miles further down into the

valley, where we came to another village, where there is another chief or headman. It was his duty to escort us to Damba twenty miles further on, but he was away ; so we had several hours' delay before we could get animals and men from the mountains to take us on. We tried to hire the men who had come from Drozer to take us into Damba, but they would not do this, saying they had no authority to escort us through the other chief's district.

ULA AND A GRASS-LAND TRIBESMAN.

Brooke and Meares went on with some of the coolies and the Chinese escort, while I remained behind to wait for the ula, keeping the interpreter with me.

It was a long wait, and by 2 o'clock only two animals had arrived. We waited on till 4 o'clock and at last I saw the other yaks coming down the mountain side, and put my bedding on an old broken-down horse that had been waiting mounted. But the old nag refused to carry me, and I felt it was much safer as well as quicker to walk. So with my bedding on the ancient steed and a good stick in my hand on we tramped down to the depths of the valley quite 2,000 feet below our starting point. After crossing an old cantilever bridge we followed the left bank of the stream for some two miles, and then turned up a ravine and up a steep spur, where we toiled for an hour and a-half, my female guide tugging on the halter in front of the nag, while I plied the stick from behind.

At last, dripping with perspiration, we reached the top of the pass. The sun had already set, and there were ten miles of rough road yet to travel, so, without waiting to take breath, we pushed on, and in the twilight overtook the rest of the party.

They had waited for the coolies, and counting on the ula to overtake them, had pitched their tents ; but while I talked with them my escort pushed on with my bedding, and was already out of sight. So, as I knew the road, and also people on the street at Damba, I gave chase, and though I did not overtake my guide I found my way to the capital in the dark, and near the entrance to the castle met two men, who took a message to the Princess that I had arrived and would like accommodation. This was Colonel Kao's aunt, who had already heard of our coming through him, so I was given quarters with my old friend of the year before. I soon found my bedding, which was in another house near by, where my escort had put up. They had a good laugh at me for getting left in the dark.

A pound of parched barley meal, some milk and hot tea were now brought in, and I don't remember tsamba ever tasting better. If my readers think they would not appreciate tsamba for supper I would recommend a twenty-mile tramp between 4 and 9.30 p.m. with a climb of 4,000 feet and several descents of 2,000 feet each. If they have not had anything to eat since morning, except a small cake made of coarse cornflour, cooked in wood ash, I will guarantee their agreeing with me that tsamba is good food when one is hungry.

After supper I was taken on the roof and allowed to choose my apartment. I took the best there was, and taking a large round basket about six feet in diameter used for sunning the grain, made my bed in it, under the projecting roof, and rolled myself in my quilt, while my worthy landlord rolled himself in a sheep-skin gown and lay on the roof near by. Needless to say I was soon in the land of know-nothing, and was only aroused by the shouts of the interpreter next morning about 9 o'clock, trying to find out where I was. The sun had been shining full in my face for some time, but I had been quite unconscious of it.

The rest of the party had not fared so well. They had pitched their tents in a swampy place where there was some wood, but it was so wet that it would not burn, and the ula with their bedding did not overtake them; so they were left to pass the cold night with what they had on them, and the next morning came in half frozen and very hungry.

An empty house, or kung kwan, was put at our disposal, and we soon made ourselves comfortable. A little later the ula all turned up, so we had bacon and eggs and fried scones for breakfast, and a bucket of milk was brought in by my old host, and that morning we feasted.

Here, again, the people gathered around us for medicine; and as Colonel Kao was to arrive with his younger brother, who is to be put under the charge of a Lama here to be prepared for the Tussuship of this State, when his aunt dies, we waited another day. In honour of their arrival there was to have been a great dance; the country swains and the maidens came in from the mountains dressed in gay colours, and had already gathered on the green in front of the castle, when three men rode in on horseback, and said some brigands had driven off a large herd of cattle. At once the interesting party broke up, and in groups of fives and tens were seen hastening away to guard the passes, and to try to capture the thieves and redeem the animals.

After spending a pleasant two days here we passed on to Cheoser, the capital of Chosschia, where another aunt of Mr. Kao's resides, and is the wife of the Tussu.

We had got the Colonel to send word over the evening he arrived that we were coming and to arrange for our entertainment.

On leaving Damba, we descended a steep hill, and after travelling four miles came to the banks of Tachin.

The only means of getting to the other side was by means of a coracle, a craft the appearance of which is not inspiring. It is made of a very slim frame of willow branches, woven together and covered with a raw hide, is about four feet in diameter and three feet deep, and will hold three people. I have seen four natives, who were used to these skiffs, cross in one. All hands huddle down in the bottom with their legs curled up in a most uncomfortable position, and it is fatal to move after the craft is shoved off. As for ourselves, we shot up stream in the back water until we struck the current, when the coracle was sent swirling round and round in the vortex and bobbing like a cork on the waves. One moment we were down in the trough with the feeling that we would surely be engulfed, for the waves seemed much higher than one's head; the next we were riding the crest of the waves, but all the time being carried down stream at the rate of fifteen to twenty miles an hour. Just below the landing stage the river foamed through some boulders and cut the shape of the letter S. To a stranger it looked as if we must surely be carried on to the boulders. But the ferryman, by means of his paddle, steered and dragged the coracle forward in a wonderful way and safely landed us, and it really needs much more skill to manage one of these crafts than it does a birch bark canoe.

The Journey to Chosschia.

We now found our way to the town of Cheoser, where the Chief had set apart a house for our use. The courtyard was soon filled with Lamas and laymen, old women and young maidens, all anxious to have another look at the stranger. But all were friendly, and one after another I saw them point to me and say "That is the man who passed through last year." Some of my former escort came forward and saluted me by falling on their knees, bowing their heads and saying "Chou-ba-le-su, kuzu demo duk-kam" ("You are welcome; are you well?").

CHAPTER XIII.

Through the Unexplored Grassland.

We had to spend three days at Chosschia waiting for ula, but it was not time wasted.

The people soon began to gather about, afflicted with all kinds of ailments. Priests and laymen, women and girls, gathered about me and had their sores dressed. Skin diseases and sore eyes were the commonest complaints, but there were many with ulcered legs, and some of both sexes with syphilis and kindred diseases. From morning till night I was kept busy, for, when I had treated all who came to our lodgings, three of the chiefs sent for me to come to their homes and attend to some sick folk who were not able to come out for treatment.

One poor woman was almost eaten up with leprosy, and her son of thirteen years lay a few yards away, reduced to skin and bone; he could not last much longer. It was most pathetic to hear their pleading for help, but I could offer them no hope. I gave them some ointment to relieve their pain and appease their minds for the time being; they seemed surprised when I told them frankly they could not recover. The mother I judged to be about thirty-five years of age. She had heard somehow that I was able to heal the sick, and had sent her eldest son, who was a young Lama of about eighteen years of age, to bring me up. All the chanting of the Lamas and their so-called holy men had not been able to work the miracle of healing, and now she believed that the foreigner could do it. I shall never forget that face of sorrow as she pleaded with me for help, and pointing to her youngest child, a little girl of about five years, said: "If I could only live until my baby was old enough to look after herself, for who will care for my baby?" The tears ran down her cheeks, and the eyelashes of others in the room, for some reason, were not dry. The husband, old Tibetan as he was, kneeled down beside his wife as tenderly as any foreigner could have done, and whispered to her, "Do not worry about the baby, I will care for her." The mother did not quite despair, and she insisted that I should accept presents, which she commanded her husband to bring to me, and made her son, the Lama, carry to my room. I think this was the saddest case I have ever attended on all my journeys in China and Tibet.

From this home I was escorted from house to house, and had to attend to not a few female cases, about which I had not the least idea that they would ever consult a foreigner.

Taken to the palace itself I found a poor child that had fallen into the hot ashes. The flesh was almost falling off the bones of one arm and part of the shoulder, and the stench was something tremendous; but, after a great deal of work, I removed most of the filth and scab, thoroughly cleansing the sore, and it was wonderful the improvement, even in three days. The father and mother, who at first would hardly submit to my using water to cleanse the sore, were so surprised at the result that they sang our praises far and wide, and more than one person asked me to stay in their country, as they had never had any one to care for them like this before.

Even the Prince was so pleased that he consented to let us travel across the Grassland where no foreigner had ever been allowed to pass, and sent one of the chief's sons, whose home I had visited, to escort us to Damtung, the capital of Gaishechia.

From this point Mr. Meares went south, down the valley

of the Tachin, with the coolies and most of the stuff, while Mr. Brooke came with me. We packed what we thought we would need upon the horses and yaks that were brought in to convey us westward. A tent, a few camping articles, bedding, clothing and books, a good supply of flour and some bacon—for there was nothing to be procured *en route*—comprised our outfit.

When all was ready we set out—one party for Mongung, the other for the Unknown beyond. The whole street turned out to see us off, and we received many kind farewells and much advice about being careful on the road, for in this country even their own people never know when they may be surprised by a band of villains. Our interpreter from Tsakalao went back from here, not understanding the language beyond this point. So we started out with quite a stranger, the son of one of the chiefs to whom I had given medicine.

This young man proved himself a very good guide and interpreter, but he had neither the cunning nor the experience of my friend who had just turned back. We passed up a wide valley that was mostly used as pasture land for the milch cows of the town. Great boughs of wild white roses clung in clusters of bloom over the stone walls that surrounded the fields. The birds were singing, all Nature seemed at peace, and we were happy at the thought that kindness and a little knowledge had won our victory over ignorance and superstition.

The year before it was with the greatest difficulty I had got into this place, and the people were not friendly. On one occasion Mr. Edgar had arrived there, and had to fly almost for his life; now we were the friends of the people and their rulers, and were travelling under an escort and with documents written by the Prince himself, stating that we were his friends and must be protected and escorted safely through his country. I also had a letter on my person to the Prince of the next State asking that he would receive us. Our success was even greater than we had dreamed of.

A BOWER OF WHITE ROSES NEAR CHOSSCHIA CASTLE—MR. BROOKE FEEDING DOG ; INTERPRETER ON LEFT.

We rode north-west up the valley for about three miles, then turned south-west up the side of the mountain, where we toiled for some hours, first through a rank forest, then at

8,000 feet, coming out on a great grass slope facing south. A little later we came to a long stretch of cultivated land. We put up for the night in a small village called Rengack, where we were comfortably housed. There seemed to be an epidemic of sore eyes all through this country and I had a number of patients. The people here, fifteen miles from the capital, had heard of our doings at Chosschia, and flocked about us freely. Goitre seems to be a very general complaint all through this country, and it is common to see people—women especially—going about with a great pouch hanging under their chin. I could not discover the cause, but rather think it is the mica which is so plentiful about here, and which, washed down by the melting snows, may be found in the sparkling water that ripples down every mountain side.

There was no salt or brackish water about. The natives themselves attribute the trouble to drinking snow-water. I noticed that where the surrounding mountains were largely composed of mica shist there goitre was most prevalent.

Another day's march brought us to the first tents in the grasslands. Up till 10 a.m. we marched on through fields of waving barley. We were now 9,000 feet above sea-level, but by reason of the southern aspect and the sandy nature of the soil, the crops were well advanced, and would soon be ready for the sickle.

On crossing a small stream down which a road leads from Yukoh we here turned south-west, and started up the north-eastern slope of Mount Zibzier. When we crossed the stream we were over 10,000 feet above the sea-level. Here we entered a forest, and for four miles the path ran through as wild a track of country as one could wish to travel in.

By noon we had come out on the Grassland. We laboured up the slope, passing a number of small lakes or basins kept full of water from the melting snow, and at length reached the top of the pass—12,460 feet high. We found here the usual obo or pile of stones in which are inserted poles with prayer-flags attached.

From the top of this pass the whole country lay open before us. We could see for miles to the south, west and north away over the forest, and far to the east over the country we had just travelled through. On the mountain lower down we could see little black specks through the glasses feeding on the slopes, and knew that we were nearing the herds.

Five miles down a gradual slope brought us to the camp where the Chief lived. Not far away a number of other tents were pitched, and the mountain sides were literally covered with thousands of yak grazing. A few small calves were tethered near the tent, and a huge mastiff, the inevitable sentinel of every Tibetan's tent, whose deep bass bay make the very slopes vibrate, warned the stranger to approach with caution.

On arrival our interpreter went in with his letter from the Prince, for here we were to change our ula. We waited some time and, when he did not invite us in, walked up to the tent, raised the flap, stepped in, and sat down about the fire in Tibetan fashion.

The tent was about twenty-five feet long by fifteen feet wide, shaped almost like the bottom of a Chinese boat when turned upside down. The sides of the tent were so arranged that it could be rolled up in warm weather, and in the centre of the roof of the tent was a long slit that could be thrown open to let the smoke out, or closed over at night to keep the snow and rain out and the heat in. In the centre burned the usual argol (dried manure) fire, for wood had to be carried on yak from the forest ten miles away, and they only used it for starting the fire.

A large pot of tea was boiling and a bucket of milk stood

near by; and as they never wash these wooden buckets in which they milk the yak, and keep the milk while the cream rises, there was a thick coating of dirt and sour milk both inside and out. However, one must not look too closely at things in a country like this, though, to be sure, there is no need for a magnifying glass to enable one to see dirt, or a microscope to discover bacteria. The milk is boiled and then put in wooden vats, when it sours almost immediately, but the people claim that they get more cream that way, and make more butter. After I saw how they skimmed their milk I was convinced they were right, for they put in a great deal of the curd with the cream, and this curd mixes with the butter in some way, and, as they do not wash the butter after it is churned, it is about half curd. Sometimes, when I have washed the butter before using it, most of it has run off in the water in the form of butter-milk. On other occasions I have used Tibetan butter which was almost pure milk-fat and of a very good quality; but a good plan is always to use a knife and cut carefully through it, first one way and then another, and so remove the long yak hairs which are so abundant in the butter, especially in that made in the springtime, when the animals are casting their coats.

The Chief promised to send ula the next morning, and passed us on to Acree, where we found the large monastery of Muska Cumba.

The monastery was built of stone, and was the only place where there was any attempt at fixed dwellings. The inhabitants all lived in tents, which they pitched wherever they could find the best pasture for their herds, and in winter they all fed in the lower valleys in the neighbourhood of the monastery, 12,137 feet above sea-level.

We had some little difficulty in getting lodgings in the temple, but after a short time the Lamas allowed us to put our things in the porch of the gold-roofed temple, and lodge there for the night. We were able to distribute a few books among the Lamas, but could not get much information from them, though they were much more friendly when we left. There were several private residences in connection with the monastery, and we saw a number of women and children.

At 10 o'clock next morning the ula turned up, and we packed our things, paid the drivers from Chosschia for bringing us thus far, and proceeded on our journey. The country continued of the same undulating character, all grass. Many herds were pasturing, especially on the higher slopes above 12,000 feet, where they graze in the summer months, the lower valleys being reserved for the winter pasture lands.

That night, after crossing another pass 14,000 feet high, we reached a monastery called Kimlung, which was about the same size as Muska, having about 200 Lamas and 100 lay families.

At first the Lamas were not friendly, but on our showing our letters and saying that if we informed their Tussu of their unwillingness to give us shelter for a night he would not be pleased, they consented to allow us to stay in a large room connected with a private residence, and later brought us wood and were amicable. A number of people came from the tents for medicine. I extracted some teeth, which was a great surprise to the Lamas; but the owners of these annoying decayed pieces of bone were very grateful at being relieved of the source of their pain, and brought presents of milk and butter, which they insisted we should accept.

One more hard day's march brought us to Damtung, where the Tussu of Gaishechia lives. It had been raining nearly every day since we left Chosschia and was still at it when we arrived at Damtung. Of course there were dry spells each day, but in this country one minute the sky is black with thunder-clouds, and an hour after is bright blue.

When we reached Damtung it was pouring, and we were wet through, and were glad when, after some little delay, we were shown to a house near the castle. We gathered round a fire in a smoky little room, cooked our supper, dried our clothes, slept, and awaited events of the next three days.

CHAPTER XIV.

IN THE LAND OF THE CATTLE THIEVES.

WE were the first foreigners who ever have visited Damtung, and we found it a compact little town, well fortified by physical conditions, being built on the projection of a mountain where two swift streams join, both of which it would be most difficult to ford. For, while the streams were not over three feet deep, except in flood time, yet they came rolling down at such a rate that it would carry men or animals clean off their feet. Now it was a roaring cataract on both sides of the capital. The photograph will give a better idea than I can make with my pen. Indeed, my pen utterly refuses to portray the beauties of this rare and wonderful scenery, so I must trust to the illustrations for that, and confine myself to the simple story of what took place on the march, day by day. When we first arrived the people looked on us with suspicion and were very shy, but they were not long in changing their attitude. Our interpreter told them of what we had done in Chosschia, and before 9 o'clock next morning I was invited to see my first patient, who was lying dangerously ill in a house close by.

He was a man of about thirty years of age, nearly six feet tall, and although he had a big strong frame, he was reduced to skin and bone. I found he had been suffering from fever for twenty days, and, having recovered from that, was now suffering from another complaint which was the result of fever. He could not have lived many days longer unless he got relief in some way, for all the remedies that they knew of had failed.

A simple operation by means of a syringe and some warm water was all that was required, and to the amazement of the natives the man immediately began to recover. I prescribed egg and milk, and though we only remained here three days, my patient had so far recovered that he was able to sit up and walk about a little.

The report of what I was able to do for a poor cottager was not long in finding its way to the ears of the Tussu. At 2 o'clock he sent one of his servants to invite me to his palace, which is the high building near the tower seen in the photograph.

On passing a large courtyard where the cattle are housed at night I ascended two flights of stairs, passed two tigers which were kept in a cage on one of the landings, and then on through a long corridor. A yellow silk curtain was lifted and I was ushered into a room about twenty feet square, in which was a table and two chairs. In the centre of the room was a brazier, and therein a charcoal fire burned and the inevitable teapot boiled.

On a wooden bed, curtained with yellow satin, reclined a miserable looking creature, whom they introduced to me as the Prince or ruler of the State. His feet were at right angles to his body, and could not be straightened out. The pain was so excruciating that he had taken to the pernicious habit of opium-smoking in order to get relief. His hair was in a knotted mat, his face distorted to such an extent that he looked more like a beggar than a prince, though his surroundings were otherwise.

On examination I found that he was suffering from inflammatory rheumatism, and that he had been ill for about two months. I had with me none of the medicines that are usually prescribed for this trouble; but as became a quack who had at last achieved a royal patient, I felt I must do something; so going back for my medicine case, and hunting

THE CASTLE AND TOWN OF DAMTUNG, WHERE THE AUTHOR HEALED THE CHIEF.

it through, I uttered this prescription:—To start with, a good dose of salts; 10 grains of quinine morning and evening; massage for the legs for six hours a day (if the patient could stand it), and this last I illustrated by taking my turn at the work for the first half-hour. We had brought methylated spirits for preserving such insects and reptiles as we might secure on our way, and this was freely used in the process of massaging, with vaseline later, to keep the skin from being too much irritated. At 9 p.m. I went up to the castle again, painted the knees with iodine, and, wrapping the legs in flannel, told the royal patient that he must go to sleep.

Next morning, shortly after 9 o'clock, I was called to the palace, as the Prince wanted me. I followed my guide into his presence. On entering I noticed a heavy cane near the Chief's bed and rather wondered whether it would be used on me; but I had not to wait long to see what it was for. Almost immediately the Chief seized the cane, threw off the covering and swung out of bed, and, in a manner hard to describe, hobbled across the room and back to his bed again. This was the first time he had been able to put his feet to the floor for nearly three months, and I have never seen a child more delighted with a new toy than this Tussu was over being able to use his legs.

I forbade his attempting to do this for a few days, and unbandaging his limbs gave them another good massage, and repeated yesterday's prescription, then left his people to continue the rubbing. On pulling the legs lightly to try to straighten them I found that they already relaxed to an angle of about 20 degrees.

The Prince's wife and daughter now came into the room and prostrated themselves on the floor to thank me for what I had done. Indeed, the cure was more rapid than even I had dreamed it could be, and to them it seemed a miracle.

I returned to our abode, and awaiting the ula which had to be brought from the mountain (a day's journey away), we were not idle, for the people kept flocking about all day. Already word had reached some of the country people ten miles away, and in they came to see the magician thus suddenly alighted in their midst. Patrons of all descriptions and all ages flocked about, and I was kept busy from morning to night. All fear of the foreigner seemed suddenly to have vanished, and they were as free in making known their complaints as if I had lived in their midst all my life. That night the Tussu sent down one of his retainers to know if I cared to choose a wife from the fair daughters of Gaishechia, saying I was invited to come up to the palace to choose one from the scores of eager faces which, from our humble position on the roof of our lodgings, I could see peering over the parapet of the castle. Needless to say I thanked the Chief for his kindness and thoughtfulness, but informed him I had a wife at Chentu. "Oh!" said the emissary, "but a Chinese woman is not like our women, they stay in the house and have small feet, so that they cannot walk. One of our women would go with you, carry your load, cook your food and do all kinds of work." Again assuring him that this was not necessary, I gratefully dismissed him.

When we arose next morning we found the ula had at last arrived, and, while the yakmen were packing the things on the yak, Brooke and I went up to say good-bye and see how the patient was progressing. As soon as we entered the room he sprang out of bed, and, with the aid of his stick, walked around the room almost in an upright position.

We were almost as delighted as he was at this sudden recovery. The Prince called for paper and ink, and wrote down the foreign names of the remedies used, using the Tibetan character, and then wrote down my name and address at Chentu.

We got a photograph of the huge mastiff kept to guard the palace, and then said good-bye.

THE GUARD ON THE ROOF—TIBETAN MASTIFF.

Three months later the Prince sent some of his people all the way to Chentu, twenty days' journey, with presents to me, and a message that he had quite recovered, and that I was welcome to his State whenever I chose again to visit him.

When all was packed we set out to visit the famous robber district of Yukoh. The only name that is written on our maps to convey any idea of what that stretch of country is like is the word "Goluk" or "Robbers," while on many maps it is left entirely blank. The inhabitants are known to the Chinese as "the great cattle thieves," and many of the neighbouring tribes fear these pillagers. The Prince of Yukoh is married to a sister of the Prince of Chosschia, and the Yukoh prince's brother is married to the sister of the Prince of Gaishechia, and by means of these marriage ties they try to live at peace with each other; but despite this bond of marriage the herdsmen of the different States often have feuds with each other about the boundary line of their pasture lands, and sometimes take possession of each other's herds, if they happen to stray over the boundary. A feud of this kind took place between the herdsmen of Yukoh and Chosschia on the northern border, a few days after we passed through.

On our way to Yukoh we followed the left hand stream shown in the photograph, and after four hours' travelling through wooded land, which we entered about a mile from the capital of Gaishechia, we came out on grass land again, and four hours more brought us to a small temple and a few tents.

The priest was quite differently dressed from any I had ever seen, having long hair, like a Taoist, done up on the top of his head. He had a wife who lived in a tent close by. Their images were very similar to those usually found in Buddhist temples, but it was reported that their books differ.

This was the only priest of this order I had met with in all the journey, and I am not prepared to say just what branch of the faith he represented. He was not a Bon, at least not as we find Bons in the Tachin valley, in Bati and Bawang States, where they have adhered to the primitive form of

Bon Nature worship. I was told that this was a sect found only among the herdsmen, and now almost extinct, being superseded by the Red and Yellow sect.

In the porch of this little temple we spent the night, camping early, as it had rained hard all the afternoon. About 5 o'clock a Lama, the brother of the Gaishechia chief, overtook us, riding a big white horse. He had five companions all armed to the teeth. They had been sent by the Prince to escort us, and hand us safely over to the brother of the Yukoh Tussu, who was camped some ten miles further up the valley. We were now camped at the boundary line of the two States, Gaishechia and Yukoh.

This escort had good horses and rode on to the camps that night, while we decided to pass the night where we were and go up next morning.

It was 10 o'clock when we sighted the camp and the herds grazing on the slopes. By 11 o'clock we drew up in front of fifty-six black tents all pitched on a level flat between two streams, which here could be easily forded. Our Gaishechia Lama was accompanied by two of the Yukoh Prince's brothers, one a Lama, the other married to the sister of the Gaishechia Chief.

Their servants brought Tibetan rugs along, which were spread on the ground, and we were asked to be seated.

We found that our escort had arrived late the evening before, and had been attacked by the great ferocious dogs kept to guard these tents. One of the escort had been badly torn by one of these dogs, and I made shift to dress twenty-eight nasty wounds, some of them on his face, others on his arms, hands and legs. This occupied nearly two hours. Next the Chief's son, a lad of fifteen, was brought with a bad foot, and when he was attended to we were urged to pitch our tents and spend the rest of the day with our friends.

The whole encampment gathered about and lent a hand,

and in a very short time all our ula was unpacked, our tent erected, and we were led off to visit the Chief in his tent. There was nothing to distinguish this from any of the others, only it was pitched almost in the centre of the encampment. Inside it had more comfort in the way of rugs and cooking utensils; but they all ate the same kind of food and lived practically in the same way.

CAMP OF THE PRINCE'S BROTHER—YAK IN FOREGROUND.

In the evening quite 5,000 head of yak, sheep and horses were driven in. There was no enclosure, but the yak were tethered to long lines made of yak hair and pinned to the ground. The sheep gathered toward the centre of the encampment, and at dark the dogs were let loose. They scampered round the outside of the camps, kept the herds together, and kept off wild animals from the flock. All night long the deep baying of these ferocious brutes resounded in the still night air, and warned the stranger that the safest place was inside his tent. On several occasions a pack of dogs came so close to our tent that we thought they were going to attack it, but they scampered off again without harming us.

Next morning we set out for the capital, which we found to be quite thirty miles further on. We tramped up to the watershed, between the head-waters of the Kwanyin, and the stream that flows past Gaishechia, and empties into the Tachin near Romi Chanku. The pass of Gerhubdumdoh we found to be somewhat higher than the other we had come over, and we got into a heavy snowstorm near the top.

After crossing the pass we found large herds on the other side belonging to the inhabitants. These herdsmen seem to group together in parties of from ten to fifty families, each with their own tent made of black yak hair. When the yak are brought in at night the animals are thrown and their feet tied by a rope. Then a number of people gather round and pluck the hair out in great handfuls, continuing until all the long hair is plucked out. The poor creature groans at every tug that is given, and it is no light pull that extracts a handful of hair from these yak. At 5 o'clock, in a pouring rain, we reached the capital of Yukoh State, and were almost carried away while crossing the stream that flows past the monastery.

At first we tried to secure lodgings in the monastery itself but did not succeed, so pitched our tents in the pouring rain, and made our beds on the wet grass. With great difficulty we secured some wood and cooked some food. We had not eaten anything since morning and had had a long march. A Lama, the Tussu's brother, had gone up another ravine to bring word of our arrival to the Tussu, who was also out in a tent with his herds, so that we had no one to herald our arrival, and had to wait till late in the afternoon of the next day before he arrived with ula to take us on.

This Lama was a very sullen-looking priest, and if it had

TIBETAN NURSE-MAID AND BABY.

not been for the Gaishechia Tussu sending his brother along we should not have fared so well as we did. We could do but little here, though we met people from other States who were friendly.

In the Land of the Cattle Thieves.

The next morning we set out on a 30-mile march to Dawo, and pressed on over the same rolling grass land. Some two miles from the capital of Yukoh we passed a hot spring where there was mixed bathing. On the opposite side of the stream we saw a band of the famous cattle raiders, returning with their plunder of about 200 head of yak, which they were forcing on at the point of their long lances. These would be taken to the Tussu's tent, and, after he had taken his share of the booty, the raiders would be pardoned and the remainder of the plunder would be theirs.

It is hard to imagine a more fiendish-looking lot of men than these nomads of the grassy slopes. According to the maps this country is all within the Szechuan province, but the Chinese official has to ask leave if he wishes to travel in these highlands, and the inhabitants would think as little of plundering him as they would the ordinary merchant. One might undertake a journey in the hope of trade.

We were benighted and had to camp on the plain, and the next morning about 8 o'clock reached Dawo, a large monastery on the great north road to Tibet.

CHAPTER XV.

THE TRAFFIC OF THE GREAT NORTH ROAD.

ON arriving at Dawo we found a large monastery which contained about 3,000 Lamas, and close by was a small village of about fifty families. We got rooms in a large new gochuang, belonging to the people of Mantze State. A gochuang is a house built by a tribe for the accommodation of their people, while passing through on business.

In large centres like Tacheinlu, each tribe has its own guest-house. This one we found to be very roomy and, as it had just been reconstructed, it was quite clean. Upon examination we discovered that most of the houses were new and several others in the course of construction. When we inquired why these houses were being rebuilt, we were told that some three years previously a great earthquake had destroyed nearly all the buildings, and killed most of the inhabitants. The monastery, which is about half-a-mile away, had also been shaken, and some of the cloisters in connection with it fell, yet the temples and many of the cells were unharmed.

These monasteries along the main road are also great warehouses or tea stations; much of the tea shipped into Tibet travels over this road, and is conveyed from stage to stage by local animals. A great part of this work is done gratis, while on some occasions a small fee is paid by the monastery for carrying the tea from one post to another. I saw hundreds of yak loads deposited at Dawo while I was there.

BLACK RIVER BLACKSMITH AND HIS WIFE.

The Traffic of the Great North Road.

We thought of passing down through Chantwei, a track of country that is bounded by the Horba States on the north, by Dergi on the west, by Chala on the east and by Litang on the south ; so far as I know, Chantwei has never been visited by any European.

We found a Mohammedan military official here whom I had met some years before. He called and was most friendly. We made very cautious inquiries about the condition of the country to the west, and found it was governed from Lhasa, the official being changed every three years. About fifteen years ago these people rebelled against the Chinese, who asked the Tibetan troops from Batang to help them to put down the rebellion. It ended in the Chinese handing the government of the country over to Lhasa, as the inhabitants were all Tibetans, on condition that there should be no raiding along the big roads. An official was appointed from the Holy City with the title known to the Chinese as Tsangwang, or Tibetan king, but his term of office is only for three years, so that he is not a king actually, though the Chinese call him by that name.

The new representative from Lhasa had just taken over office ; from the reports we got he seemed to be quite an obstinate man, who intended to compel the Chinese to hand back the country taken by the Chinese troops when the Litang monastery was sacked about seven years ago.

It would be interesting to know just how many troops inhabit the country of Chantwei. Report has it that there are 80,000 men capable of bearing arms, but this must be greatly exaggerated, though it was given to me as the result of the census recently taken.

By 6 o'clock a.m. our ula to convey us to Tachienlu had arrived ; but late the previous evening Mr. Ma had agreed to send his interpreter with me over to the Tussu to see if it were possible to get through Chantwei. We postponed our journey. Mr. Ma promised to send up the interpreter for me, so I waited till 9 o'clock, but he did not appear, and I went over to see what had happened. I was told that early in the morning the interpreter had gone across the river to arrange an audience and had not returned. I was none too pleased with Mr. Ma, and told him I knew what the answer would be, but he assured me it would be all right, and that the interpreter would soon be back; accordingly we waited. It was 12 o'clock when they sent word that the Tussu would not receive me, so I went over to Mr. Ma, and told him what I thought of his plan and its result. He expressed his regret, but assured me he had done his best. Knowing that it is the business of these officials to stop travellers from entering a country of this kind, I said, "If you will allow me, I will go across the river and seek an interview with the Tussu and return before dark." Whether he thought that I was "bluffing" and that I would not dare to cross the river in the coracle, I don't know, but he replied, "All right, you may go, but it will be impossible for you to get an audience." He wanted to send his interpreter along, but I refused his aid, seeing that we had a man of our own. So, immediately setting out, we succeeded in crossing the Ngachu, which was divided into several streams.

The valley is quite wide here and the water is high, necessitating three portages before we crossed the other bank, and it took us a full hour to cross, for we were carried far down the stream. Consequently it was almost 2 o'clock when we found ourselves outside the palace gate.

I sent in the interpreter with my letter from the Chosschia and Gaishechia Tussus.

In a very few minutes I was invited to enter and was shown to the seat of honour.

The Tussu, in this case a female, entered. She was a woman of about forty. One of the retainers poured out a cup of tea and handed it to her, which she passed on to me with a very polite courtesy. She then sat down and talked for a little on local affairs. I found she understood Chinese very well, though Tibetan was the language spoken by the people. Presenting her with a Waterbury watch, which she accepted, I then very soon made known the object of my visit, first stating that the Princes of Chosschia, Gaishechia and Yukoh had given me ula and a letter or passport, which I submitted to her and stated that I would like ula now to pass through Chantwei. At first she tried to put me off, saying that if the Tussu of Kongser, who lived on the other side of the river, would give me a letter and ula, she would do the same. My reply to this suggestion was that it was very difficult and dangerous work crossing the river, but that if she would just write her letter and give it to the interpreter, who was a relative, he would carry it and, should the Tussu of the Kongser refuse, I would send him back with her letter. So she wrote the order for ula and also a letter to the Chief or Lhasa representative of Chantwei. We left, thanking her, and feeling that part of the task was accomplished.

On recrossing the river, we went direct to the Kongser Tussu, and found him a most sullen, insignificant man. Presenting my credentials, I at once stated my business. His reply was, "If you can get a letter and ula from the Tussu of Mantze I will give you one." My reply was, "I have that," and presented her order. He studied it for a few minutes, then called for pen and paper, and wrote the order for ula and a permit to pass through his territory.

Now that the difficulty of gaining admission was overcome, I returned to the gochuang with something of the feeling of victory in my breast.

Mr. Ma was quite surprised at my success, and so was Mr. Brooke, as he felt that the Chinese official had done us at last.

Now that we had got permission to go, and the ula was in, we began to query if it were really right to go on. We had no Scripture left either in Tibetan or Chinese, neither had we any mapping paper, and it seemed a useless tramp to go through a country like this, able to do nothing.

I was due at Chentu by a fixed date, and if we took this journey it would probably lead us through Derge, which would mean a two months' journey and perhaps more; we decided that it was best to go south to Tachienlu, and attempt this journey at some future date. Thus halting between two opinions we had our ula again changed for Tachienlu, and started south the next morning. We were then on the northern road between Tachienlu and Lhasa, over which others had travelled, and which has been described by more than one. I need not detain my readers in this section of the country with more than a few glimpses by the way, that the blank may not be too great between Dawo and Tachienlu.

From Dawo to Tachienlu is about 510 li (or 135 miles). It is called seven stages for a horseman, but we did it with ula in that time, including waiting for relays, though that was not considerable on this road.

About two miles south of Dawo the Nga River turns west and disappears in the mountains. All along its banks a foot-path is reported to exist, but in some places it is almost impassable and really dangerous. We followed up a small stream that flows into the Ngachu, near the point where it disappears into the gorges of Chantwei. The road was 50 to 100 feet wide most of the way, and we met large caravans of yak laden with tea, one day 500, another day 200, besides passing large herds grazing on the grassy plain.

The tea was piled in great heaps in front of the light tents. These tents are made of ordinary grey shirting which people take on the road because of the convenience in transit.

We soon passed over into Chiala State, for Dawo is located

just at the corners of Matze, Kongser and Chiala States. Three days through almost uninhabited grass land brought us to Tailing, where a fierce battle was fought between the Tibetans and the Chinese troops in 1903, when the Tibetan monastery was destroyed by the Chinese troops. Tailing has long been a military post and there is quite a long street composed of one-storey, flat-roofed, wooden houses, most of which are new, as the former buildings were destroyed by the

ENCAMPED FOR DINNER—AUTHOR ON LEFT, MR. BROOKE ON RIGHT.

Tibetans. The Chinese have made the Tibetans build the present new ones as punishment for the outbreak. When the Chinese troops re-took the place from the Tibetans, they sacked and destroyed the large monastery, carrying away many valuable copper and bronze utensils; in fact everything that the Lamas left behind, when they fled before the troops. This loot was taken to Tachienlu and sold, and was readily bought up by the Mohammedans and Chinese traders, who carried on quite a business. Most of the soldiers had no idea of the value of most of the articles they had secured, and if they had, it was imperative for them to dispose of the stuff for what they could get, as they could not carry it with them on the march.

When we passed through, the temple was almost restored, the workmen were busy painting it in most brilliant colours; when completed it would look very grand indeed. The Lamas were very friendly and showed us all over the place. Before the late war they would have refused to admit foreigners within this Holy enclosure.

The cause of the trouble was that the Chinese were coming in large parties to dig and wash for gold.

Near Tailing we met 500 yak in one caravan, laden with tea, going westward.

I kept count of the animals that passed up during the two days we spent at Dawo, and also on the way down, and allowing three days for our journey from Dawo to Tailing, the average number of loads that passed up was 200 per day. Each load averaged 120 catties, which would amount to 24,000 catties per day, allowing sixty days in July and August, when there are very few loads shipped from Tachienlu on account of the heat, which neither the yak nor the inhabitants of the higher plateaus can endure. If we accept the statement that 24,000 catties of tea are carried up this road by yak and mules for consumption in Tibet, for 300 days in the year, we find that 7,200,000 catties of tea are carried over this great north road. If we look at Sir Alexander Hosie's carefully worked-out report, founded on the statistics he was able to obtain at Tachienlu, we find that he estimated the tea passing through Tachienlu every year at 8,533,000 catties, and the value to amount to 948,591 taels. My rough estimate of what passed over the Great North road, viz., 7,200,000 catties, would leave 1,333,000 catties to be conveyed over the western route to

CHINESE TEA-COOLIE CARRYING 370 POUNDS OF TEA.

Litang and Batang and other local routes. This would allow for about six times as much of the tea for Tibet to be carried over the Great North road; and find its way to the heart of that great country.

On a very fair basis, Sir Alexander Hosie has been able to compute the quantity of tea passing through Tachienlu,

HOT-SPRING NEAR YUKOH—AND MIXED BATHING.

and I believe he is well on the safe side, as no doubt some tea finds its way through which is not registered on the official books; and we may add to this amount the tea that finds its way into Tibet through Songpan, Mongun and Tsakalao, which is not less than one-quarter of that passing through Tachienlu, or say 2,133,250 catties. Almost as much more finds its way through India and Russia. I know that along the Kansu border and Kokonor district the Hankow brick tea is almost universally used, so that the total amount of tea finding its way into Tibet by other routes may be safely estimated as being equal to the quantity entering from Szechwan, that is, from Tachienlu, 8,533,000 catties; and from Kwanhsien, 2,133,250 catties; would give a total amount from Szechwan of 10,666,250 catties. Allowing that much more finds its way into the country from India, Russia, Yunnan and Kansu, 10,666,250 catties; we may estimate the total quantity of tea annually consumed in Tibet from all sources to be not less than 21,332,500 catties.

If we next allow three catties of tea per person, we arrive at a population of 7,111,166 souls. Now this is a very poor way of getting an estimate of the population; but I believe that research will prove that that quantity of tea finds its way annually into the country. And while the Tibetans are great tea drinkers, yet they boil their tea until every particle of tannin is extracted, and they also use a family pot, so that a pound of tea will go a long way with them; and when we take men, women and children into account, and also that it is a cold country, I believe that three catties each is not too small an estimate of the consumption per head.

When we passed through Tailing, it was reported to us that there were 350 Chinese engaged in the goldfields, along the valleys and streams, which are very numerous here. The whole country is hopelessly broken up, and streams run in every direction of the compass. Groups of gold diggers, varying from 10 to as many as 100 men, were to be seen, all busily digging up the sand and gravel near the water's edge and washing it.

The great snow mountains towered up in the south-east. The most northerly peak is Tapaoshan (Great Peak Mountain),

CAPITAL OF YUKOH.

also called Dabashan, which is the name given to cattle thieves. The Yukoh raiders sometimes come as far south as this and surprise parties crossing to the Tachin Valley. There is also a road from here to Romi Changku, a Chinese military post, at the junction of the Tachin and Siaochin Rivers. Tapaoshan towers up 25,000 feet, and is quite conical in shape at the peak. A little south of it, in the same range, is Haitzeshan, so called because of numerous small lakes found about its base.

At 4.30 next morning we struck camp, and followed the stream down twenty li and came to Pame, on the big road, where we had breakfast and changed our ula. One of the men had come on here the night before, so the ula was all ready for us.

The people were most friendly, and set tea, butter, curds and tsamba on small tables about fourteen inches high, while we sat on benches of about the same height. Chinese customs were to some extent making themselves felt. As soon as the thunder-storm, which came on with terrific force, had subsided, we set out for Barchonku, which we found to be 11,567 feet high, and here we again changed ula. There was a little cultivation about, especially in the valley just below the house of the Fupei Fu, but most of the country was grassland, and it was very cold at night.

On the way up I heard of a strange kind of cat, of which they gave the most wild description, calling it the lion-cat. I got one of the escort to go back with me to see this strange animal, and after riding five miles we found that the reported lion-cat was nothing more than an ordinary house cat. Its hair was long and fuzzy-looking on account of the cold climate.

On the way back we had one of the most severe thunderstorms I have ever been out in, but it is wonderful how quickly the weather changes in this part of the world. One minute you bask in brilliant sunshine, the next are pelted with rain and hail, and so severely that it is almost impossible to live in it. Six miles farther on there were about fifty gold diggers at work in the bed of the stream. Each gang was composed of fourteen men, which was subdivided into two parties of seven. Each party dug a hole along the river's bank. Before digging far, they get below the water in the stream, the pit keeps filling up, and the miners bale it out with a hand ladle. In one place they were working a bamboo pump, and three men were working a small rod, with a sucker on the other end, but they only succeeded in pumping out a stream of water about half-an-inch in diameter. It was more like milking a cow than draining a mine, only the quantity of water did not in any way seem to be reduced. Three men worked the rod, while four stood by and smoked or looked on. They changed places frequently though there were no signs of perspiration on any of them. This was reported to be a good pit, if they could only get it drained. When enough fine sand is collected in the bottom of one of these holes it is carried in buckets to the stream, ten paces away, and washed over a board some three feet long by eighteen inches wide, which has grooves cut in it to catch the gold.

The stream has a fall of about two feet in every ten feet run, and it would have been the simplest thing in the world to have had a proper trench and sluice-way for washing the sand; but John Chinaman likes his own way of doing things and only laughed at me when I suggested something better.

It was almost dark when I reached Porchangku, to find the party all comfortably housed.

The country was similar to that we had traversed for the past two weeks, only more rolling, with high peaks immediately about.

At last we came in sight of Tachienlu, and received a hearty welcome from the missionaries located there.

The China Inland Mission have had a station here for

nearly fifteen years, and the Foreign Christian Mission of America have been at work for about six years, and were then just moving on to Batang, another eighteen days' journey further west, where they were opening a new work.

We were well looked after during our short stay, and it was indeed pleasant to reach a Mission Station and kind friends after our wanderings.

CHAPTER XVI.

UP THE TUNG RIVER.

AFTER our long journey over a very rough country, where we had to live almost entirely on the local produce of the land, which was barley meal and butter, it was good to find ourselves once more sitting around a table on which a white cloth was spread. Better still, the table was amply supplied with such luxuries as strawberries and cream, home-made bread and butter, and many of the other delicacies that may be found in an English home, and this although we were on the very borders of Tibet. But wherever the Western lady goes she soon adapts herself to local conditions. What is still more important, she puts her wise hands on the local produce, and with a little manipulation transfers it into delicacies which are far more appreciated by the traveller who has been roughing it than a preparation of the same kind would be under much more favourable conditions.

And here is a reason why so many travellers write of the missionary as living in luxury. On most occasions, when he visits one, it is after a long trying journey on which his supplies have run short, and he has been reduced to what he can pick up on the way—sometimes very meagre fare indeed. He then arrives at a station, and the missionary's wife, wishing to be kind, brings out her preserved fruit which she has laid by for special occasions, and in fact puts herself out to entertain the stranger and make him feel at home: often to find herself and her family written up in some book as a missionary household which lives in luxury, with nothing to do but entertain passing strangers.

We were fortunate enough to reach Tachienlu in the strawberry season, when the mountain sides were covered with beautiful, wild, red, luscious berries. The native children go out in parties and gather these berries, and sell them on the street for less than a penny a pound.

The cattle that graze on the mountains about the city were driven in and milked, and the milk can be bought for

DOWN THE TACHIEN-LU RIVER.

about a penny a pint, so that while strawberries were a great luxury to us, they had been the common dessert of missionary homes for some weeks. Even China and some parts of Tibet are not such bad places to live in during some parts of the year, especially when people know how to adapt themselves to circumstances, and to make the best of what is available.

We spent one and a-half days in Tachienlu, which is a small but very important border town. To this city hundreds of

Tibetans come daily, some from the very heart of Tibet, as well as from all parts of the border States, and here is the great depository of the Chinese Tibetan frontier. Taking the average train of tea coolies, we find that about 125 arrive daily throughout the year, each coolie carrying a burden of about 200 catties (or 366 lbs.). During the busy season there are as many as 400 coolies arriving per day; in the slack season very few are seen along this road. But, since Tachienlu is the terminus of the Chinese coolie line of transportation, it is also the point from where the yak caravans are made up.

Commercially Tachienlu is of great importance. From the heart of Tibet hides, wool, deer's horns, musk and gold dust all find their way, and these are exchanged on the street of Tachienlu for tea, cotton goods and haberdashery of all kinds, such as are used in Tibet for bartering purposes.

The stranger, simply passing through the place, might dismiss it as a dirty military outpost. The streets are very narrow and, if one turns out early in the morning, they will be found extremely filthy, especially in the summer months. The shops look insignificant, as little can be seen in them but copper kettles, pots and pans, used by the Tibetans when travelling; and cloth, needles and cotton thread, a few old swords and relics from monasteries which the Chinese troops have looted, complete the display.

The Lu River comes rolling through the centre of the town, bisecting it. This river is spanned by three suspension bridges, over which foot passengers, animals and caravan traffic pass to and fro. The town is paved with stone throughout, the houses are built on wooden frames, with movable wood fronts, mostly painted brown, but some of the walls are built of stone. The architecture is a modified Chinese Tibetan style found all along the frontier.

The finest building in the place is the Ming-chen Ssü. This title was given by the Chinese to the Tussu of Chala State, which is bounded on the east by the Tung, on the west by the Yalung Rivers, on the north by Matze and Gaishechia, and on the south by the Huang Lama's district, whose headquarters are at Mili, a ten days' journey south.

We called to see Ming-chen Tussü, but unfortunately he was not at home. We entered a large compound surrounded by a high stone wall, enclosing lofty, semi-Chinese buildings, with sloping roofs and covered eaves. The roof was decorated by several gilded pinnacles.

The poor-looking residence of the Sub-prefect, who also fills the position of commissary, is close by, but looks small and insignificant in comparison.

The Tussu has been politely asked to remove to his summer residence, which lies ten miles to the south-west, as his city abode will be required by the Warden of the Marches. This may be only a temporary arrangement, but the Chinese policy is an aggressive one, and the day is not far distant when they may be able to dispose of the services of the Prince of Chala, though his residence may prove useful for housing the Chinese officials, his successors. At present this once powerful Tussu is only a tool in the hands of the Chinese. He is useful to them in securing transport for their military supplies. His people are groaning under the heavy burden thus imposed on them, for hundreds of animals are required daily to forward the supplies and ammunition to the troops which are scattered along the frontier.

We must now return and have a peep into the monastery which is close by. We entered a large room and were received by the secretary. After tea and refreshments he led us to the general assembly room, from the gallery of which we had a fine view of the service that was being conducted. On an elevated seat, on which was a silk cushion, sat a lad of about sixteen years. He was an incarnation of Buddha. In two rows down the centre of the large room about fifty lamas sat, all with bells and dorgies (thunderbolts) in their hands, which they waved about and kept time to the weird chant. Candles and butter lamps burned on the altar, causing a most peculiar light and effect as we looked down on the worshippers, some of them apparently most devout, while some of the younger members of the party were quite frivolous and inattentive. We were careful not to attract their attention that we might see the ceremony under ordinary circumstances.

However, we must now go back to the gochuangs and see what is going on there before we take our departure. I have in a former chapter explained that a gochuang is a kind of guildhall, where the members or friends of a clan lodge.

In Tachienlu there are many of these, and the people coming from the interior always put up in their own guild, and through the managers of these guilds they buy their tea or other articles of import to Tibet. The articles brought from the interior for the most part also go through the hands of these indispensable gochuang managers. In other words, they act as the middlemen between the Chinese merchant and the Tibetan trader from the interior. It is only by remaining in these gochuangs for some days that one gets some idea of the business that goes on in such a place, for from the street nothing can be seen of what is going on inside these enclosures.

We said good-bye to Tachienlu friends and continued our journey, following the main tea road as far as Wassukou.

The river was a seething torrent all the way, and falls almost 3,000 feet in six li (fifteen miles). In several places we were marching right in the spray, that was dashed far over our heads, as the water beat its surf in white foam against the boulders. Very little cultivation was to be seen after passing two miles below Tachienlu. About some of the houses by the roadside a small patch of vegetables or tobacco was to be seen, but such cultivation was so limited as to be scarcely worth mentioning.

Wassukou stands on the right bank of the Lu River, just above its junction with the Tung. Here we spent the night. It was quite early when we arrived, so we went down to the river to watch the natives fishing. The system of angling adopted was one commonly used by the Chinese in swift-running streams, where the fish is caught when passing over the shoals.

SOME OF THE PEAKS OF THE DABA RANGE.

The fishing gear consists of a long bamboo rod, with a fixed iron ring at the tip, a reel is attached to the fishing rod, sometimes the line is wound between the thumb and forefinger and over the elbow, two hooks are attached to the line a few feet apart, and a small lead sinker is made fast about six feet higher up. The line is thrown out into the current, and let run through the iron ring, the current being swift the line is carried away, then drawn up over the rapid again. The hooks catch in the side of a fish that is struggling to get up the rapid, and in this way large fish are sometimes caught, but it requires a lot of practice and patience to be at all successful. I have seen fish 7 to 8 lbs. landed in this way, but I have also on other occasions watched the fishermen work away for an hour and never get a fish.

Near Wassukou we met the Sub-prefect, who was out examining the road that was undergoing repairs before Chaoerhfung, the new Warden of the Marches, should arrive. The change was quite noticeable between Tachienlu and this point, but it would not be very lasting, for a lot of loose earth was placed over the rough places, which a good shower of rain would wash away.

In many places boulders which had been washed down and almost blocked the road were removed, and in other places they were immovable. The road was built up with stones so as to allow chairs and mules to pass without any difficulty. Two thousand men were reported to be at work on the section controlled from Tachienlu.

From Wassukou we passed over a chain bridge spanning the Lu River. This bridge was built of thirteen chains, the links of which were about twelve inches long, made of three-quarter inch iron. These chains were built into stone masonry, and made tight by means of primitive windlasses, one to each chain, and turned by inserting an iron crowbar into holes bored in the log. When the chains were jacked tight, the windlasses were built over with masonry. It was a very good bridge, but there was a deal of vibration.

We travelled up the right bank of the Tung for four miles, where we arrived at Kutze, and took shelter from the pelting rain in the old Tibetan temple. There we found an ex-Lama, who had been turned out of the Lamasery on account of a fight he had had with another brother of his order, so he said, but I should judge there was a more serious charge against him. The temple was a fine building, though the Lama in charge of it only visits it twice a year. Owls and bats have taken possession of the place and roost on the idols. In the daytime the rafters of the temple were literally covered with bats. The lower storey of the temple was kept locked, but from the gallery to which we had access we could see the gilded faces of the huge idols in the dim light. The work about the altars was of fine workmanship and in good condition,

HERB-GATHERERS OF LIANGHOKON.

bearing testimony to the fact that at one time there were many devotees in this section of the country.

The temple was quite unique in its architecture, very different from anything we had seen on the whole journey. It had two round houses built out on the roof like turrets, which gave the place a very fine appearance.

At Kutze there was a single rope bridge, worked by the ex-Lama, who was certainly an expert at performing on the tight rope; he tried to persuade us that this was the best place to cross, but we learnt that there was a ferry boat some distance higher up the stream at a place called Chiang Tsui (river's lip), and there we found a very frail and small boat in which we managed to get across safely.

Here the river bears to the west and we went up a small stream and over a mountain to avoid a very difficult gorge, through which it would have been almost impossible for our coolies to have passed, even if we could. We spent the night 2,000 feet above the river bed, and had a magnificent view of Paomashan (race horse mountain) to the south of Tachienlu, which is quite 25,000 feet above sea-level.

The country is picturesque and there is considerable farming carried on along the valley and slopes. The people belong to Yutung, where a chief lives, but he is really subject to the Muping Tussu.

On passing over the spur, after a climb of 2,000 feet, and a descent of nearly as much, we came down to the bed of the Songlin River, a tributary of the Tung; this we followed to one of its sources.

At Heiku we found quite a large Bon or Black monastery, and purchased some of their books. I was sorry not to have a copy in Tibetan to give them, and even the few copies of Chinese Scriptures I had picked up at Tachienlu had all been disposed of.

The people were most friendly, though no foreigner had ever been here before. We spent the night in a water mill a little farther on, just before entering one of the finest forests I have seen for a long time. The people were busy grinding flour till nearly 12 o'clock, but at last the water was turned off and we went to sleep.

Next morning we dipped straight into the dense forest. For the first five miles the trees were not very large, but for the next thirty miles they stood as straight as church towers, and many of them measured six feet on the stump, or eighteen feet in circumference. I have never seen anything to equal them outside of a British Columbia forest.

Years ago an attempt was made to raft timber down from here, but the rapids were so difficult that there was much loss of life and timber, and the enterprise was abandoned. We spent one night in this forest, and the next day, at 4 p.m., we arrived at the place where we had hoped to meet Meares, for we had sent a runner on ahead to escort him from Hannin, where we expected him to be, and bring him to us at Linkou. He had left for Mongun before the runner arrived, as we were two days later than we had expected. So after waiting two days Brooke went across to Mongun to join Meares, and I went on my way eastward through Muping to Chentu.

This was a very rough piece of country. The road was built out on bamboo poles, stuck in mortices in the perpendicular rock, sometimes sixty feet above the stream. I arrived home on the last day of July, 1908, in the hottest weather that had been known in Sechuan for twenty years. After the cool mountains of Tibet, the heat was enough to prostrate one, for the thermometer rose to 105 in the daytime and never was below 95 at night for quite three weeks.

CHAPTER XVII.

Two Gold Streams.

From the junction of the Kermer with the Kwanyin River at Damba the united stream flows almost due south to Romi Changku, and is called the Ta Chin or Great Gold Stream. At Changku another large stream, called the Siaochin or Small Gold Stream, joins it, and from that point to where the road leading to Ningyuenfu crosses it the river is known by the name of Tatuho or Great Ferry River. From there to Kiatingfu, where it joins its waters with the Ya and Min Rivers, it is known as the Tung or Brass River. These are all local names, and may be very misleading and confusing to the traveller as well as to the reader—never sure of just what river he is travelling on, or reading about, unless these points are borne in mind.

A little information as to how these names came to be used and why they exist may be of interest.

We will go back to the source of the stream and follow them down again. Kermer is a Tibetan name, given to the branch of this river that rises in the Kermer Mountains or plateau, a range that divides the waters of the Tung from those of the Min River or Fu, as it is called near Songpan. This river runs through the pasture lands and camping grounds of Upper Kermer, Middle Kermer, and Lower Kermer. These three settlements are on the southern slopes of Ngaba State. We now follow the stream down through the States of Somo, Drukagi and Runga, to its junction with the Kwanyin River. The latter river forms the boundary line between

Runga State and Chosschia. Kwanyin is the largest or longest of the two streams, the true source of the Tachin or Tung River. Some of its tributaries rise in the Baian Tukmu Mountain in the Goluk Range, which divides the waters of the Huanghu from those of the Yangtze. It derives its name from a large Lamasery called Kwanyin Cumba, which is built

A MONASTERY IN BATI ON THE GREAT GOLD RIVER.

on its banks, about three days' journey north-west of its junction with the Kermer. One of the Kwanyin's tributaries rises on the northern slopes of the Dabo range, and flows through the centre of Youkoh State. This branch we followed for several days, and crossed it almost at its source.

We must now return to Chosschia and trace the Tachin

River. From the junction of the Kermer to Kwanyin Rivers it runs through a valley which has a rich gold deposit. Great quantities of this precious metal have been washed from the sands along the banks of this stream, and also from deep tunnels sunk into the bank near the river's edge, where deposits of silt have been made sufficient to turn the stream from its former channel. This is the case also with the Siaochin, and from their gold deposits both of these streams derive their names.

From Hsu Ching, a strong military outpost and the most important town in the Tachin valley, the Chinese have taken possession of most of the land along the river, though it has cost them a great many lives to do it. In the time of Chen Lung fierce battles were fought in these valleys, and the famous Tussu Solo Wang was subdued. Two small States further south—Bati and Bawang—still retain their hereditary Tussus, where the old cult of the Bon, a primitive form of native worship, yet exists, and is still the State religion. Buddhism, therefore, has never been fully established here, but it is steadily making its way.

In the Siaochin valley there is only one small native State left—Ojen or Wokji—which is still governed by an hereditary Tussu. The rest of the valley is directly under the Chinese officials stationed at Mongun. They employ native headmen, called respectively Peifu and Chienfu, *i.e.*, the head of 100 families and the head of 1,000 families, and these are hereditary offices, and are a remnant of the old Tussu system. This system the Chinese are trying to adopt throughout all this country and Tibet. Chaoerhfeng, the present Warden of the Marches, may be able to accomplish their policy, but not, I fear, without a struggle on the part of the tribesmen.

It was in these valleys that Meares was travelling while Brooke and myself were on the long journey described in the former chapters, and here I may summarise his wanderings, as he told us of them.

It was decided that he should go south with the coolies and their baggage while he went toward the Tibetan frontier, and we hoped to meet at Changku by a certain date.

He travelled down the fertile valley of the Tachin among cornfields and beautiful scenery. The river's banks were covered with flowers, over which fluttered gaudy butterflies,

GROUP OF TRIBESMEN IN THE TACHIN VALLEY.

while brightly-coloured parrots flashed among the trees, which were abundant along the water's edge. It was evening when he reached Hsuching, a Chinese military outpost. The official seemed pleased to see him, and invited him to dinner.

He found plenty of fruit for sale on the streets. This district is famous for its pears, and later in the year they are even shipped to Chentu, an eighteen to twenty days' journey.

Continuing down the river, at noon the next day he came to another coracle ferry. The river was running in high flood and it took some time to cross.

They were still fourteen miles from their destination, but the ferryman volunteered to take Meares and his interpreter down by river in an hour ; so they struck a bargain. They took their seats in the bottom of the walnut shell, and were off at the speed of an Atlantic liner. The craft bobbed up and down, turned round and round, while the boatman, in a half-kneeling position, endeavoured to steer the raft off the rocks with his small paddle.

They shot a number of cataracts, and at last came to a place where they heard a tremendous booming and roaring. The boatman worked his boat to the shore, and landed to have a look at the rapid.

First, he thought it was impossible to shoot this, then he said he would try, and off they went again. When they reached the big waves which surged quite ten feet high they were hurled into the air, then twisted round and round in the eddy, until the whole world seemed to be swinging ; next they disappeared into a hollow and the waves broke over each side of their tublike craft.

The escort covered his face and cried bitterly, but the boatman worked away with his paddle, and soon they were in smooth water again, continuing their trip to the large monastery just above Tsonghua, where they arrived in three-quarters of an hour from their starting point.

The writer having made this same journey the year before, can vouch for the sensational experiences of the trip.

Tsonghua is also a military outpost, but all these officials have both civil and military power.

From Tsonghua they went over the pass to Mongun, the largest and most important town in this section of the country. There the Brigadier is located, and there it

A CHINESE MANDARIN.

was Meares hoped to store their extra baggage and supplies.

Soon after leaving Tsonghua they started up a steep mountain and toiled on all day in pouring rain, and at 7 p.m. reached a herdsman's hut, where they put up for the night.

Next morning it was still raining, but they set out to top the pass, which they reached at 11 o'clock.

Though it was the middle of July the snow was still lying deep on the top, and they all felt the effect of the altitude a good deal. This pass is over 16,000 feet high. Most of the coolies collapsed, and, if they had not been able to hire some medicine diggers to carry the loads over, they would have been stranded.

On the other side of the mountain they found a large glacial valley covered with grass and decorated with flowers.

On the upper slopes there was a deep soft carpet of edelweiss, adorned with a profusion of large red, yellow and blue poppies. Lower down, the slopes were covered with cowslips and other flowers like primroses, besides many other varieties, the names of which were unknown.

Scattered through the valley was a number of herdsmen's tents, and large droves of yak were grazing on the rich pasture. Below this they came to timber land, which is rather a rare thing in this part of the country, where the mountains are for the most part destitute of trees.

They reached Mongun in a heavy rain, to find the bridge had collapsed, leaving only one log to connect the buttments on either shore. With much difficulty they got across and very soon reached the street, where they found an inn and plenty of Chinese food for sale.

After paying off all the coolies but three, and stowing the baggage in the official's yamen, they set out for Changku, a town three hard marches south-west, situated near the junction of the two gold streams. The first day they had no difficulty, but the river was rising fast, and, for the next two stages, the path for much of the way was submerged by the swirling stream. It was impossible to climb the steep cliffs that hemmed in the valley in many places, so there was nothing for it but cautiously to wade through the submerged places, a most difficult task for the coolies with their loads. It was rather chilly work, thus wading in the ice cold water, for the melting snow was pouring into it from the surrounding heights. They at last reached Changku, to find a man waiting them with a letter from Brooke, saying that he was going with me still further west, and that we would not be back for some weeks. So Meares filled in the time by visiting the tribes of Bati and Bawang, who live on the west bank of the Tachin, north of Changku.

Marching up the right bank of the river for ten miles they came to the capital of Bawang, where there is also a large monastery, and the residence of the Chief is near by.

They were soon invaded by a crowd of truculent, ill-favoured looking Lamas. These they tried to entertain, but they only grew more insolent and began throwing stones, and it was with some difficulty they escaped without a row.

They marched on to Bati, passing the famous black temple which is the headquarters of the Bonba cult, but were not successful in gaining access to the temple. Mr. Edgar, so far as I know, is the only foreigner who has ever been inside it. The priests would not allow me to enter this temple when I passed through last year. Meares reached a small town on the right bank opposite the Tussu's residence, but the river being in high flood it was impossible to cross. While Bonba is the State religion, there is also a number of the Red and Yellow cults about, and they have a monastery near the Bonba temple.

The banks of the river are rich in alluvial gold, but no one is allowed to collect it except the Lamas, and these only for gilding the temple roofs. When they find a large nugget they are supposed to put it back in the earth, that it may increase and multiply.

From here Meares returned to Mongun by the route just travelled, where he arrived without further adventure, except that on one occasion a huge stone, which got loose

THE PICA NIN OF ISO—CROSS BETWEEN YAK AND COW.

from the mountains, came tearing down into the valley and crossed the road just in front of them, leaving a line of sparks behind as it bumped on the rocks.

From Mongun he next set out for Hannin, where he hoped to meet us on our way back. Hannin is a pretty little place, nestling in the mountains at a height of 10,000 feet. A Chenfu or centurion is responsible for the good conduct of the people there. After waiting some days and hearing no word of us he returned to Mongun, where a runner from Mr. Brooke overtook him, saying that he had arrived at Lianghokou, a place three days south of Mongun. Meares sent back word that he would wait at Mongun, and there Brooke joined him.

After a few days' rest they continued northward toward Tsakalao; the weather was very hot, and all the maize fields were burned up for want of rain.

Everywhere the people were beating drums and cymbals and burning incense, imploring the gods to send rain. If they had only settled down to a few hours' hard work many of the fields could have been irrigated from the streams which flow everywhere down the mountain side.

All along the river's bank were to be seen the remains of gold diggings which had long since been abandoned. As far as Lianghokou there was a good deal of cultivation. A number of Chinese have emigrated into this valley and have taken native wives. One Chinaman had rented a mill for three shillings a year and married a native wife; her he sent to the mountains to dig medicine, while he ground the corn. They followed the right-hand stream which rises in the Hongchiao Pass, and after camping for a night in a deserted herdsman's hut, they crossed the pass, and lodged in the medicine digger's hut on the eastern slope of the mountain. The day they crossed the pass it was raining, so the view they had hoped for was unobtainable.

One more day brought them to the road over which we had passed on our way up two months previously. Two more uneventful marches brought them to Tsakalao. As they intended to rest for a few days they pitched their tents on the river's bank some distance from the town.

Some large walnut trees afforded splendid shade from the hot sun. Here they held a spring cleaning. First, they washed themselves, then all their clothes, and then made the coolies do likewise. This was not an easy matter, for although it was hot in the sun the water was very cold. But one man undertook the task, and the rest all followed like a flock of sheep.

They went over the pass by which Meares had come in when returning from his takin hunt in May, and camped near the salt-licks, hoping they might again meet with a takin, for Meares was anxious to photograph a live one. Brooke spent two days and nights waiting for one of these strange creatures to appear, but vainly; there were plenty of tracks about, but the creatures that made them were nowhere to be found. They changed places and Brooke went on the hunt, while Meares took his bed to the salt-lick and waited to get a photograph. For three days he waited without result. The fourth day the rain fell heavily, and during the night a stream came down under the rock where he was camped. The rocks were loosened by the heavy rain, and began rolling down the steep hillside. When daylight broke he picked up his wet bed and cleared out, but on reaching the main stream he found that the log which spanned it had been washed away.

After wading down the side of the torrent for some distance he met Brooke, who had come out to find him, and they were able to fell a tree across the torrent, and thus bridge it. The weather continued wet, so sending one of the hunters back to Tsakalao for mail, they awaited his return. Two days later he arrived with a big bundle on his back, and they rushed at him and seized it, hoping to find the long-expected letters and papers. On tearing open the parcel they found nothing but bacon. This mail had been sent to Colonel Kao for them, but he had had to leave home, and being desirous to keep their letters in safety, had locked them in a box. So after the hunter had partaken of a meal he went back again for the letters, and two days later returned with such a bundle of mail that it took some time to read it.

After spending several more days in a fruitless hunt after the takin they came on to Chentu, and made preparations for their journey southward through China and India, where they hoped on their way to pass through the Rema and Lisu tribes.

CHAPTER XVIII.

MANTZE RELIGION AND CUSTOMS.

MY readers may ask, Who are these Mantze and in what way are they different from the rest of the people of West China? I must admit that this is a fair question, and so far I have only been telling you about the experiences of individuals who have travelled through their country.

From scraps of history which I have been able to gather and translate, as well as from reports given by the people themselves, I have come to the conclusion that the people known as the Mantze are emigrants from Gari, a place just north of Siklim, near Camba Dsung. Over 800 years ago they were invited by the Chinese to come over and help them subdue the fierce warlike tribes of the Upper Min or Fu River, who were constantly raiding the Chinese along the plain, and, when pursued, retreated into the mountains out of reach.

Three thousand of the Gari mountaineers, many of them with their families, came over to help and subdue the raiders; and were given the promise of free homesteads on the land previously inhabited by the people called Changmin, who were the original inhabitants. Fierce battles were fought, the Gari emigrants attacking from the rear, while the Chinese troops came in from the plain.

The Changmin were driven back, and the land they occupied was ceded to the strangers who had recently arrived from the head waters of the Brahmaputra, on condition of their being loyal to the Chinese Government.

Hereditary titles were given them and they were left in

control of these mountainous regions, if only they would check the raids of the aborigines, and render tribute to the Chinese Government as acknowledgment of China's sovereign right over the country.

For many years there was a fierce struggle carried on between the Changmin and their new enemies, the Mantze or Garionian, who had crowded them back and taken possession of their lands.

To enable these invaders to withstand the fierce attack of the Changmin, strong stone stockades were built on the spurs of the mountains, where the natural surroundings afforded the greatest amount of protection. We find many of their chaitze or forts built in such positions that very few men would be needed to defend a whole fort. This also accounts for the great towers, like factory chimneys, which we find everywhere, and which were used for two purposes; firstly as beacons, in case of a sudden raid, when a fire was kindled on the top of these great towers, and friendly villagers would come rushing to their aid; secondly, for storing their valuables and grain. The cattle were driven into the lower storey and were shut in by great heavy doors. In case of being hard pressed, the inhabitants took their final stand around this tower; and when compelled to take shelter, retreated up a ladder or temporary scaffold that led to the second storey of the tower, and defended that through the turret holes, and by casting stones from the top on their enemies.

It was this most uncertain and strenuous life that made these people such famous warriors, and accounts for the name given them by the Chinese, "Manpuko," meaning "Cannot be overcome"; Mantze means "One who cannot be overcome," and originally they were thus looked upon by the Chinese. Later the character applied to an unruly tribe, which means "barbarous—unruly," was used in writing of them, and is now used by the Chinese in contempt, and is much resented by the tribesman. But there is no other Chinese term to distinguish them from the Sifan, employed in reference to the ordinary Tibetan of Central and Northern Tibet.

These people came from the upper slopes of the Brahmaputra, where that form of nature worship known as the Bon or Bonba, also as the Black Cap cult, existed. They were slow to surrender their sceptre to the aggressive Red and Yellow sects of Buddhism.

To-day, in addition to the large Buddhist monasteries found established in this country, many of which have made a compromise with the Bonba and retain many of their hideous idols in the temples, we find the orthodox Bonba in Bati and Bawang, and also along the Tung River, between Wassukou and Romi Changku. The priests are distinguished by their dress, as shown in the photograph. They turn their prayer wheels the opposite way to the Yellow and Red sects, and their teaching is looked on as not only heterodox, but most wicked; yet much of it is accepted by the people and winked at by the Lamas.

The Bonba is a pre-Buddhist, indigenous Pantheon, and the idols of the cult are the most obscene and vulgar conceptions of an earthly and foul mind. Yet the people worship before these obscene and even fiendish models, offering them blood and spirits, as well as all the cereals produced on the land; herbs, tobacco and poisons are especially offered. They insist on the maidens wearing nothing more than a string round their waist, into which is tucked a small lamb skin or tassel made of yarn, which hangs to the knee.

After their first child is born they may wear skirts, as the gods have purified them.

The priests of Bati and Bawang States, where the old Bon cult is still the State religion, teach the people that, if they divert from this ancient custom, the gods will grow angry with them, and they will all die off. In winter time they wear a coat woven from yarn made of yak hair, which keeps them pretty warm. In the summer months the valley in which they live, in fact the whole valley of the Tachin, is very hot.

The neighbouring tribes have long since discarded this custom and all the females wear plaited skirts.

The black priests wear a conical black hat, similar to that of Mother Hubbard, and very similar to the dunce cap the Chinese crier wears when he runs in front of an official chair. There are not a few Bon symbols found in Chinese architecture; for example, the two poles, with a box, much the shape of a grain measure, affixed about two-thirds up each pole, found in front of every yamen and temple, is a relic of nature worship which is not unknown to the Bonba.

Buddhism has made many concessions to the Bon, and where it really has established itself in the Mantze States, it has done so by yielding substantially to the wishes of the people, and allowing them to retain much of their old belief and customs; though in many of the States Buddhism has really succeeded Bonism, yet it is a Buddhism different from that of most parts of Tibet. Colonel Waddell states in his invaluable book, "Lhasa and its Mysteries" (page 381), that the Black Cap is not unknown, even at Lhasa. He writes: "They have no literature, and utter their sayings orally. The leading oracles in Lhasa are the Nachung and the Karmashar.

"The chief oracle is attached to the principal State monastery, Dapung. For, notwithstanding its un-Buddhist character, this gross form of heathen sorcery was so deeply rooted in the minds of the people that that crafty ruler, the first Dalai Lama, brought it into the order of the Lamas. In doing this he was doubtless actuated, as were the Roman governors, by the obvious political advantages of having so

SUNNING RICE ON THE CHENTU PLAIN.

powerful an instrument for the Government service entirely under the control of the priests.

"Those who are masters in this art bear the title of 'Chief of the Wizards,' and not only do they perform at stated festive ceremonies, when they dance frantically to quick music in the midst of clouds of incense, burning from large swinging censers, but they also take it upon themselves to frighten the people into paying sums of money to the temples, and the up-keep of the Lamas, who live on the fat of the land, and make the people believe that they are the only medium through which the gods can be approached."

Demon possession also forms part of the programme. On one occasion I witnessed a most impressive ceremony while I was waiting for dinner in a village, and everything was perfectly quiet. Suddenly we saw a demon-possessed priest dressed in scarlet robes with a black, conical-shaped hat on his head, and in his hand a sword dyed red in blood. He seemed to throw himself down the hill from the temple, then leap in the air brandishing his sword in a most fantastic manner; then he seemed to roll down the hill, head over heels, and land on his feet, striking with his sword first in one direction then in another. At last he reached the street and drew near us in a most aimless way. His face was painted red, and he certainly looked hideous enough to have come from the lower regions. He rushed up to the street and stood opposite me for a minute, not more than five paces away; my men all screamed and some got under the tables, others ran for their lives. The whole street was in an uproar. I made sure he was a Boxer and drew my revolver. When the old lady in whose house I was dining saw it, she threw her arms around me and cried, "Don't shoot, he is my son. The man across the way has borrowed money from the temple some years ago and will not pay it back, and the idol has borrowed my son's body to come down and chastise him; he will not hurt you." I assured the old lady that she need not fear for me, that so long as he kept his sword at arm's length away he was quite safe, but he had better not come too close.

After a few leaps in the air he went to the house opposite, where the man who owed the money lived. The poor wretch was so frightened that he lay prostrate on the floor. The would-be demon marched up to him, threatening to smite him with the sword, waving it wildly in the air, while the prostrate man on the floor pleaded for mercy, saying he would surely return the money. The demoniac never spoke throughout the whole performance, and with wild leaps, came out of the house, staggered up the street and then ran up the hill to the temple like a madman. In all my wanderings on the Tibetan border I had never seen anything like it before, my coolies and helpers said they never did either. Judging from the secret the old lady gave me, the whole thing was arranged and the priest just worked himself up to a great state of excitement, which, together with his attire and blood-stained sword, made a most impressive sight.

Buddhism has gained much ground in many of the fertile valleys, and on prominent hills we find large monasteries containing from 500 to 1,000 Lamas. The one near Miala is the largest I know of in the country, which claims to have about 2,000 names on its register.

The feudal system that prevails has held the lands in the possession of the lords or Tussus, who have in turn let them out to their people on condition that they render certain services to them as lords, and also hold themselves ready to serve the Chinese Government through the lords, if they should be called out. The lands thus not belonging to the people, they could not borrow money on them, nor will them over to the monasteries, as is done in some parts of Tibet.

Yet the Lamas have not missed any opportunity to get possession of the people by threats of the evils that will befall them if they do not support the monasteries and the Holy Lamas, who are the only medium between God and man, and they also teach that without a Lama there is no remission of sins.

The plan adopted is to have a Lama succeed to the Tussuship; and, once that is accomplished, the whole State is in the power of the leading Lamasery, and the people have to bump their heads at the feet of a vassal lord and Father Superior; and at the same time pay their dues in kind to the monastery for the use of their lands, and in fact for the right to exist at all. Once the State falls into the possession of the monastery it rarely or ever emerges from its grasp again; for while the nearest heir should succeed, whether male or female, it is always arranged by the powers that be that their heir, if he be a male child, should early enter the Lamasery, while if a female, her chances of reaching maturity are very poor indeed. There are ways and means known to these spiritual fathers of a superstitious people of disposing of any obstruction that might come in the way of the coach of State.

The Lamas aim at keeping the people in ignorance, but some of them are beginning to see what the Lamas want is their money. The worship at the temple is largely performed by the women, though some of the men also make pilgrimages to these Lama strongholds to perform their periodical prostrations before the fiendish-looking idols; but many of them have confessed that they do not believe in the supernatural powers claimed by the Lamas.

The Lamaseries are the only seats of learning, and the layman who wishes to learn to read must put himself under some priest and study Tibetan writings, the only literature known to them. The Black Cap, or Bon, also use the Tibetan script, but the text of their books is quite different from the orthodox Lamaism. Their books are very difficult to obtain; I was able to secure one copy only, and that was from a young priest who sold it to me, when his superior was absent. He carefully bound it up and made me put it in my baggage, saying if his superior got to know of it he would be expelled from the temple. I have not yet been able to satisfy myself as to the teaching contained in this particular scripture of the Bon cult; but a most interesting subject still remains hidden away in closely guarded documents and parchments, some of them written on a paper manufactured from a kind of willow or dogwood, while others are on a preparation of birch bark.

The Tussus or chiefs intermarry in their own circle. The son of a chief always marries the daughter of another chief, so that they are hopelessly mixed in their relationship. Every Tussu is the brother, cousin, uncle or aunt of all the others, so that the hereditary rights may be passed on from one generation to another. It is a more difficult operation to disentangle some of these mixed-up marriages than to take to pieces and build up again the most complicated Chinese puzzle.

The young man may have something to say about the choosing of his bride, and often pays a visit to a relation's home to enable him to make his choice, but usually the parents make the choice and all the arrangements. A Tussu may have more than one wife, but the children of the first wife are the legitimate heirs. Should there be no offspring by the first wife, the second wife's children naturally fall heir to the hereditary property and title.

In the common ranks it is quite different, however; the young men and women mix freely in the home and in the fields, where they work side by side. They make their own love matches, and then make their intentions known to their parents. Should their parents object to the wedding the couple sometimes elope to a neighbouring State, and by paying a small fee may be pronounced man and wife by the Tussu, and may either become citizens of his State or return to their own home. A divorce may be had by a small payment to the Tussu by either party, with the complaint that the pair cannot live happily together. In some States the old Bon custom of marriage is still in force.

The betrothed goes to the home of her would-be husband, and lives with him for three days, after which she returns to her parent's home, where she remains till her first child is born; and as a period of two years is allowed, this custom leads to lewdness of the most open form, as girls thus betrothed are practically profligates, and have to sleep on the open flat roofs of the houses, with a ragged piece of felt rug for a mattress and often only thin covering.

The greatest possible shame is for a woman to be barren. When her child is born she takes up her position of wife and mother. Presents are exchanged in proportion to the position of the parties concerned, and sometimes a feast is made, but that is often dispensed with in the common ranks.

Though the standard of morality set by the Bon is so very low, yet in some parts, where Chinese sobriety has to some extent moulded a new social life, we find things quite different, and the traveller will see very little of the custom described above at the present time, except in the Bati and Bawang States.

To obtain a true idea of the social life of this people in most of these Federal States, you must again come with me on a visit to the home of an hereditary Colonel. I will try and be brief, yet make the visit as comprehensive as possible.

On arrival we shall be met at the door by the Colonel, and probably his wife, a very pleasant lady of about forty years. Next we shall be ushered with great state through the main doors into the yard in front of the building, into which all the cattle and horses are driven at night, and round which all the granaries, store houses and stables are located.

Now we climb up a steep staircase to the second floor, on

which the reception and guest rooms are situated. Being shown into a large room, we are invited to take a seat around a table and have a chat with the Colonel. A sweet home-made wine will be served to the guests by the Colonel's wife if she is acquainted with her guests or wishes to show them special honour; or it may be served by her handmaid or slave, who wears her mistress's bracelets and neck ornaments for the occasion. Tea is also provided for those who refuse to take this sweet wine, made of fermented barley.

The Colonel tells us of his experience while fighting with Heishui, the people of the Black River, under the humped-backed chief we met at Matang, who have been amusing themselves by raiding in the country north of his domains. He had to call out 1,000 of his militia, and go out to crush them. The Colonel is full of what took place on the field and will amuse us for some hours, if we have time to listen to an account of the guerilla warfare that is carried on between these tribes. But we must confine ourselves to their religion and customs.

While we are thus seated in the guest room, a tall stately lady and her two daughters, one aged ten and the other thirteen, come gracefully into the room, all wearing beautifully embroidered skirts and jackets, a beautiful home-woven sash tied around their waists, a blue kerchief on their heads. Their hair is plaited up in two long braids, crossed on the forehead and covered with rings of silver, crusted with coral and turquoise. The daughters are a little shy at first in the presence of strangers, but soon get over this and become quite natural and more like European children, which is very striking after the affectation and false modesty of the Chinese.

A little later the servants announce that the meal is ready. Wheaten cake, macaroni, stewed venison and some sweet-meats are served, and more sweet wine for those who care for it is offered by the servants on bent knee.

At sunset the servants return from the fields, driving in the cattle, sheep and horses for the night.

As each servant comes in they approach the mistress of the house and salute by dropping on one knee, and she has a kind word for each of them, both male and female. When the daughters wish to address their mother, they perform the same graceful act and present their request.

A HAPPY FAMILY.

We are reminded of customs that prevailed in the Europe of another day. When the children come in from the fields they drop on their knee and salute their parents ; the servants and slaves do the same. They all live under the same roof and eat the same food. There is the greatest friendship and familiarity between the children of the lord and the slaves' children, who all play together, yet they never take liberties or forget their position.

The servants are free from worries, they live in a fine house, have all they want to eat and wear. A little pocket money is given them on occasion. They have little inclination for city life, and everywhere you hear their merry songs, making the mountains resound. A happier people it would be hard to find than the family we have just visited.

Their evenings are spent round the big kitchen fire, about which they sit and chat, sing or join in a family dance, as they feel inclined.

Since we are old friends, we may be specially favoured by an invitation to the family kitchen for an evening's entertainment.

We are led through a corridor up another flight of stairs, into a large hall at the back of the castle. The room is about forty feet long by twenty wide; down the centre is the fire-place, with three large iron pots set on tripods, and under one of these a good fire is burning, and corn-meal cakes are baking in the ashes. Ranged on shelves round the walls are all kinds of beautiful copper and brass utensils, glittering like gold in the torch light.

The slaves open some of the old chests and get out some fancy clothes and masks. They are going to act a play. It is about a man who was jilted by a girl and who ran away into the forest and became a monkey. The chief was out hunting one day and almost shot him, but just discovering in time who he was, brought him back safely to the girl, and they lived happy ever after.

After the play they will give us a specimen of their native dance.

The girls all line up at one end of the row and the boys at the other. Some have strings of bells, and the dance is half a play, representing the chief of a neighbouring State coming to ask for help in a war he is carrying on. The girls say good-bye to their sweethearts, and as they dance round and round the fire, they first act a scene of good-bye, and later one of welcome to the boys on their return. The whole performance is most graceful and attractive. The Colonel's wife is mistress of ceremonies, and her two daughters and daughter-in-law are by far the most graceful performers and set the pace.

This is their way of spending a happy evening and entertaining their special guests.

A jar of sweet wine is set in the centre of the room, some long bamboo tubes, a little thicker than a straw, are set in the pot, and the thirsty go forward and take a few sucks through the tube and return to the ranks.

It is now late, and we must retire, but the performers, though they have worked hard in the field all day, and must turn out at sunrise in the morning, urge us to stay for the next scene, and if we want to see the play finished we may have to wait till daylight.

The mistress of ceremonies says "Enough," and all is quiet. Refreshments are served from the pot she has been watching with one eye, while with the other she has seen that each one played his or her part properly.

After a good bowl of vermicelli and venison soup, we retire to our room, which is next to the Colonel's, and sleep soundly until we are awakened early next morning by the merry laugh and tread of the servants as they drive the cattle to the grazing ground, or take their departure to the fields, from which they will not return till sundown.

It took some time thus to gain the friendship of this people, but now they claim me as one of their own and say, "You are so different from what we had heard about foreigners, you are one with us." Their home is open to the writer and his home is open to them, and they never fail to find it when any of them come to Chentu.

CHAPTER XIX.

The Caves of West China.

After spending some little time at Chentu, making the necessary preparations for a second journey, Messrs. Brooke and Meares started off again with the intention of going south to Ningyuenfu, a city lying between Lololand and the Tibetan frontier.

From there they intended to make a tour into the country marked on the maps "Independent Lololand," and then turn north-west and travel towards Batang, thence turn south-west in the direction of Rima, and try and cross that country if possible.

Unfortunately, their interpreter, a man they had engaged from Shanghai, developed heart trouble and had to be sent home, and as they were in this way stranded I let my adopted Chinese boy, who spoke very good English, go with them as interpreter.

They left Chentu on October 29 in two small boats. The party consisted of Messrs. Brooke and Meares, two interpreters—*i.e.*, one English-Chinese speaking interpreter and a Chinese-Tibetan speaking one—besides two cooks, seven pietze or back coolies, five ordinary coolies, a headman and three chair-bearers.

The party with all the baggage filled the two small boats; but the river was in good condition for a down trip; and as the boatmen rose early each morning and plied the oars all day, they were carried quickly through the fertile Chentu plains, passing under a number of beautiful old sandstone bridges, and the third day arrived at Chiatingfu, where they disembarked, and went overland to Omeishan, the famous "Mount of Pilgrimage" in Western China.

To Omei come pilgrims from all parts of Szechwan province and also from some of the neighbouring ones.

Every year during the winter months, thousands of Tibetans make pilgrimages to this sacred mountain to worship at the summit, where Buddha is supposed to cast his halo of glory over them.

This strange phenomenon has been described by more than one writer, but many people have made the arduous climb to the summit of Mount Omei, and after waiting some days to see the wonderful sight have gone away disappointed.

But the fortunate have seen the almost miraculous effect of the sun shining on the clouds that rise from the valley, in which their own shadow was reflected and magnified many tens of times, for the glory of Buddha is only to be seen when the sun is in a certain direction, and when there is a mist rising from the valley. To stand thus on a pinnacle 11,000 feet high, and look over a cliff, with a sheer drop of many hundreds of feet, and see reflected in mid air—arrayed in all the colours of the rainbow—the image of oneself magnified to the size of some tremendous giant, is a sight not to be missed if it comes at all within one's reach, and there is little wonder that the Buddhists have attached a miraculous meaning to the strange appearance.

The party only spent one night in Chaiting, and set out for the famous mount early next morning. A march of fifteen miles through a most beautiful valley brought them to Omeihsien. On the way they passed the adopted home of the white wax insect, for this wonderful little creature is carried all the way from the Ningyuen Valley in the early spring and deposited on a species of ash tree that is plentiful in this district. On these trees it deposits its wax, which is gathered in the autumn, melted and moulded into cakes of about 10 lbs. each, and exported to all parts of China; a considerable quantity of it also finds its way to Western countries. This is one of the chief industries of this section of the country. A strong, coarse kind of silk is also raised and manufactured, and these are the two special productions of the valley; but in so tropical a climate cereals and foliage of all kinds are abundant.

On reaching the little city of Omei, which is situated just below the mountain spur, they entered a long suburb on the eastern side. The city itself is little more than a quarter of a mile square, and the whole place is covered with trees and seamed with mountain torrents, which give it an appearance almost park-like.

The next day they passed up the bed of a torrent and through woods that gradually thickened into forest; and, passing a number of temples, they reached at last the long stone stairs that lead up the mountain side.

After climbing for some time they arrived at the Temple of Fuhusze ("Tiger-taming Temple"), where they had breakfast.

The next climb was a steep one of about 14,000 feet up, through pine groves intermingled with nanmu trees, some of which had grown to the size of two and a-half feet in diameter, and quite 150 feet in height. This nanmu is a wood much in demand for furniture, and compares favourably with walnut in appearance when polished, but is much softer.

Most of the buildings on Omei are temples, in which live some 2,000 monks.

So far they had only climbed a spur on the mountain, and had to descend into a valley again before making the steep climb that leads to the summit.

The most remarkable piece of work they found on the mountain was a huge brazen elephant in a shrine at Wanienssu (Myriad Years Monastery).

Mr. Meares writes of it thus :—" Here we found an interesting building. The style looked Indian. The lower part was a cube thirty feet square, which graduated into a circular dome, all beautifully made in brickwork.

"Inside the temple was a massive wooden cage, and in the cage a great bronze elephant of Indian workmanship. The

THE HONG CHIAO PASS.

elephant had three tusks and bore on its back a figure of Buddha in a lotus blossom, and is supposed to be placed on the spot to which Buddha came when riding on his white elephant."

Mr. Baber wrote thus of this same piece of workmanship :—" Just below it, in a kind of hostel, is a statue of Buddha twenty-five or more feet high, of a very rude and archaic style, reputed to be the oldest idol on the mountain. It is said to be bronze, but I took it for pure copper. Nothing could be learned of its age. A more artistic work is found in a temple behind Wannienssu, in a separate shrine. Passing under a dark archway we enter a hall, in the middle of which, as soon as we could see through the dim religious light, we observed a kind of palisade, and inside it an elephant cast in magnificent bronze or some such composition, nearly as white as silver. The surface is, of course, black with age and the smoke of incense, but I was able to judge the colour of the metal by inspecting a patch which had been worn down by a practice of devotees who rub coins on it, and carry them away as relics. The size of the image is that of a very large elephant, that is to say, some twelve feet high ; its peculiarities are that it is somewhat too bulky, that the trunk seems rather too long, and that it has six tusks, three on each side. With these exceptions, if exceptions can be taken, the modelling is excellent, and a glance shows that the artist must have studied from life, for the folds of skin on various parts of the body and the details of the trunk are rendered with great truth and success, though with a certain conventionalism. The creature has been cast in three sections—the belly and legs forming the lower, and back uppermost. The contour of the belly is complete, but on stooping underneath one sees that it is hollow and that the exposed edges are about five inches thick ; in some parts the metal is a great deal thicker. Each of his feet stands on a bronze lotus, and on his back the mammoth bears, in place of a howda, another huge lotus-flower, in which is enthroned an admirable image of Buddha, cast, I was told, in the same metal, but thickly gilt, his tower of glory towering to a height of thirty-three feet above the floor. Though generally called a Buddha, the image represents P'u-hsien P'u-sa (Samantabhadra Bodhisattva), the saint who is the patron—or patroness, for the Chinese credit him with female permutations—of Mount O. The monks told me that P'u-hsien descended upon the mountain in the form of an elephant, and that the casting commemorated the manifestation. But it may more probably bear an allusion to the well-known vision in which the mother of Buddha saw before his birth a white elephant with six tusks.

"The fane which encloses the casting is not less curious, being a hollow cube, covered with a hemisphere and roofed with a pyramid. The walls of the cube are twelve feet thick; the floor of the interior is a square of thirty-three feet on each side. The square becomes modified into a circle as the courses arise, by a transition which is gradual and pleasing but impossible to describe clearly without a knowledge of technical terms. Speaking clumsily, the four walls each terminate in a semi-circular outline, the summit of each semi-circle touching the circumference—*i.e.*, the base of the dome—and the four corners are each filled with three masses of brickwork, the surface outline of the central mass being an oval pointed at both ends, and the two others spherical triangles. The faces of all three are concave. The circumference of the dome is thus evolved from a square without any awkward abruptness, and it is only on trying to describe it geometrically that the arrangement begins to appear puzzling. To the eye the architectural process of squaring the circle is perfectly simple. The dome, however, springs from a rim which stands a little back from the circle thus formed, and so gains a few additional feet of diameter and increased lightness of appearance. The vault is to all appearance a hemisphere, very smoothly and exactly constructed. The whole edifice is of brick except, I think, a few insertions of stone blocks in the lower courses. The walls contain a series of ledges, on which are placed a number of small images said to be of silver. The only light which enters is admitted by the two arched doorways before and behind the elephant.

"The outside of the shrine cannot be seen, as it is enclosed in a timber building, which entirely covers it. Clambering by means of this envelope on the roof I found, instead of a cupola, a confused heap of brickbats, the *débris* of a low, four-sided pyramid which seems to have been faced with porcelain tiles. The timber casing was absurdly added by the monks to protect them from the weight of the winter snow, a fair indication that the shrine was not built by Chinese. So solid a building would probably stand fast even if the whole mountain were upset on to it. The precaution has gone far to defeat its own purpose, for the wooded husk has been twice burned to ashes, damaging not only the roof but the tusk of the elephant as well. It is said that they were melted off by the intense heat. The present tusks are a feeble restoration built up of plates and bands.

"With respect to the age and origin of the shrine and its contents, the most authentic information is found in the Ssu-ch'uan Topography to the following effect :—'The Monastery of "Clear Water P'u-hsien" on Mount Omi, the ancient monastery where the patriarch P'u served Buddha, dates from the Chin dynasty (A.D. 265-313). During the T'ang dynasty Hui-t'ung made his hermitage there. It was named "Clear Water P'u-hsien Monastery" under the Sungs ; Wan-li, of the Mings, changed its style to "Saintly longevity of a myriad years." The "Hall of Great O" stood in front, facing which was the "monument of Illustrious Patriarchs of the South," on the left the "monument of Sylvan Repose." The buildings included a series of seven shrines, the first of which contained a "P'i-lu" (?) the second seven Buddhas, the third a Deva king, the fourth a guardian deity (Chin-kang), and the fifth a great Buddha ; the sixth was a revolving spiral constructed of brick, enclosing a gilded bronze image of P'u-hsien, sixteen feet high, mounted on an elephant. In the beginning of the Sung dynasty (A.D. 960) orders were given to set up a bronze shrine and a bronze image also, more than 100 feet high. Under Wan-li, the Empress-mother directed the shrine of P'u-hsien, namely, the spirally-constructed edifice, to be carefully and thoroughly restored, and had the elephant gilt.'

"The existing building is obviously the 'revolving spiral'* here mentioned, and the awkwardness of the term, which conveys no idea to a Chinaman, is another proof that the builders were not Chinese. A name has had to be invented for an exotic form of construction, and there is, so far as I am aware, no other instance of a true dome of brick or masonry in China. It seems safe to conclude that the builders of P'u-hsien shrine, as well as the artist who designed the castings, were Indian Buddhists."

My friends were told that in another temple there was a mummy of the priest who had made the road up the mountain. Never having heard of a mummy in China Mr. Brooke was curious to see it, and by offering a small sum in money he prevailed on the priest in charge to climb on the altar and undress the figure, which turned out to be made in clay and rather badly finished. They reached the top of the mountain in a pouring rain, but got comfortable quarters in a temple on the summit, and were tired enough to sleep soundly amid the periodical banging of drums and clanging of cymbals.

* In the name "revolving spiral" we seem to have another allusion to such structures as are mentioned in the note on page 25. In the present case there may have been some wooden structure, formerly pivoted in the dome, that revolved. The suggestion of Hindu builders does not help to solve the puzzle of the dome. The description of the square building, with pendentives and circular dome, rather suggest work like that of the Indian Mahommedan of the Deccan in the sixteenth century (see Fergusson's "Indian and Eastern Architecture," page 560).

When they awoke next morning the whole mountain was covered in a blanket of snow, and as it was cloudy and there was no chance of seeing the Buddha's glory, they inspected the temples, and then hurried down and slept that night four miles from Omeihsien.

They were very much disappointed in the temples; many of them had the appearance of having been burnt down and very recently rebuilt, and seemed to have small historical interest. Many of them looked more like broken-down barns than temples. The weather was very wet; it was not the time of year for pilgrims to visit the sacred shrines, and many of the temples were closed, and this may account to some extent for the impression they received. There is no doubt that in this region there are many historical landmarks, for though the Lolos do not visit this mountain since it has become the strong tower of Buddhism, yet they claim that their three deities once made their homes there.

But we must pass to the ancient caves that are found in this part of the country. These are most numerous along the banks of the Tung and Su Rivers, and they are also found in other parts of the country on the sides of the hills; but usually they are dug out of the sandstone rock along the rivers' banks. And here I will give Mr. Meares's description of what they saw in the caves :—

"On our way back to Chiating we stopped for a few days to explore the caves which are situated near the road.

"We took up our quarters in a little Chinese hut, and hardly had we settled down when a Chinese pedlar came up to us and said, 'Do you remember me? I am the man who had a pain in the night in the inn at Fupien,' and he was very pleased to meet us again.

"In the rolling hills of this district thousands of dwellings or tombs have been hewn out in the red sandstone cliffs.

"All these caves are similar in plan, but differ considerably in size and ornamentation, doubtless in proportion to the rank and wealth of the owner. Some had only one small

TERRA-COTTA PIGMIES.

entrance running into the face of the cliff, while others had large verandahs with three or more caves opening from it.

"Let us take as an example one of these large caves.

"Some distance up the face of a cliff of red sandstone (on the face of which some hieroglyphics may still be seen), and approachable only by steps cut in the cliff, large enough to hold the toe of the foot, a large cavern has been hewn out, evidently with the help of a metal instrument, as the marks are still sharp and clear.

"In the cliff above the cavern a gutter is generally cut to shoot off the rain water, and sometimes imaginary animals are cut above the doors, evidently the crest of the owner. This verandah may be thirty feet long, twelve feet wide and ten feet high, and the roof is supported by two large pillars which had been left when the rock was cut away; there is very often a large cooking place between these pillars. This verandah is cut with square corners, and running round the top there is always a pattern, which is the same in almost all the caves. This looks very much as if it were built in imitation of the beams of a house, and a small model of a dwelling which I found in one of the caves had similar work on it. Above the central door on both sides of it are often carved figures of deer and horses. On the left side of the verandah a small cave is sometimes cut, evidently for a dog, and in one case I saw a carved stone dog in it. Generally these caves open from the main verandah. The one on the right is usually about thirty feet long and straight, and was evidently intended for servants or animals. These caves generally had an outer and an inner doorway, the first a few feet from the entrance, the second about twelve feet further in.

"The caves were about six feet broad and six feet high, and sloped gently upwards. The doors were solid buttresses, left when the caves were cut, and were about five feet six inches high by four feet wide; in these buttresses were grooves to hold doors, and sockets and grooves to hold crossbars. The two larger caves had two or three similar doors.

"About half-way along the larger caves were recesses cut in the walls. On one side was a large trough cut in the solid rock and evidently used for holding water. A small gutter was cut round it to carry off surplus water and the edge was much worn. Below it was a shelf for holding pots. In some of these troughs were round stones which had signs

TIBETAN INTERPRETER COMING OUT OF THE CAVE WHERE THE TERRA-COTTA PIGMIES WERE OBTAINED.

of being constantly heated in a fire. On the other side of the cave would be a similar cave, covered with a huge monolith which would take ten men to move, and inside some of these sarcophagi were coffins made of one piece of earthenware, with tight-fitting covers. These coffins were all empty, except for a little mould. Further in were small sockets near the roof, which had evidently been used for poles to support a curtain, and past this the cave generally opened out into one or two recesses large enough for rooms; these also had sockets for curtains.

"At the extreme end of the caves was a small shelf two and a-half feet from the floor, and two or three small cooking places cut out of the solid rock at a lower level beside it. Near these cooking places were the remains of cooking pots, which fitted the fireplaces. The terra-cotta figures and other remains were generally found on the floor below the small shelf, or in the large recess. They cannot have fallen from the shelf, or they would have been broken into a thousand pieces.

"Some of the caves are quite open and visible; others have been silted up by wash from the hills, and it was by digging into these we found most of the things, while others had been flooded and the figures were buried in the mud. Other caves had small openings much worn, which led into further caves at lower levels, and one could emerge again into daylight some distance from the point of entrance; while some of them were quite dry, and the figures could be seen just as they were left by the original inhabitants. In one case we found portions of a life-sized head with the cheeks painted red, and a black moustache and side whiskers, and, as may be seen from the photographs, the types are entirely different from the Chinese or aborigines of the present time.

"The modelling of the animals is much more artistic and correct than any modern Chinese work.

"As we were pushed for time we could only spend three days exploring the caves; so much still remains to be done.

"The authorities at the British Museum have no clue as to who these people were, but as some of the things are almost identical with objects found in the ancient Japanese dolmans, it is possible that these people emigrated to Japan at some remote period."

CHAPTER XX.

Chiating to Ningyuenfu.

After finishing their investigations in the caves our friends travelled north-west along the border of the Ya to Yachowfu. The Ya is a very shallow and fast-flowing river, and on this account the Chinese have constructed some very ingenious rafts by which they navigate it, and carry on them quite large cargoes, both up the river and down as far as Yachowfu. These rafts are made of giant bamboos, which are from four to six inches in diameter at the thick end. They taper off very gradually, and some of these poles reach a length of seventy to eighty feet. The bamboos are lashed together side by side; each pole is heated and turned up in front, and when the rafts are completed they look like giant Canadian toboggans, being about eighty feet long by fifteen feet broad.

As these bamboos are hollow and full of air, a raft will carry several thousand pounds, and only draw a few inches of water. They are quite flexible, and glide over the rapids and even over shallows without injury.

The principal traffic on the down journey is wool, hides and deer horns, which find their way from Tibet; also iron, copper, lead and coal, all of which are mined in considerable quantities in the neighbourhood of Yachow, and beyond.

When returning, they carry wine, sugar, cotton and piece-goods, which are the chief articles of import.

For anyone who is fond of duck shooting, a good plan is to go to the Yachow and there hire a raft to Chiating. These rafts are not the most comfortable looking crafts, as the only shelter afforded is a bamboo mat hut, usually erected near the centre of the raft. A few boards are elevated about a

RAFT ON THE YA RIVER ON WHICH MR. BROOKE AND MR. MEARES JOURNEYED.

foot above the bamboo to keep one's feet out of the water, though in crossing some of the rapids the spray will still insist on coming through. Yet even ordinary passengers, who are in a hurry to reach Chiating or some other port down the stream, do not hesitate to take passages on these rafts, and even the missionary ladies often take advantage of this quick and easy mode of travel; so that the sportsman who is anxious to see thousands of mallard, widgeon, divers and almost all kinds of water fowl within close range, will not mind a wet foot, or even being dumped overboard, if he can secure 85 to 100 duck during the trip of a day and a-half.

I know of one cool-headed missionary, who had taken passage on one of these giant toboggans, and was standing outside drinking a cup of coffee when the raft gave a lurch, a swirl, and he was sent overboard to partake of a cold bath. But managing to catch hold of the raft with one hand and keep his head above water—for it was in a place where the water was deep, just below a rapid—he contrived to hold on to his cup of coffee in the other hand, and, when helped on to the raft again, continued sipping his coffee as though nothing had happened.

All along the river fishermen may be seen at work with cormorants. They also fish with nets, and frequently catch the giant salamander, a huge newt, which often reaches a length of ten feet, and weighs from 60 to 100 lbs.

A peculiar fish, called by the Chinese wa-wa-u ("childfish") is sometimes secured near Yachow. It is reported to have arms, and to come out on sunny days and lie on the rocks in the middle of the stream sunning itself. I heard of this fish first in the autumn of 1902, but thinking it was only a Chinese tale, paid but little attention to it. My boy, who was with Messrs. Brooke and Meares as interpreter, mentioned it to them, and they tried to secure one but were not successful. They spoke of it to Mr. Openshaw, the American missionary at Yachow, who, though he had lived there for many years, had never heard of the "childfish." His cook, however, being consulted, declared that there was such a fish and bought one next day in the market. Mr. Openshaw put it in alcohol; I have not heard what became of this specimen, and was not fortunate enough to see one myself.

Yachow is a busy thriving town, beautifully situated on the banks of the Ya, and hemmed in by high mountains on three sides.

It is a great centre of the Tibetan tea industry. Tea grows on all the mountains in the neighbourhood and is carried by coolies into Yachow, where it is dried, prepared and packed in long bamboo baskets for the Tibetan market.

While at Yachow our friends engaged a raft and started out on a duck hunt. It was a lovely morning and the raft floated quickly down the river. Ducks were not very plentiful near the city, but they picked up quite a number. At one place they shot two teal, one of which was only wounded and floated down in mid-stream. The raftsmen rowed hard, endeavouring to overtake it before it reached an island which divided the river. They got near enough to get another shot at the teal, but it was too late to pull out of the cataract. A terrible current was whirling them into its fierce jaws, the waters leaped over the rapid and piled up against the rocky banks. Just below and in their course, great black, jagged spikes split the green waters into rushing, tearing streams of white foam. The raftsmen were frightened, but did not lose their heads. The raft shot over the rapid like an arrow. The men at the bow and stern oars now began rowing furiously, swerving the bow of the raft up into slack water, so that the stern swung round, just shaving the rocks. They swept stern-first for a few seconds and again the raft swung round, before they took the final plunge, bow on. The waves splashed up to their waists, and the raft wriggled over the sunken boulders like a snake.

They continued down the river for about ten miles, then walked back to Yachow. On the way they came across some snipe near a village, and after shooting several, the villagers collected in hundreds to watch the sport, and as it was im-

BRINGING RAW TEA TO BE PACKED AT YACHOW.

possible to convince them that what hurt snipe would also hurt them, the sportsmen had to give it up and return to Yachow.

They continued their journey towards Ningyuenfu, but before they had gone very far it began to rain and so continued all day. The continuous line of coolies marching along this road soon tramped it into thin mortar, and the round boulders, with which it was paved, were so slippery that it was almost impossible to keep one's feet. Hundreds of coolies were passed, staggering under their heavy burdens of iron, lead, copper, fuller's earth, coal and raw tea, all of them obtained from the surrounding mountains.

It was difficult enough to tramp this road in dry weather with such loads as these men carry, but with the road in this condition it is quite dangerous, and even as much as an ordinary pedestrian empty-handed can do to travel on. In places there were pools of blood, showing where some unfortunate wretch had fallen under his burden and cut himself on the sharp stones.

Along this road there are wayside inns every two or three miles for the accommodation of the tea coolies, who only travel from seven to ten miles per day. This road has been recently repaired for Chaoerhfung's troops and supplies to pass over, but in rainy weather the fresh clay that had been placed to fill in the holes between the boulders only added to the difficulty of travelling it.

The second day they reached the foot of Tahsiangling, and stopped for the night at Huangnipu, a street with about 100 families, where travellers generally rest before ascending the mountains, as the accommodation at the inns on the way up is very poor indeed.

Half-way up the mountain they found it covered with snow and the path very slippery, being coated with ice; so, strapping iron plates with sharp spikes on the soles of their boots, they struggled on through the bitterly cold wind that was blowing, and were rewarded on reaching the top by a magnificent view of the Tibetan mountains, which from this pass opens out before the eyes of the traveller if it happens to be fine weather when the top is reached.

On the east slope of the mountain it is nearly always raining or snowing and the foliage is very dense. Near the top vegetation almost ceases, except for a very coarse grass found on the slopes. On looking westward there is scarcely a tree to be seen. The view that opens before the observer is expansive. The cliffs are composed of red sandstone, and even the cultivated fields have a reddish tint as far as the eye can see.

Away in the distance, contrasted in the blue horizon, the white-tipped mountains and the eternal snows of Tibet fill in the background.

The west side of Tahsiangling is covered with a coarse grass, intermingled with jagged cliffs and deep cut gullies, through which small streamlets trickle.

Passing down from the summit the first two miles are quite gradual, but beyond that the descent is very steep, and after a drop of 3,400 feet, the travellers found themselves in the little town of Chingchihsien.

This is a most insignificant little town, nestling near the foot of the mountain, and the only thing that it is noted for is its place at the junction of the Ningyuen and Tachienlu roads, though most of the Tachienlu traffic does not come into the city, but takes a short cut across the mountain, thus lessening the distance by about three miles of rough road.

All the way up the pass they overtook hundreds of coolies wending their way slowly up the mountain, laden with great loads of tea. Fourteen bundles is about the ordinary load, and each bundle weighs from 14 to 18 catties, and, if we take 16 catties as the average weight of a bundle, we find that each load will weigh 224 catties (or 298 lbs.). On some loads I have seen eighteen packets, which would be equal to 384 lbs., and it is a common thing to see boys of from fourteen to eighteen years and sometimes girls, too, carrying loads of 150 lbs., toiling wearily up the pass. These loads are carried all the way to Tachienlu, a distance of not more than sixty miles as the crow flies, but quite 140 miles by the main road, which also makes a V on the map, and passes over two high mountains, both of them approaching 10,000 feet. Near the top they

CARRYING TEA OVER THE DAHSIANGLIN PASS FOR TIBETAN TRADE; AVERAGE WEIGHT CARRIED 200 TO 400 POUNDS PER HEAD.

met coolies with loads of parrots on frames, and others with packs of hunting dogs, coming from the Ningyuenfu Valley. The parrots were on their way to Chentu, and other cities in Szechwan, where there is a good market for them, and the dogs are for the Wassu and Muping hunters.

These little hunting terriers are bred by the Lolos, and a

good one brings a very handsome price for China. I have known one to sell for as much as three guineas.

All the way up on the slope to the south-east of the town and about half-a-mile distant, is the old site of the Lolo capital. Nothing is now left to mark the place but a few trees and some stone heaps. Few of the inhabitants even know that it was once a Lolo stronghold. At the present time there are no Lolos located north of the Tung River, at least not in the Chingchi Valley.

From Chingchihsien the road runs south through a fertile valley well irrigated from the numerous streams that rush down the mountain sides. Fruit of all kinds is plentiful, and oranges and pears are a speciality. Rice is grown on the terraced plots in the valleys, and other cereals, such as peas, wheat, barley, oats and buckwheat, are grown on the slopes; but the whole aspect of the country is most barren, especially in the winter months; not a tree adorns the hillsides, except for an occasional willow grown by the side of an irrigation ditch, or near some of the villages, where they have been planted and cared for by individuals.

The demarkation of the natural vegetation and tree producing country is noticeable. On the west side of the pass it is sunshine for most of the year, but the prospect is bleak and barren, with scarcely a tree to adorn the hillsides, while just a few miles to the east the sun is only seen for a few weeks in the year, nothing but rain and mist all the time; and there are places where the dividing line is quite abrupt, and a few paces will carry one from the rank foliage and mist, into the treeless grass lands and bright sunshine.

They spent the night at Fuling and the next morning crossed the Tung at the Tatu, or great ferry, from which this reach of the river derives its name of Tatuho (a great ferry river). It was on the banks of this river, and only a few miles further up that that Shih Takai, the leader of the Taiping rebellion was defeated and 7,000 or 8,000 of his followers were killed on the field, while he and a few hundred of his men were captured.

The credit of crushing this conquering army that was devastating China and defeating the Imperial troops at every point of contact is due to the united efforts of the Lolo and Sifan tribes, who know their country, and knew how to beguile their enemies into a position, where there was no possible way of escape. When the rebel army was in the deep ravine which leads to the ferry at Tzetati, the Lolo and Sifan tribes surrounded them, and by cutting off the supplies of this great army, soon reduced them to the point of starvation. So steep were the sides of this gorge into which they were penned, that it enabled the Lolos to roll down stones and tree trunks and pour poisonous arrows on a penned-up, helpless mass of humanity. Though the Chinese General took much credit to himself for this crushing victory, he did little more than stand with his men on the opposite bank of the Tung, and destroy any raft or craft that was unfortunate enough to reach that bank. It was the Lolos and Sifans that surrounded them and drove them to their doom.

On crossing the ferry of Tatu, the traveller plunges into a narrow glen between two treeless hills. The valley is full of great boulders, washed down from the mountain side by the freshets, and among these the road winds about in its zigzag course up the mountain.

The fields and hillsides were cultivated even on the steep slopes, but the grain was all harvested, and the aspect was very bleak.

After climbing to a height of 2,000 feet above the Tung, in a distance of four miles, the road immediately drops 1,000 feet, zigzagging its way down the steep mountain side until it reaches a mountain torrent, which disappears into a wild gorge to the west, cutting its way through limestone rock and joining the Tung about ten miles above the ferry.

The road follows up the left bank of this stream. A few ricefields are seen near the river's edge, and a little cultivation on the hillsides, but there does not appear to be much to attract the farmer, yet all along the stream watermills are kept turning, which shows there must be grain to grind.

The mill wheel lies horizontally, and the water is admitted by a small water race and strikes the fans of the wheel which

BAMBOO RAFTS ON THE YA RIVER.

offers its face to the current. The millstone is attached to the other end of the wooden shaft, and revolves on the same axis as the water wheel. The road continues on through the valley, and is made dangerous by falling rocks, which come rolling down from the heights, when loosened by the rain, or on the slightest other provocation. Often one of these boulders come rolling down the steep mountain side and pass through a caravan of mules, picking one or two out of the pack, passing on as though it had met with no obstruction until it lands in the torrent bed far beneath the road or path. After passing the village of Tawan (great turn) the mountains close in upon the stream leaving barely sufficient space for a narrow path. In places the rock actually overhangs the road so that one has to bow the head if riding, in order not to be pulled off. The cliffs rise to a height of about 200 feet, almost perpendicular or slightly overhanging, then fall away and continue to rise to the height of 1,000 feet. Wild tales are told of the attacks on caravans and lonely travellers by the Lolos in this gorge, and the place is certainly weird enough to make one feel that an enemy might be lurking anywhere along the march.

The stories told me by my escort, when I travelled through this wild place, were enough to make the hair stand on a timid man's head, but I saw no one more ugly than my informants and certainly none that looked more like outlaws, for the escort that was given me at Chingchihsien contained the most dilapidated specimens I have seen for a long time. However, as my journey was three weeks later, Brooke and Meares might have had a better lot.

On emerging from the gorge a plateau is entered, the highest point of which is the watershed, 7,200 feet, lying between the Tung and a small river, locally called Nga Rung, which is a Tibetan name. This river rises in the Siao Hsiang-ling, flows past Yueh Hsiting, and enters a gorge which opens out of the Yueh Hsi valley from where it flows in a north-easterly direction until it enters the Tung. It forms the border between independent Lololand and the semi-Chinese Lolo country through which the high road passes.

Along the road there is a mixed population of Lolos, Tibetans and Chinese. Most of the black-blood Lolos have left their

LOLO CAVES ALONG THE YA AND TUNG RIVERS.

former estates this side of the Ngarung River to their serfs, who have become Chinese subjects. These semi-subjected Lolos have a nominal chief, who is supposed to be a pure black blood, but he is not recognised by the chiefs in independent Lololand, and he really holds his position by appointment from the Chinese Government.

All along the road the Chinese have established block-houses, which are guarded by militia composed both of Chinese and subjected Lolos, but in spite of these guards, robberies are committed frequently along the main trade routes, and it is not safe to be out after nightfall.

Two days' march over this plateau brings the traveller to the valley of Yueh Hsi, in which is the Chinese city of Yueh Hsiting, quite an important centre, as from this place a large section of country is governed.

In a kind of prison or hostel in connection with the Yamen are to be seen a number of hostages who may be seen also in our photographs. These hostages come from various parts along the border, and are representative leaders or chiefs, who take turns of imprisonment to go pledge for the good conduct of their tribes. These chiefs are paid a nominal sum by the Chinese Government for thus serving a period in durance, and after serving a term of three months they are allowed to be relieved by other representative men of their tribes. This is the only hold the Chinese have on the tribes from the interior of Lololand.

After leaving Yueh Hsi the road continues up the left bank of the stream and leads over the Siao Hsiangling with a very steep ascent. Every five li (or mile and a quarter) there is a guard house, and two or three soldiers escort the foreigner from post to post. The road over the pass runs through very wild country, and it would be an easy matter for the Lolos to surprise travellers if it were not for the sharp look-out kept by the scouts posted all along the road. Even in spite of this vigilance, parties are often surprised and individuals carried off to be sold as slaves.

The day I came over I was benighted near the top, my coolies made such slow time ascending the mountain.

When I arrived at Chupanying where there was a centurion stationed in charge of 100 soldiers, he insisted that I should stop the night with him, as it was impossible to do the five miles that separated us from the usual stopping place. He lived in a tiny little guard house, but quite comfortably. Just as we were sitting down to supper, which he provided, there was a great shout which rang through the mountains, then three shots were fired. At this time there were only five men in camp, the rest were posted on duty along the road. In a moment all five were armed with their Mausers and fixed bayonets, and a cartridge belt buckled round their waist. They rushed out into the darkness, and Mr. Li, the centurion, seized his broad sword and went with them. I wanted to join, but to this he would not consent, and warned me that I must remain inside.

Calls were exchanged all along the line, and word arrived that it was only a false alarm given by one of the pickets near the top of the pass. However, night and day they are kept on the alert during the winter months, for it is in the winter when the Lolos are not busy in their fields that they do most of their pillaging.

All the way to Loku a good number of Lolos are to be seen along the road, but they are friendly and are either bringing faggots to the small towns and military camps, or are returning empty after delivering their burdens.

Just before reaching Loku, the road leads through the famous gorge where the Taiping robbers were blocked and forced to turn up the Mienning Valley, and so were trapped to their doom.

The road is cut out of the side of the rock and is just wide enough for two animals to pass. A block house is placed at a commanding point, great doors are mounted so that it is impossible to pass up or down when these are closed, and a very small force could defend the position.

From Loku the road runs down the left bank of the Anning River through a fertile valley inhabited by the Chinese.

HAWKING PARROTS FROM THE NINGYUENFU VALLEY TO CHENTU; PHOTOGRAPH TAKEN ON VASHINGLIN, 10,000 FEET ABOVE SEA-LEVEL.

The climate is ideal, but the unfortunate people always have the fear of being surprised some night by their Lolo neighbours.

Ningyuenfu is a snug little town built on the side of a beautiful lake, the outlet of which runs into the Anning River.

The city has quite a history, but no records are to be found in the archives of the Yamen there; they have all been sent to Yachow and Chentu for safe keeping. The present city wall is only eighty years old. The old city having been destroyed by an earthquake, a report has it that it stood where the present lake now is.

That there was a terrific shaking here is quite evident from the huge clyptomeria trees that are still being dug out of the mountain sides, where they have been buried for a 100 years at least. Some of these trees are three and four feet in diameter, and a coffin made from a good tree is worth from 300 to 500 taels (or from £40 to £60), which is a lot of money to a Chinaman, and of course only the wealthy families can afford it.

The country at the present time is very bleak, and only near the waterways or on an occasional hill small trees are to be found, and there is very little shrubbery about. Fuel is very expensive, as it has to be carried a long way.

On arriving at Ningyuenfu Messrs. Brooke and Meares had some difficulty in finding a respectable inn, but they met the Rev. Mr. Rudd, an American missionary, who invited them to the Mission Station. The Rev. Mr. and Mrs. Wellwood, who were then in charge of the station and of the work in the district, were away at the time visiting out-stations, but Mr. Rudd made it very pleasant for our travellers.

Some days were spent in exploring the lake and city and in trying to find out something about the Lolos before Mr. Brooke undertook his last—and fatal—journey.

CHAPTER XXI.

INDEPENDENT LOLOLAND.

STRANGE to say, almost in the heart of the great province of Sechwan lies a small section of country some 70 miles wide by 120 miles long, which is probably one of the few remaining tracks of country which still retains its independence and is still unexplored—even the latest intelligence maps mark it a blank.

Little is known about it except that a great mountain range runs through it from north to south, cutting it almost in two halves. The Chinese border towns on the west are Huili Chow, Ningyuenfu, Lichow, Loku, Mienshan, and Yueh Hsi; on the north Opien Ting; on the east Mapien Ting and Luipo; and on the south by the Yangtze River.

The Nosu—*i.e.*, black bloods—who are better known by the Chinese name Lolo, are a fierce warlike people who claim to have in their veins the blue—locally, black—blood, which their name indicates. Their forefathers came from Hunan and played no small part in the early history of the Chinese Empire. They have, however, been gradually surrounded and hemmed in by the Chinese, until nowadays we find them confined to the track of country above mentioned.

Although thus surrounded they prove a veritable thorn in the flesh to the Chinese who have to live near them, as well as to the Chinese Government, and they have been the means of disgracing more officials and showing up the weakness and rottenness of Chinese officialdom more than all the Censors in the kingdom.

The Chinese attempts to subdue the Lolos, especially during the last twenty years, have been a farce; there has been no organised plan, no united effort. True, officials have been appointed to the task; much money has been squandered, and many lives lost, but every attempt has been an utter failure, its only result to line pockets of officials in charge of the operations, to discourage the Chinese Militia, and to encourage the Lolos in their raiding and insubordination.

LOLO CHIEF'S HOSTAGES.

To explain all this I will give a rough idea of how these Chinese expeditions are conducted.

In the first place the Chinese Government sends in officials who know nothing about the Lolos or their country; after all these years of warfare they have not even a map. The orders are to subdue these disturbers of the peace. The official takes over his seal, collects the Militia, consisting of local farmers who have to supply their own weapons, which consist of antiquated muzzle-loading fuse guns, bamboo poles with iron heads which they call lances, and old swords covered with the rust of years. With these untrained men and useless weapons he marches against the Lolos, to beard the lion in his den.

The Lolos, who are as well or better armed, have the advantage of knowing their country. Their very existence depends on their defence of the small track of territory which they call their own, and in defence of it they are prepared to fight to the death. Their motto is, "The man who is afraid to die for his country is not fit to live." The Chinese motto is, "He who fights and runs away may live to fight another day"; and John prays to the gods that there may be a way of escape when the time comes for him to run.

Take, for example, the latest Chinese expedition against the Lolos. During last winter the Lolos had become more and more daring in their raids and capped their outrages by attacking a village, carrying off some 300 of the inhabitants, leaving only the very old and helpless ones, many of whom they slew in their homes.

The Chinese officials thought that something must be done, so they treated with the Lolos to try and ransom the prisoners; but they did not want to spend too much money, and, as the Lolos asked a large price for the young and strong captives, the officials only bought back some of the old ones, who were cheap, and left the others to their fate. This did not satisfy the friends of the captives. Representations were made to Chentu, and the officials were recalled and new ones sent to take their place. They arrived at Ningyuenfu in July, 1908, and by the Ninth Moon had made preparations to chastise the unruly brigands.

This time, the General, a very fair officer as they go in China, asked for foreign drilled soldiers and modern rifles;

so they sent him 400 foreign drilled soldiers. Modern rifles are valuable and cannot be risked in warfare, so he was compelled to make up the balance of his force with 3,000 farmer Militia.

The force collected at Ningyuenfu, but before going to the front they had to christen the flag. The day for this great event was fixed, and an unfortunate hostage from the district in which the war was to be waged, was led down to the parade ground, where hundreds of spectators and the army of 3,400 men were assembled.

The victim was tied down to a bench and a bucket being placed to catch the blood, his throat was then cut from ear to ear in the same way as men kill a sheep.

The flags were then dipped in the blood, and the heart and liver were taken home and cooked and eaten by some of the soldiers to give them courage.

When their courage had been thoroughly aroused the whole army marched out bravely to Tasin Chang, about ten miles from Ningyuenfu. They presented a brave and formidable appearance, as there were no Lolos in sight.

The Taotai and Colonel thought that Tasin Chang would be a good place to make their headquarters, as there is a good inn and 200 Chinese families, and they could buy vegetables and meat there, and make themselves fairly comfortable. The soldiers were sent to the front and after some weeks of hard marching had advanced twenty miles.

They were 3,400 strong, and had a Gatling gun besides, so they felt very brave as they had as yet seen none of the enemy, and had been marching on a good road.

They had now been some time in the interior, and had no heads to send out to their superiors to prove their great achievements, battles fought and victories won; so to fill up this blank they caught some of the slaves of a friendly tribe, cut off their heads and sent these, with the report that

WHITE-BLOOD LOLOS.

they had won a victory over their enemy, whose country, in fact, was some twenty-five miles further on.

This was too much for the friendly tribes near Kohchoh-ling, so a few days later, under cover of a thick fog, fifteen of the Lolo warriors charged into the middle of the Chinese camp, war-whooping and cutting right and left with their short swords; they killed some eighty of the Chinese braves and the fifteen escaped unhurt into the thick fog.

The Chinese were so surprised that they forgot to fire their guns or use their bayonets or even their spears, their excuse being that they were afraid to hurt one another.

A short distance away 1,000 Lolos attacked another part of the camp but were not successful. Their plan was to surround the Chinese camp and to kill off all the soldiers, but they were met on a pass by part of the Chinese Army, and about eighty fell on both sides.

However, the Chinese had had enough, struck camp, and fled toward Tasin Chang, the news of the Emperor's death arriving about the same time, so they were able to save their face. But the Viceroy, who had his spies in the country, got the true story and all the officials who had anything to do with the affair were at once recalled; and the brave little pedlar, who drove a brisk trade with the soldiers, now sits in the Prefect's chair, though it remains to be seen if he will be able to manage things any better than his predecessors. Strange to say the Lolos claim a victory, and are now daring and energetic in their raids on the poor farmers.

It was just a few weeks after the Chinese troops returned from their attack on the Lolos that Brooke entered the country.

He took with him his Chinese-English interpreter, also his Tibetan interpreter, three coolies with light loads, and the Futou or foreman.

Their first intention was to go to the border of the Lolo

country and get acquainted with some friendly chief, if possible, and find out something of the country and its people.

He knew if the Chinese officials suspected his plan they would surely stop him, so he quietly slipped out of the North Gate of the city, and by going up a quiet path got clear away, without anyone knowing even which way he had gone.

Mr. Meares was left at Ningyuenfu to develop photographs and make ready for their journey toward Batang when the party returned. They had learned that there were friendly Lolos to the north, and Brooke started out, hoping to find one of them, and telling his companion that he might be only two days away or he might be two weeks. Day after day Meares waited in vain for the party to return or some word to arrive of their whereabouts. When I reached Ningyuenfu some three weeks later I found him in a most agitated state of mind. He and Mr. Rudd met me on the road as I approached the city and told me the position. I feared the worst, but thought it was possible that Brooke might have got safely through the secluded stretch of country, and had had to return by one of the roundabout ways. That would take at least five weeks for the round trip, and there was no way of getting a letter or messenger across. To inform the Chinese would probably get the party into trouble even if they were quite safe, for the guards have been known to make it very difficult for any one trying to break through their lines and enter this country. Mr. Wellwood was expected home any day, and as he was personally acquainted with the officials, and also with some of the border Lolos, we all thought it was best to wait for him.

I was also anxious to see Wellwood, so delayed my journey westward a few days.

While I waited, I got in touch with some of the friendly Lolos, and tried to find out if they knew anything of the whereabouts of the party. They professed their ignorance, but agreed to send out men to inquire and report to us on their return; but though they learnt what had happened they refused to inform us, being afraid.

By the time Wellwood returned we had given up hope, and he and Meares went at once to the Chinese official and reported Mr. Brooke's delay.

The Prefect, who was expecting to be relieved any day, for he had already been dismissed for the failure which he

TWO LOLO CHIEFS, HOSTAGES AT YUEHHSI TING.

and the Taotai had made in subduing the Lolos in the previous autumn, was quite indignant at the party attempting the journey without first reporting to him. He said if he had known he would not have allowed them to go in; but, of course, they had known this, and that was why they had not reported. Mr. Meares, through Mr. Wellwood, engaged native spies and sent them into the country, and they brought out the first report of what had really befallen the party.

This account differed in some details from the reports we got later from the two survivors (after they were ransomed by the Chinese military official Mr. Yang of Tsoying also called Sanchiangkou, a military post on the Mupien side), but was true enough to the facts.

After Mr. Wellwood returned I remained three days, and then, deciding that there was nothing I could do there, started out for Mienninghsien ; but on reaching Loku, feeling I should go up to the Lolo border and see if I could get any word of the missing party, I turned east instead of going north, landed at Kan Shang ying, and there made friends with the Chinese military official, getting later in touch with one of the most influential black chiefs, who agreed to go security for my safe journey to Chaochoh, the Lolo capital or centre. I had very little difficulty in making this arrangement. The chief said they had heard no word of Mr. Brooke and his party, but assured me they would be all right, as most of the people were friendly to foreigners.

All the arrangements for my journey to Chaochoh and out viâ Ningyuenfu being completed, the chief and his party left me.

The guide was to come next morning at daylight to lead the way to the next chief, but next morning I waited till 9 a.m. and neither my guide nor the chief appeared. As I did not want to let the Chinese officials know my intentions I kept quiet. About 9.30 the old chief came into my room, and squatting on the floor, said after a little ado that he could not be security for me, and asked me to give up the idea for the present. Some of the tribes *en route*, he added, were at war and it was impossible to cross the country. I could not understand the cause of his sudden change of attitude but felt that all was not right.

After trying in every way to assure him that I was not afraid, and that we could get round the tribes who were

LOOKING OVER THE WALL OF NINGYUENFU; SHOWING ROUTE FOLLOWED BY MR. BROOKE.

fighting, but finding this no use, and the old chief quite firm; I had to give up the idea of advancing—at least from this point—and returned toward Lòku.

We had not gone more than four miles when my Lolo interpreter told me the cause of the chief's changing his mind. He said two men had come from the interior, arriving at Kanshangying just after the chief left me the evening before, and had brought word that Mr. Brooke and party had been cut to pieces by the A-heo tribe, and that the people in the interior were quite excited over it. This was just like a Chinese, and I suppose a Lolo as well, to keep back the facts until the opportunity of finding out more had passed.

I had not to wait long until the report was confirmed from another source, and a little further down the valley I met a runner with a letter saying that the scouts they had sent out had returned with the report that Mr. Brooke and party had been cut to pieces. Mr. Meares begged me to return to Ningyuenfu to try and help him, as Wellwood had to go out to Chiatingfu to their conference. I returned at once and found that other messengers had come in with reports, which did not offer any hope for the isolated party.

About the same time a telegram arrived from Chentu from the Consul and my wife asking me not to continue my journey westward as there was serious fighting in the neighbourhood of Batang.

I remained at Ningyuenfu two weeks, doing what I could to help to rescue the party or any survivors that might be held as slaves; but we could get but little satisfaction as the official would not exert himself. During this time I got acquainted with a number of Musu and Lisu people and some even from Mili, half-way to Batang; all of them offered to guide us as far as Mili.

After what had just happened, and the message that had come from Chentu, it seemed best to return and postpone my westward journey; so with a sad heart I turned my face toward Chentu, while Mr. Meares remained at Ningyuenfu to await further developments, and see if the Chinese would be able to get the bodies and bring the guilty persons to justice.

I here give a translation of the report given by the two survivors of the party who went in with Mr. Brooke—one who was the Futou or foreman, and the other one of the carriers—the rest were all put to death.

For the sake of the friendly Lolos I refrain from giving the names of the friendly chiefs, but this free translation of the report given by the survivors may be of interest.

After leaving Ningyuenfu the party travelled in a north-easterly course, passing through the territory of several friendly chiefs before reaching Chao-choh.

From one of these chiefs Brooke secured an interpreter who had travelled throughout the country.

Near Chao-choh they found a friendly chief who killed a sheep in honour of the visitor from the West and insisted on making Brooke his blood brother.

This chief invited them to travel through the country, and sent his own son to introduce them to the next chief. Thus they were passed on from one tribe to another and were well received.

They travelled five days in a north-easterly course, during which time they walked 300 li (or about 75 miles) and reached the top of the Liangshan Range at the Tafung ting Pass. As the snow was very deep and the descent steep on the east side of the pass Brooke decided that they would not descend it but return from this place.

From the top of the pass they could see the country about Mapien and even Omei shan in the distance, but by the shortest route they were still 180 li (or 45 miles) from Mapien. On this pass Mr. Brooke spent some time, mapping the

TOWN OF YUEH-ITSE-TING; THE HILLS ACROSS THE RIVER ON THE LEFT OF THE PICTURE ARE IN THE LOLO COUNTRY.

country to the east, as well as filling in the great stretch that opened out to the west and south of them.

The snow was very deep and the weather extremely cold, so during the night the Lolo guide ran away, and in the morning they found themselves without a representative man to introduce them to the next chief.

However, they continued their journey by a road that runs further north, hoping to come out at Kanshangying, the place where I attempted to enter the country. The descent was quite gradual and 2,000 feet below the peak, which they descended in a distance of five miles, and came to the first Lolo chief's hut.

On arrival they found the chief and all the representative men away, but the chief's wife was at home. In Lololand the women have almost as much authority as the men. The chief's wife asked them to wait until the chief returned, but this Brooke refused to do, saying that he must hurry, and if she could not give an escort he must go on without it; and so they continued their journey. They had not gone far when the chief's wife overtook them on horseback, offering to conduct them through her domains herself on condition that the fee was paid in advance; for they always make a charge for allowing anyone, even a Chinese pedlar, to pass through. Brooke agreed to pay the fee, which was only a small one, on arrival at the next chief's house, saying that the last man was paid in advance and had run away. To this she would not agree, demanding the amount in advance; and when it was not paid she rode off and left the party to find their own way.

Brooke and his party continued their journey without escort, and after crossing a small spur arrived at a village, where they slept in the house of the next chief.

He was quite friendly and agreed to pass them on to his next neighbour. Brooke paid 1 tael (about 3*s.*) in advance.

The chief escorted them some distance himself, when Brooke urged him to return saying that if he sent a representative man that would be quite sufficient, so the chief sent two of his slaves with them.

That night they slept in a house of one of the tribe, and while they were eating their supper a suit of fur clothing and some small articles were stolen. The people who gathered about were a bit rowdy, and in a half friendly way tried to frighten the interpreter Ho, by pretending to make him a prisoner (as in the photograph). They were also determined to see and handle the Mauser rifle, to which Brooke objected; so, putting the rifle in the sleeping bag, himself kept charge of it. They were not molested during the night, but the people did not seem very friendly.

Next morning when leaving Brooke refused to make any present unless the fur coat and other things were returned. They continued with the two slaves from the last chief as guides.

All went well until about noon, when an arrow was fired at one of the advance coolies from a thicket through which they were passing. He dropped his load and ran back. The interpreter and two slave guides held a consultation with the men who were in ambush. They came out into the road and proved to be a gang of about thirty men who had followed them from the village where they had spent the night. They stated that they were looking for some stray cattle and marched on ahead until they came to a place where the path ran through a deep gorge, where they mounted the cliff and waited for Brooke's party to come up.

Their movements were detected and the party halted while the two interpreters and the slave escort went forward and consulted with them.

A-heo then stated his business, saying that he was the chief of this district and they had no right there without his consent. The chief was invited to come down from the cliff and talk the matter over. A-heo-labow and six of his followers came down, and Brooke explained to him that he thought the escort he had was in order, and that he did

LOLO GIRLS, AGED ABOUT EIGHTEEN.

not know that he was breaking any of their rules or customs; adding that if the chief had authority to escort him through the country to the next State he would be glad to arrange with the chief for this.

The A-heo chief said that the slaves who had escorted them from the last chief had no right to pass through his territory, and that they should have been changed where they spent the night.

He at first demanded 10 taels to escort them to the next chief, but as Brooke knew it was not more than ten miles from where they were he refused to give so much, and they finally agreed to take 5 taels (or about 9*s.*), but demanded it in advance.

The attitude of A-heo and his followers did not inspire the party with confidence, and the interpreter said that they intended to rob them from the first.

Brooke tried to show him that it was impossible for his party to run away with all his coolies and things, and that he would surely pay him what he had agreed to on reaching the next chief, who had been friendly on their way up.

They seemed to have some little talk over the matter of paying in advance, and Brooke in a friendly way put his hand on the chief's shoulder and put the other hand on his own pocket, trying to show by signs that he would surely pay him the money himself on arrival at the house of the next chief. Whether A-heo-labow understood Brooke's meaning or whether he took it as an insult it is hard to say, but I think he resented Brooke's freedom, as no one is supposed to lay their hands on a chief or on his clothes. Instantly drawing his sword, he struck a blow at Brooke's head, which he caught on his left arm, receiving a bad cut, and, aroused by this treacherous assault, he drew his revolver and shot the chief. Seeing what he had done, he fired two or three more shots in the air and the chief's supporters all slipped off into the undergrowth and disappeared. Brooke called to his followers to drop their loads and follow him, knowing that in a very short time they would be surrounded and taken, and their only hope was to try and reach the next chief. They ran down through the gorge and reached a stream, and by the time they had run ten miles and arrived at Suga's house they were quite exhausted. Some of the coolies fell behind and were overtaken in the way by the pursuing Lolos.

When Brooke and his interpreter reached Suga's house they reported what had taken place and offered the chief 600 taels if he would get them out safely to Chinese territory. This he promised to do if they would give up the rifle. Believing the chief to be friendly Brooke gave him his rifle with the promise of being safely escorted to Yueh Hsiting, but no sooner had he done so than their pursuers were upon them and they were surrounded. Brooke tried to get on the top of the house, but was knocked down by a stone. Suga, who was a brother-in-law of the chief A-heo-labow, who had been shot, let his men help the A-heo people, according to their law he was bound to—and the whole party were soon cut to pieces.

But Brooke kept his men together to the last and died bravely trying to defend them; but it was more than 100 to 1, and the struggle was short.

The two men who escaped the sad fate of the rest of the party were stunned by a stone by which they were hit in the early part of the fray. After some time, reviving, they managed to creep away and hide in caves, neither of them knowing but that they were the sole survivors. They were found next day by a slave and secretly sold to a neighbouring tribe. How they were tied to one of the other slaves and were made to work all day, only given a very small portion of corn meal cake or some boiled potatoes when they returned at night, and were put in a pit in the centre of a house while the rest of the slaves slept on the boards lest they should escape—is a story which would really be amusing if it were not linked to that other and tragic story of Mr. Brooke and his party's end.

My Chinese boy who went as interpreter to Mr. Brooke stood by him to the last, and he met the same fate as his master and the others.

This report was told me by both men before they had met each other after their release. The foreman was escorted to Chentu and made his report to me before the officials saw him.

The other man reported to me at Mapien, and both stories agreed except in a few minor details which were not important. Both of them had deep scars, and one had deep cuts in his head which eighty days after the attack were not healed.

Thus ended the life of a daring explorer and born traveller.

CHAPTER XXII.

RELIGION AND CUSTOMS OF THE LOLOS.

THIS is a most difficult topic to write about, since there are many branches of these people under the general name of Miao, into which the Chinese group all the tribes of Kweichow, Yunnan and Sechuan.

Many of these tribes have their own local customs and religion, and one has to be careful to state clearly which tribe is referred to. A good deal of general information about some of these tribes can be gleaned from Chinese history, but it is difficult to be always quite sure just whom any of its compilers is referring to. However, I propose to give a few extracts from an abridged history and then to add a few paragraphs on what I know of the particular people under review. But it will be impossible in one chapter to go into much detail, and already my story has grown far beyond the original plan of this book. I trust my readers will not have grown weary of this simple narrative of adventure and travel among this ancient and secluded people.

I venture, therefore, to insert these short extracts from a Chinese history which, so far as I know, has never before been translated.

There are many tribes in the mountains and valleys of Sechuan, as recorded by many historians. After having read their accounts and comparing them with what I know and have heard of the Miao tribes, I here record what I have learned of those in Sechuan though brief yet complete. "The Miao religion dates from Panhu about 2500 B.C. Panhu killed off all the aborigines for which the Emperor Tikuh honoured him by giving him his daughter and a kingdom. He had six sons and six daughters, who became the fathers of all the Miao.

"They occupied the country of Yalang and lying between Suifu and Ningyuenfu to the border of Kweichow and Yunnan.

"These tribes are divided into the White Miao, Flower Miao, Black Miao, Red Miao, Green Miao, and each tribe has its own colour of dress. They are scattered about in villages and hamlets, and any trifling cause will start a vendetta, as the proverb says, 'They will continue their animosity for nine generations.'

"Those who live near the border governed by China are called Su Miao (ripe or manageable), while in the interior they are called Sung Miao (raw or unmanageable). The people near the Chinese border work hard like the cow or ox, yet they are very poor. The men put their hair up in a horn, and the women wear clam shells, and a hair pin about ten inches long in their hair, and in their ears long earrings. They wear a seamless cloak, having a hole for the head to pass through.

"The first day of the tenth moon is their feast day. On the first day of the new year they worship Panhu and offer fish to him in a trough or altar, and crying out in a loud wailing voice.

"When visiting an official, whether of high or low degree, he is addressed as the old Emperor.

"The Chinese are always referred to as the Han, because it was in the Han dynasty, between 201 B.C. and 23 A.D., that they were conquered and made subjects.

"The Song Miao and the Tsai Miao are the descendants of the kings of Song and Tsai, who ruled in Honan and Hunan from 1122 to 770 B.C., when their two kingdoms were con-

A LOLO MUSICIAN.

quered by Chi and Tsu a remnant of the people escaped westward and became the Sung and the Tsai Miao.

"These people are very honest and cultivate the land. The Sung tribe are the more intelligent.

"They still wear their hair in a horn on top of their heads as of old, but have changed the fashion of their garments and have adopted that of the other Miao tribes.

"When the Tsai dynasty conquered the Chow, many of the princes of Chow were sent west as outlaws and prisoners, and these became the Tien tribe, who still retain many of the Chow customs, such as the worship of their ancestors, which is performed by a procession, led by the heads of the families or chiefs and all join in a song of praise to the departed.

"The Ya Miao live in Peisha (north gorge), they despise the old and honour the young. When a man or woman is old they drive them out for sale, and even a son will sell his own father or mother.

"This tribe lives in caves, which they have hewn out of the rocks in precipitous places, some of which are as much as eighty feet up the cliff side, and to which ascent and descent are made by means of bamboo ladders or ropes, which the men and women can climb like monkeys."

Much more of this ancient history could be quoted, but it might not be of interest to the general reader, and I think enough has been given to show that there are a great many different tribes, each having somewhat distinct customs. It will be noted that the caves found in Western China were not hewn out by the Chinese, but by those tribes; not for tombs, as some suppose, but for dwellings and strongholds. While the terra-cotta figures found in some of these caves show that a different style of dress was worn by the people which made and placed these figures there more than 2,000 years ago, yet it is not proved that the caves were not cut out and once inhabited by the emigrants from Honan and Hunan, after they fled westward from Central China.

History states that many of these emigrants were princes, who were banished or had fled for their lives rather than submit to their conquerors. Their descendants claim to have royal blood in their veins and are as proud to-day as their princely forerunners may have been in the year 700 B.C.

The characters used by them prove that they were once connected with the Chinese nation. I know one man in Chentu, a student of the ancient character, who was able to recognise many of the signs used by the Lolos, but many of them were unknown to him.

We must now look at the people found in that piece of country marked on the map "Independent Lololand."

First their name :—These people are generally called Lolos by the Chinese, which is much resented by them, and even the name of Iren, *i.e.*, barbarian, is preferred. Some Chinese claim that the name Lolo arose from the custom of writing the name of their departed on a piece of paper and placing it in a basket which is hung in a certain position on the wall. This is why the Black Bloods look upon the name as an insult to their ancestors. Whatever the cause may be, serious objection is raised to the name and they call themselves Nosu, which the Chinese translate black bone, but literally it means black person, or as the Nosu interpret it "royalty." It is used in much the same sense as the term "Blue blood" is applied to aristocracy in England.

There is very little known of their religion, except that some of them worship the sun, and others oak trees and groves. When a Lolo dies his greatest ambition is to be sent to the next world in a chariot of fire. As soon as he is dead his friends gather round his remains and build a great bonfire and place his body on it. When the body has been cremated the ashes are put in a jar and buried, and his name is written on a piece of paper and put in the family basket. This basket occupies a similar position in their religion to the ancestral tablet among the Chinese.

It is this desire to be despatched in a fiery chariot that keeps the Lolo from ever going very far from home, unless travelling in fairly large parties. When a Black Bone is killed in war, either by the Chinese or in tribal feuds, a great price is sometimes paid to secure their dead bodies, in order that their friends may join in the ceremony of lighting them into the next world. That is why their dead are always carried off the field while the battle is still raging, that their bodies may be despatched with great honour and may not fall into the hands of their enemies. It is a rare thing to find a dead Lolo on the field, even immediately after the battle. It is the greatest honour for a serf to rescue the body of a chief or comrade from the enemies' camp.

If they are away from home and anyone should be taken seriously ill, or is wounded so that he has to be left behind, his companions will prepare for him a pile of wood on which they place the body, so that the sick or wounded man may light his own fire when he finds he cannot get better or is about to be overtaken by his pursuers.

The magicians, or witch doctors, of the Lolos, have great influence and are practically the only persons who can read. Their writing is very little used except for purposes of incantation. I believe they have some landmarks of their history preserved, and when some one has mastered their hieroglyphics and translated their writings we may find it clearly stated who these people are. But so far as I have been able to glean, up to the present time, I am persuaded that the Lolo Nosu are the original inhabitants of Assam, who were driven northward at the time of the Bengal invasion. They found their way into Central China and there for some time played a leading part in Chinese early history, having much to do with the introduction of Chinese writing. In some Chinese histories credit is given to the chief of one of these tribes for introducing writing into China. In the time of the Chow's, rather than submit to their conquerors, they emigrated to other regions.

So we find a remnant in West China. I have reason to suppose that the Corean is of the same stock; he has the same type of face, his ancient style of writing is similar to, if not identical with, the Lolos. Others of them found their way over to Japan, and we find terra-cotta models in the ancient caves of that country similar to those recently found in West China. All this is still short of absolute proof, of course; but from clues that I have been able to obtain I think I am on the right track.

They are certainly not Tibetan, as some people have been led to think, having nothing in common with the Tibetans, and being their sworn enemies.

I was told by a commander in the Siamese Army, whose father is a member of the King's Cabinet, that the original inhabitants of Assam emigrated northward into China many thousands of years ago, and that there is not even a remnant of that people left there. When I showed him the photographs of the terra-cotta figures found in the caves of West China, he declared that they corresponded to the relics of the early inhabitants of his country, who, when conquered by Bangal, emigrated northward rather than submit to their victors. This is exactly what they did when overcome by the Chows. This officer was an educated man, who seemed to be well up in ancient history, and it was impossible for me to follow him in the recital of his dates, which he quoted as far back as 4000 B.C.

Since coming to England I have been fortunate enough to meet an educated Corean, and this gentleman claims that the Lolo writings and customs are very similar to the ancient

Corean ones; and he was prompt to claim a relationship. I only throw these hints out for what they are worth, not being able to prove them one way or the other; but for the student of anthropology, ethnology and archæology, here is a most interesting field for his operations, and I only wish I had the necessary knowledge of the languages and the leisure to delve into the subject. Perhaps, if he should cast an eye on these pages, Mr. Andrew Lang may have something to give us from the store of his mythological knowledge.

The Lolos are very superstitious, and one needs to be well acquainted with their customs and beliefs in order to deal with them without giving offence, for once that is done three generations will not erase the grievance, which will be handed down to posterity until revenged.

If a chief or one of his family is killed, his tribe are under obligation to take the life of some one of equal rank in their enemies' camp before the wrong is appeased.

The pure Black Bloods are tall, nimble fellows; some of them are over six feet in height and scarcely any of them below five feet ten inches. The way they scale cliffs and descend mountains is a mystery to the Chinese, and some celestials credit them with the power of being able to fly.

Their chiefs wear long black cloaks made of one piece of very good quality of felt. I bought one of these cloaks from a Lolo chief; it measured twenty-four feet around the bottom when spread out; a draw string put through one end of this sheet of felt is gathered in until it ties neatly about the neck, and hanging loosely over their shoulders comes down to about the knee. He wears very roomy trousers made of Chinese white cotton, which are tucked into long white felt socks. The leg is neatly wrapped from the ankle up by a narrow black woollen bandage very neatly put on, and is similar to the putties worn by our troops.

Over the felt socks he wears sandals made of bamboo fibre,

which has a string of the same material coming over the side of the foot and toes, fastening around the ankle with a draw string.

His hair is done up in a horn on the top of his head, around which he sometimes wraps a white piece of cotton.

The Black Bone can easily be distinguished from the White Bones or serfs, who are mostly Chinese or Tibetan who have been captured by their knights and carried into slavery. Strange to say, they soon become loyal to their chiefs.

The serfs wear white, grey or brown cloaks, short trousers; and go barefooted.

A few of the more fortunate ones have white putties and sandals in the winter season.

The Black Bones are the lords and never do any work. They are fond of hunting and wandering about the mountains. They are almost without exception remarkably straight built, with slim muscular limbs, whilst some of them are robust, yet anything approaching the build of a chubby Chinaman is unknown in their ranks. Most of them have broad, deep chests as become mountaineers.

Their large oval eyes, set in an oval face, with fairly prominent cheek bones, arched but rather broad nose, pointed chin and thin, firm lips, from which the scanty beard has been plucked, set them apart as being a quite distinct race of people from any other in China. Their teeth are white and regular, which may be accounted for by the food they live on, which is largely maize bread; and it is said that they never eat roast meat, but partake of it either raw, dried or boiled. One marked feature is a tendency to wrinkles, especially in their forehead, of men past forty years of age. Their foreheads are low but broad and upright.

The Lolo gathers his felt mantle tightly around him and cares not for wind, rain or hail; he is at home wherever night overtakes him, for, tucking his mantle closely about him, he squats in a sitting position on his heels, with his back up against a rock or a bank, and gathering his cloak over his head, sleeps there, impervious to wind and rain. I have seen them, even when lodging in a Chinese inn at Haitang, spend the night in this way, even though there was a Chinese bed there if they wished to use it. In their own homes they sometimes lie down to sleep.

The Lolos are great horsemen and breed fine ponies, which when well trained are sold to the Chinese. The stirrups are so short that when riding the knees are at right angles to their bodies, yet they pace their little ponies along the sides of the cliffs on narrow rough roads at high speed, as readily as they do on the plains.

Once a year, usually in the tenth month, a great fair is held, when the clans gather from all quarters and race their ponies. This is a time of general merriment, much wine is drunk, and many of them spend the night on the race course.

The Lolo women are also tall and graceful, wear flat hats rather like tam-o'-shanters, and some of them have hats made of calico or cotton stretched on a bamboo hoop, which look almost like quaker bonnets; while round the neck a tall collar, ornamented with silver, and embroidered short jacket over a long accordion-pleated skirt, complete the costume.

The Black Bloods never marry out of their own rank, and never marry with a Chinese of any rank.

When all the arrangements concerning a marriage have been completed and the day for the wedding is fixed, the bride is escorted by her parents and some of her friends to a favourable camping ground near the bridegroom's home. The day is spent in feasting and merriment, and at night the bridegroom comes to the tent of his bride and steals her away to his own home.

The women are much honoured and a daughter is much more welcome in a home than a son; for when the daughter gets married her husband must send horses, sheep or cattle as presents to the girl's parents; when a son gets married he must send presents to his father-in-law's home.

Women have almost as much to say in political affairs as the men, and in stopping a quarrel they have much more influence.

Should there be a quarrel between two parties in a clan and one of the girls wish to stop it, she takes off her skirt and, walking backwards, trails it after her on the ground between the two parties, and if they have any honour or chivalry in them, not another blow will be struck, at least on this occasion. It has been stated by the Rev. S. Pollard that there are 20,000 of non-Chinese people in West China exclusive of Mohammedans.

It is estimated that there are 17,000,000 of non-Chinese, exclusive of Mohammedans, in all China.

These are grouped into four great families, viz., the Shan, Miao, Nosu and Tibetan tribes.

There are 5,000,000 to be found in Kweicheo province, which has a total population of 8,000,000; 7,000,000 are found in the province of Yunnan, which has a total population of 12,000,000; and over 5,000,000 are to be found in Sechuan, which has a total population of 65,000,000.

It is only within the last few years that any attempt has been made by a foreigner to come in contact with these people, and still only a very small part of this great host has come under the influence of the Missionary. The China Inland Mission have two or three men in Kweicheo who are giving their attention to the Shan and Miao tribes of that province. In Yunnan the United Methodist Mission and also the China Inland Mission have had two or three men at work among these tribes for some years, and already part of the New Testament has been translated into their language, and thousands have been won for Christ.

The change that has been brought about is really wonderful. Scores of witch doctors have given up their lucrative occupation of sorcery. The drunken Miao has discarded his wine cup: the maidens have torn down their huts of ill-fame, which they once built by the roadside, and where they, without any sense of shame or disgrace, spent their nights in merriment and debauchery.

In one place the Miaos gave 2,000 days of gratis labour to build a church in which to worship the true God, and there, on Sundays, as many as 800 will partake of the Lord's Supper at one time. Thirty thousand Hosannahs are going up daily in this one section of the country, from a people who have been despised by the Chinese for generations, until they had fallen so low in the scale of civilisation that they were but little above the brute beast.

Yet, when the love of God reached them, it lifted them from the deep pit into which they had fallen and put a new song in their lips, and set them singing such notes of joy that the hillsides resound with echoes of praise, which we trust will go on till they reverberate through every valley and hill and this despised people shall be won for God.

CHAPTER XXIII.

Rescue of the Survivors and Burial of the Murdered Explorer and His Interpreter.

When definite news was received of the fate of the party, a number of Lolo spies were engaged to enter the country and try and recover the bodies and as many of the things as could be found; also to try and redeem the two alleged survivors.

These men brought back different versions of what had taken place, and it was difficult to sift out the true from the false. It was decided that nothing should be made public until the two men who had been present were rescued, and their report made.

The spies secured a few small personal effects, a note-book and part of a letter written to Mr. Meares; but the things had been so much scattered, and most of them were destroyed, so that it was difficult to get back much.

A friendly Lolo chief agreed to bring the bodies out for a nominal sum, but there was so much quarrelling over who was to get the money that he did not succeed in getting them.

In the meantime the Viceroy sent word to the officials along the border that the bodies must be recovered, and so the local officials sent in agents, who bid against each other, until the Lolos began to say, "If a dead foreigner is worth so much, what would a live one be worth?" Finally, a man sent out by a colonel on the Mapien side got possession of the two surviving men, having brought them out for 400 taels (or about £50) ; he also paid 800 taels for Mr. Brooke's body and 600 taels for Ho's.

The Futou was sent up to Chentu under escort and came straight to me. I got his report and took it down before he was questioned by the Chentu officials, and sent a report to Mr. Meares, who was still at Ningyuenfu.

The Viceroy asked the British Consul to go to Mapien to identify the body, but he was very ill and could not. A day later he had to leave Chentu for home. And since I knew Mr. Brooke perhaps better than anyone at Chentu, the Consul begged me to go up and see what could be done.

I had not long returned from Ningyuenfu, but as it was an urgent case I did not hesitate. My wife was again left in charge of our depôt and I packed two loads of books and started out, accepting only two Fusongs out of the ten sent by the officials, thus travelling in my usual way. We went overland as far as Chiatingfu and there got boat to Chienwei, a city 120 li (or 30 miles) further down the river. From Chienwei I went by the main road, but one which is very seldom traversed by foreigners and never by myself before. There was no hurry, so we took four days to do the three stages, spending some time at the towns by the way, and by the time I reached Mapien I had disposed of most of the books I had brought with me.

On arriving at Mapien I was no longer able to escape the Chinese escort, for the Viceroy had sent word to the officials there that I was to be treated with all due respect, as I had been sent by the Consul. This was news for me, for while I had consented to go at the Consul's request, I had no idea that the Chinese were going to look on me as a deputy.

Protests were of no avail. The best in the place was put at my disposal, and a guard of red-coated braves with rifles were appointed to escort me about on the streets. To this I objected, not allowing them to go with me except when I called on the Prefect and other officials, which I had to do, as they all came to my inn a short time after I arrived with a full retinue. Mr. Yang sent down an escort of eighteen men to escort me up to Sanchiang Kou. This is the most western outpost of Mapien, and only twelve miles from where Mr. Brooke and party turned back. To this military station the prisoners and the bodies of Mr. Brooke and his interpreter were brought by the Lolos, but they would not deliver them up until the money had been paid over.

Though it was eighty days from the time the murders had been committed until the time I examined the bodies, yet they had not decayed, for they had been frozen all the time; for at Sanchiang Kou fires were needed and furs were worn all the year round.

It was indeed a sad and trying ordeal for me to look on the remains of my friend, who had left our home in October full of life and vigour, thus mutilated and laid in a Chinese coffin; but I had no difficulty in identifying his body.

The corpse of my adopted Chinese boy lay in another coffin alongside. It was impossible to keep the tears of sorrow and regret from rolling down my cheeks.

I have been in some trying places during my sixteen years in China, but none that told on me more than this.

The thought of all my narrow escapes flashed on me, yet God had spared me and taken one who had only been in the country for such a comparatively short time.

It is all too sad to write about, and yet I feel that it is only right that my readers should know what it all meant to me and to others, who have to take their lives in their hands and go forth into the dark corners of the earth.

I saw the coffins nailed and sealed, and then left them to be sent on to Chentu by the Chinese official, and took a short cut across the Lolo country, coming out on the Tung at its highest point of navigation; from there I took boat and came down to Chiating, and travelled the main road home without any incident of note. The country travelled through was most interesting and quite new, but this is not the time or place to describe it. I may just say that the Lolos were making nightly raids on the Chinese along their border, and one night I stopped at a place where they came next door to where I was sleeping, sacked the house and carried off two persons.

About 2 o'clock in the morning I was awakened by a terrible row and the call of "Murder! murder!" I was sure it was in the same building in which we were lodging, for there was only a thin mud partition between them and us.

Bounding out of bed I barred the back door with some old benches. The whole place was in a turmoil. The soldiers who were encamped across the road were called out; but before they got to the house, the Lolos had done their work, and had taken some silver and carried off two young people, leaving the father and mother, who were about fifty years of age, wounded in the home, and had made their escape. The soldiers fired a few shots after them in the darkness but did not hit any of the Lolos.

This is a nightly scene at some points along the border, and the traveller who enters Lololand must be prepared for the consequences; the only safe way is to stick to one's security and never move, unless the Chief or some of his relatives personally escort one.

On returning to Chentu I found that Mr. Meares had arrived three days before me, coming direct from Ningyuenfu, where he had remained after I left, hoping to do something for the recovery of the survivors and, if possible, to get the body of his companion. This was a most trying time for him, and if it had not been for what was going on in the surrounding country the time would have passed even more slowly than it did.

The Lolos were asserting themselves everywhere. Reports kept coming in from many places along the borders of nightly raids being made on the isolated settlers.

When I was coming home, at one place near Lichow, a city only twelve miles north of Ningyuenfu, the Lolos had come down the night before and destroyed a whole village, carrying off over thirty captives. Next morning a detachment of the local Militia were sent up to the scene. They were ambuscaded and surrounded, and only seven wounded men returned to tell what had happened to the party, most of their rifles being captured by the Lolos. This aroused the Chinese General, a man of about seventy years of age, who, because of his experience in days gone by, had been sent to relieve the retiring General since the latter had made such failure of things the previous autumn. As a matter of fact the retiring General was a very capable man, but could not do much, his hands being tied by his superiors. For the Taotai and Futai, who are both civil officers and really the masters of the situation, if there is any credit to be obtained for any achievement, they claim it; but, if any blame them for any failure, they try to put it on to the military officer; so that to be a General in this part of the world, at least, is not the most desirable position.

The new General mounting his sedan chair—for he was too old and feeble to ride a horse—called out his men; and with fluttering banners and long spears adorned with tassels of yak hair (dyed red) dangling from their spear sockets, all straggled off in a long procession 500 strong. On reaching Lichow they camped for the night, and next morning set out for the ruined village to find the Lolos who had done the damage some three days earlier. Of course there was no one to be seen, so the old General led his men up to some isolated Lolo huts not far distant and set fire to them. But when they were returning from this achievement a band of Lolos pounced upon them, no one could tell how or from where they came; the Chinese soldiers were just passing through a gorge and got badly cut up, and the General just escaped being captured in his chair.

He returned to Ningyuenfu and called out all the soldiers and Militia, leaving Ningyuenfu unguarded, and led his men back to Lichow and in by the same route to attack some Lolo village where he had been surprised a few days previously. The Lolos got word of his plans and retired, taking everything with them, so that the Chinese found nothing but a few empty huts to burn, which would not take the Lolos more than a few days to restore. Their houses, near the Chinese border especially, are no more than a few poles set on end and covered over with wild grass. In some places they have fairly comfortable shanties, but they make no elaborate attempt at building. In this respect they are quite different from the Mantze.

While the Chinese General was thus pressing into their country with his entire force the Lolos divided into two parties. One went south by a small road and commenced pillaging and burning Chinese villages just outside of the city of Ningyuenfu, and came almost beneath the very walls of the city. The city gates were kept closed and the merchants and citizens took their places on the walls, with clubs and stones to defend the city, should an attack be made. Another band of Lolos attacked the small town of Mienshan three days to the north. Thus the General was forced to return and defend these places, and the Lolos again retired to their strongholds. This is the kind of thing that goes on all the time. Meares went out and got some photos while they were looting, and watched the operation from a secluded point on one of the hillsides of Ningyuenfu.

In a few days all was quiet again, but many disturbing rumours were afloat. In the midst of such rumours and excitement the Rev. R. Wellwood and his wife have lived for the last six years, until relieved on the eve of their departure on furlough by Mr. and Mrs. Rudd, who are still holding on and doing good work, in spite of the turbulent atmosphere in which they live. Some French fathers have been toiling for years in this valley so full of eruptions.

Meares' journey back to Chentu was without event until he reached Chingchihsien, where he met the Nepalese Ambassador. I give his story in his own words :—

"I could get no quarters in the town, so went to a small hovel higher up the street, and after my meal I went and called on the Ambassador, whom I found to be a very pleasant old gentleman and who spoke perfect English.

"Next morning I started off with my cooiles before daylight, and on going to the door to see them off I found the Ambassador waiting to see me. He wore a long silken kaften, and wound round his head was a sacred scarf, which barely covered a golden plate, bound to the top of his head. He was attended by one Gurka, who held a saddled horse. He immediately approached and embraced me, and began to cry bitterly, saying that he was dying. He declared that the Chinese were conspiring to poison him, and had been drugging his food for several days past ; then finally, during the night, they had been trying to kill him with chloroform. He threw himself on my protection, and asked that I should take him to the British Consul at Chentu. Inducing him to come into my inn I tried to soothe him, and after a few minutes some of his Gurka officers arrived, but as soon as he saw them he seized a pistol and tried to shoot them. With some difficulty I managed to get the pistol from him and quiet him. A little later a Chinese official came to call, but he at once seized a large hammer that was lying in the room and tried to kill him. Just managing to catch the Ambassador in time I tried to pacify him until we got the official safely out of the house. After the official left he grew much quieter,

THE AUTHOR IN CHINESE DRESS.

and told me many interesting things about himself and his country. Now that he seemed more composed I slipped out of the room and went to the telegraph office to send a wire to the British Consul at Chentu, stating the case and asking what steps I should take, saying that the Ambassador insisted on returning with me to Chentu. I received the reply that the Consul had left Chentu. Going down to the inn where the Ambassador was lodging I found his officers in a great state of agitation. They could only speak Hindustani; but fortunately I was able to talk to them, and found them all very nice men; they said that they were quite sure that the Ambassador had quite gone off his head, and that they could do nothing with him.

"After a lot of consultation we decided to telegraph to the Maharajah of Nepal, asking him for instructions. So I wrote out a long telegram, saying that the Ambassador had become strange, and insisted on coming to Chentu and abandoning the expedition.

"On taking the message to the office the clerk said that he did not know where Nepal was, or how much the telegram would cost, until he received particulars from Chentu. I got the officers to come up to my inn to see the Ambassador; they told him in my presence that no one ever thought of poisoning him, and all swore that they would protect him with their lives, saying that 'if he insisted on leaving the mission they would never dare to return to Nepal, and that they would all disperse and become religious mendicants.' After a lot of persuasion the Ambassador agreed to do what I recommended, and finally decided to continue his journey to Dachienlu, where he would find other Europeans. So I escorted him back to his inn, marching down the street arm-in-arm, and stayed with him till late at night. He gave me some presents and a photograph of himself, and begged me to take any of the ponies I fancied; but I insisted I was leaving the country, and did not need any of them. They were all most anxious that I should accompany them on their journey along the southern road to Lhasa, where they were to stay a month before going on to Katmandu. It was the chance of a lifetime; but I had other work to do and had to refuse their offer, and slipped back to my inn. Next morning, starting off early, we climbed the great pass, which was covered with snow almost from the bottom. The top was a sheet of slippery ice, and both myself and my pony had many bad falls. However, we crossed without accident, and continued our march to Chentu, where I stayed in the hospitable home of Mr. and Mrs. Fergusson's.

"A few days later Mr. Fergusson returned from Mapien, saying that the coffins were on their way, and would arrive in a few days. So we made all the necessary arrangements, and when word came that they were approaching the city we went to meet them at a large temple, one mile outside of the city gate, where the officials had made arrangements for receiving them. Every respect was shown, and they insisted on having it carried overland with escort, with all the honours that is usually paid to their high officials. Next day the funeral took place in the foreign cemetery, a beautiful place a few miles from Chentu. I felt this was, indeed, a sad ending to all our hopes and the projects we had made together, and I had lost my best friend."

It only remains for me to add that the Rev. H. H. Taylor of the Church Missionary Society conducted the funeral service. A stone engraved with the words "*Lieutenant J. W. Brooke, F.R.G.S., killed by the Lolos on December* 24, 1908," marks the spot where his body rests.

FINIS.

INDEX.

Index.

Index.

Index.

Index.